2/20

san juan island
LIBRARY

*In Memory of
Stuart Miller*

Praise for Stan Hochman

Stan was a true friend and confidant, always willing to lend an ear, give advice, and, if need be, use the far-reaching power of his pen to poke the hornet's nest. He was a torchbearer for social justice. No pretense. No BS. He was as real as they come. Stan Hochman was the truth.

—**STEVE BANDURA,** Director, Philadelphia Youth Organization; Founder, Anderson Monarchs Athletic Club; Trainer, Mo'ne Davis

I've never laughed harder in my life than with Stan on *Daily News Live* during the early days of Comcast SportsNet. Whenever he appeared on the show, I knew there would always be passion, intense conversation, and, most times, laughter.

—**MICHAEL BARKANN,** NBC Sports Philadelphia

Whenever I get into a bind or have a dilemma, either professionally as a sportswriter or personally, I take a deep breath and say, "OK. How would Stan handle this?"

While I miss Stan all the time, I always smile whenever his name comes up. I mean, really, who else in the world could write this anecdote about Richie Ashburn so darn well?

Ashburn was trying to explain to Harry Kalas how hitters felt about particular bats. "When I was going well with a particular bat," Ashburn lectured in that Nebraska twang, "I wouldn't trust leaving it around the clubhouse if we were on a road trip. I'd take it back to the hotel and go to bed with it. In fact, I've been to bed with a lot of old bats."

Kalas gulped, and returned to the action.

Here's to you, Stan.

—**ED BARKOWITZ,** Sportswriter, Philadelphia Media Network

When I turned sixty, someone paid me a compliment. "You don't write old," she said. It made me think of Stan, an exemplar in so many ways, including this one. In a career that spanned more than half a century, Stan's writing style, like the man himself, remained sharp, current, and vital. I miss him terribly.

—**LES BOWEN,** Sportswriter, Philadelphia Media Network

Stan was a celebrity, but I was shocked to discover how down-to-earth he was. How approachable, how kind, how "normal" he was. He was a man whose company you wanted to be in, hoping some of his greatness would rub off on you. He was the epitome of class.

—**JOE CONKLIN,** Stand-up Comedian; Corporate Banquet Speaker

"Iconic" and "luminary" are two words used much too frequently in twenty-first-century America. But they perfectly capture the gift that Stan was to the *Daily News* and to all who knew him. I can't say I'm impressed by much, but I always felt in awe when I was in his presence— master writer, a renaissance man.

—**MICHAEL DAYS,** Vice President for Diversity and Inclusion, Philadelphia Media Network; Former Editor, *Philadelphia Daily News*

Stan was a good and decent man who was extraordinarily talented, caring, sensitive; had a great sense of humor; and understood what life was all about.

—**FRAN DUNPHY,** Former Head Men's Basketball Coach, Temple University

Stan was the real deal. An excellent writer whose words didn't obscure what he was trying to say. Tough but fair. And very, very insightful. He set a standard that we all reached for.

—**PAUL HAGEN,** Columnist, Philadelphia Media Network

Stan Hochman was an extraordinary man with exceptional talents who lived an exemplary life. We were blessed to have him touch our lives, and we are all better persons for having known him.

—**JOE HAND JR.,** President, Joe Hand Promotions

When Joe Frazier came back from the Olympics after winning the gold medal in 1964, there was no bag of money waiting like there is now. Stan found out that Joe was broke, and he got the word out, and Joe's five kids got everything they wanted for Christmas.

That's the kind of man Stan was.

—**JOE HAND SR.,** Boxing Promoter

Somewhere, Stan is smiling. The Phillies Urban Youth Academy, a glistening baseball diamond in FDR Park, is a reality. Its greatest champion was Stan Hochman. It took four years of planning and dickering among city politicians, Phillies functionaries, and Major League Baseball's autocrats. The only person outside that group: Stan Hochman. Stan often said he hoped he would live to see its completion. He almost made it. Stan's dedication to improving the lives of children is his greatest legacy.

—**MARCUS HAYES,** Columnist, Philadelphia Media Network

The integrity of the man and his work was unmatched. The Stan Hochman transaction was a three-way relationship among the columnist, the athlete, and the reader based on honesty at its core. The athlete was rarely surprised at what Stan wrote, even if he didn't agree with it. Stan always said his goal was to be tough but fair, and he succeeded for half a century.

He would play the curmudgeon when it worked for him, or for a laugh, but that wasn't him. Stan was an enthusiastic cook, and he knew a good wine, and he liked ballroom dancing and the theater. Mostly, though, he was Gloria's husband, Anndee's father, and Sasha's grandfather. Gloria and Anndee are both accomplished writers, and you can't believe the way he lit up when he talked about them. Beyond the tough columns or the Joe Conklin impressions, that's what people will remember most.

—**RICH HOFMANN,** Former Sports Editor, *Philadelphia Daily News*

Stan's writing, his unique style, his ability to find the truth were unequaled in his profession. He was the kind of person we all hope to be: loving, compassionate, committed to making the world a better place. Stan knew that sports was more than a box score, more than winning or losing, but his stories and columns were accounts of real people struggling to achieve, and sometimes laughing and crying along the way. In the community of communicators, Stan was really the MAN!

—**LARRY KANE,** Broadcast Journalist

Stan was somebody I wanted to pattern myself after. The most important thing he taught me was to let the subjects mostly do their own talking. And how can you not appreciate a man who's smart enough to insist that he was only the third-best writer in his family? What a writer! What a man!

—**MIKE KERN,** Sportswriter, Philadelphia Media Network

Stan had a crustiness about him. He didn't suffer fools well and hated a phony. He could sniff it out in ink in a manner that would eviscerate the frauds and the powerful. On the other side, Stan loved the underdog and would write a story well enough to make you cry.

—**GLEN MACNOW,** Talk Show Host, SportsRadio 94WIP

Stan was the heart and soul of the *Daily News.* Editors would rush to read his copy because they knew it would be well written, error-free, and compelling. He was quite simply the best columnist the paper ever had.

—**TOM MAHON,** Sportswriter, Philadelphia Media Network

In the early 1960s, Stan made the *Daily News* sports section a "must-read" for young readers such as myself. Over the next forty-five years, it was a pleasure to get to know him personally. His passion to develop Philadelphia's Urban Youth Academy is just one example of his dedication to our city and its youth. He was a Philadelphia treasure.

—The late **DAVID MONTGOMERY**, Chairman and Former President, Philadelphia Phillies

If there were a worldwide sports journalism Hall of Fame, Stan Hochman would not only be included; he would have a whole wing named after him. He had more integrity in his words than the entire new Blog and Baloney universe.

—**AL MORGANTI,** *The Morning Show,* SportsRadio 94WIP

Stan was able to walk that fine line between being a reporter and a sports fan. He was able to get the real story and deliver it in a way that made you want to get up every morning and look for his column.

—**FRED SHABEL,** Vice Chairman, Comcast Spectacor

Throughout his journalism career, Stan was a writer who had to be read. Throughout his life, he was a man whom everyone would have done well to emulate.

—**MIKE SIELSKI,** Columnist, Philadelphia Media Network;
Winner of the first Stan Hochman Excellence in Sports Journalism Award
from the Philadelphia Sports Writers Association

Stan regaled me with stories of covering the Ali-Frazier fight at Madison Square Garden, one I had listened to as a boy on a transistor radio. I sat motionless, afraid to breathe, as Stan talked in that often-mimicked raspy voice, keeping me spellbound, hanging on every word. But what really cemented our relationship was the way I witnessed Stan treat his sweetheart, Gloria. He adored his wife. Cherished her. Stan was chivalrous. He was kind and gentle. True manhood. It's why I always called him "Stan the man!"

—**VAI SIKAHEMA,** NBC News Anchor

Stan was a great journalist. I feel blessed to have had him as someone I could go to for mentoring. Even beyond his unsurpassed talent was an insightful and caring human being who would talk with you about the status of the world and things each person could do to help make it a better place for all of us.

—**JOHN SMALLWOOD,** Columnist, Philadelphia Media Network

A Hochman column was a thing of beauty delivered in a flash. Day after day, Stan wrote—and spoke—with depth, intensity, and uncommon good sense. He was the finest all-around sports journalist Philadelphia has ever seen.

—**ZACK STALBERG,** Former Editor, *Philadelphia Daily News*

Stan Hochman
UNFILTERED

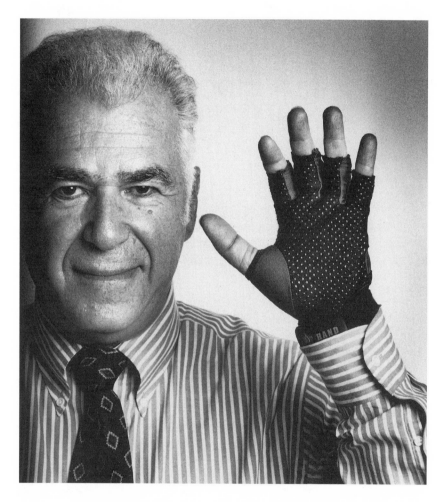

TEMPLE UNIVERSITY PRESS
Philadelphia | *Rome* | *Tokyo*

50 Years of Wit and Wisdom from the
Groundbreaking Sportswriter

Stan Hochman
UNFILTERED

Foreword by Angelo Cataldi

With a Message from Governor Edward G. Rendell

Edited by Gloria Hochman

DISCARD

TEMPLE UNIVERSITY PRESS
Philadelphia, Pennsylvania 19122
tupress.temple.edu

Library of Congress Cataloging-in-Publication Data

Names: Hochman, Stan, author. | Hochman, Gloria, editor.
Title: Stan Hochman unfiltered : 50 years of wit and wisdom from the
  groundbreaking sportswriter / foreword by Angelo Cataldi ; edited by
  Gloria Hochman.
Description: Philadelphia : Temple University Press, 2019. | Includes
  index. | Summary: "This book collects Stan Hochman's best newspaper
  columns from his fifty-year career at the *Philadelphia Daily News*,
  showcasing his wry perspective on baseball, boxing, basketball, hockey,
  football, horse racing, tennis, golf, and more. Each chapter is
  introduced by a major figure in the featured sport."— Provided by
  publisher.
Identifiers: LCCN 2019014205 (print) | LCCN 2019980980 (ebook)
  ISBN 9781439917008 (cloth : alk. paper) | ISBN 9781439917022 (ebook)
Subjects: LCSH: Sports—United States—Miscellanea. | Sports—
  Pennsylvania—Philadelphia—Miscellanea. | Sports journalism—
  Pennsylvania—Philadelphia.
Classification: LCC GV583 .H6155 2019 (print) | LCC GV583 (ebook) |
  DDC 070.4/497960974811—dc23
LC record available at https://lccn.loc.gov/2019014205
LC ebook record available at https://lccn.loc.gov/2019980980

♾ The paper used in this publication meets the requirements of the American
National Standard for Information Sciences—Permanence of Paper for Printed
Library Materials, ANSI Z39.48-1992

Printed in the United States of America

9 8 7 6 5 4 3 2 1

For

Anndee, Elissa, and Sasha Rose

Jacob, Dylan, and Scout

Contents

PART II HORSE RACING

PART III BOXING

PART IV FOOTBALL

PART V HOCKEY

PART VI BASKETBALL

PART VII STAN'S WORLD: OUTSIDE THE LINES

Photo gallery follows page 134

Foreword

ANGELO CATALDI

IN THE FINAL YEARS of his extraordinary life, Stan Hochman often thanked me for providing the final act of his career, his three-year tenure as the Grand Imperial Poobah of Sports on my WIP radio show. I had to keep reminding him that it was I who should be thanking him for the wit and wisdom that he provided on a weekly basis.

Since his passing, I have said so many times on the air how much I miss him, and not just for his pithy commentary as the Poobah. I miss his unrivaled versatility, his clever turns of phrase, his refreshing worldview, and especially his courage to point fingers and name names.

I'm going to send the sportswriters in this city a copy of this book, because it captures everything that made Stan Hochman great—and exposes all that is lacking in many of his successors.

Above all, Stan suffered no fools—and if there's one thing we can always say about Philadelphia sports, it is that we never lack the kind of clueless clods upon whom Stan feasted. My favorite was the weekly skewering he gave to Norman "Bottom Line" Braman, the greedy used-car salesman who owned the Eagles in the 1980s and 1990s.

Stan feared no one. He did his job with only his readers in mind, and this commitment came through in every brilliant column he wrote. What I never considered was where these potent opinions came from, a mind that was every bit as sharp in Stan's eighties as it had been for all the decades that had come before.

Every Wednesday during the Poobah years, I would send Stan the questions of the week, the biggest issues that had arisen in Philadelphia sports over the previous seven days. Sometimes, he would script his answers, although his gruff delivery always seemed spontaneous. I cannot deny that, at times, I would slip in something that was not on the list. Stan never—not once—came up short. Often, those responses were his best.

There is so much more I could write about Stan, but these words are only keeping you from reading more of the entertaining, provocative work of a far better writer, and a far better man.

Savor every word of these columns. They represent the work of a wordsmith with no peer, a loyal family man, and a person I was honored to call a friend.

A Message from the
Honorable Edward G. Rendell

S TAN WAS SO POPULAR AND SO LOVED because he was just like the Philly sports fans: cantankerous, angry, opinionated, and incredibly knowledgeable. But he loved our teams. Some time ago, I wrote a column for the *Daily News* about the appropriateness of booing. Stan called me and said, "Boy, we should do a book together on when fans should boo and when they shouldn't." I'm disappointed we never got to write that book.

Stan also liked to have fun. He was hysterical as the Grand Imperial Poobah on WIP's *Morning Show*, with Angelo Cataldi. If I heard he was going to be on in fifteen minutes, I'd push back whatever I had scheduled and tune in. He always made me laugh.

Stan was just like the rest of us, only smarter. Just like the rest of us, only funnier. Just like the rest of us, only more honest. I think you'll see that as you read this memorable, to-be-savored collection of Stan's work.

A while back, I was talking to someone about Stan, and I said, "If God is Jewish, he'll look and sound just like Stan Hochman."

Introduction

GLORIA HOCHMAN

S TAN WAS THE QUINTESSENTIAL Renaissance man. He loved cool jazz and soulful singers, chilled chardonnay and sizzling lamb ragout, Shakespeare in the round and theater with Mark Rylance. He was passionate about social justice and harmonious race relations, a society where drugs meant antibiotics, not heroin. His sometimes-gruff exterior concealed a cushy niche for the well-being of children, whom he was certain thrived on praise and unconditional love. Most of all, he adored his family. When he baked wild salmon and poured fine wine for us—for me; our daughter, Anndee; our daughter-in-law, Elissa; our granddaughter, Sasha—he declared himself the luckiest man in the world.

You'll see all of that reflected in his writing: his meticulously crafted words about Pete Rose and whether he belongs in the Baseball Hall of Fame; Jackie Robinson and his struggle to become the first black baseball player in the big leagues; the tragic 1972 Summer Olympics in Munich, where thirteen Israelis were killed in a chilling blot on the world's showcase for sports excellence; his unique take on Joe Frazier and Muhammad Ali.

You'll see references to mental health; the inner workings of athletes who grew up poor and deprived; the toll of a hidden illness, such as gambling; the strength and determination that can result in the construction of a field where kids with Down syndrome, cerebral palsy, and other disabilities can play ball.

Stan often said to me, "I write about fun and games. You write about life and death." We talked at the dinner table about how it all came together, and Stan's writing was laced with the results of those talks. He was more interested in how athletes felt, what their values were, how they lived their lives, what made them tick than he was about how many runs they scored or punches they landed. He wrote to hit a nerve, to challenge the way people thought and felt and dreamed and lived their lives. Even when he was days away from death, he smiled when Rich Hofmann, then the *Daily News* sports editor, told him that his column on Dick Allen's belonging in the Baseball Hall of Fame, one he had written a couple of days before entering the hospital, had been the most-read feature in the paper the previous week. It was one of the last columns he wrote, and I believe that message from Rich soothed him, told him that his readers got it, that his life's work counted.

Throughout our marriage, I was mesmerized by how much Stan knew about so many things. No matter the category, he could answer every question on *Jeopardy*. His knowledge of sports, every sport—baseball, football, hockey, horse racing, boxing, golf, tennis—was endless, and his recall, even for events that had happened fifty years earlier, was astonishing. He wrote quickly and easily, often a column, a sidebar, and a story in just a couple of hours.

As I read through more than seven thousand columns and stories to select the ones I chose for this book, I smiled, and then I cried. And I continued to be dazzled by his way with words. I think you will be, too.

With glorious memories and with so much love,

Gloria Hochman

Stan's "Zingers"

I F YOU WANT TO READ SCORES AND STATISTICS, you won't find them here. If you want the inside story into the hearts and minds of the major sports stars of the twentieth and twenty-first centuries; if you want to be center stage at the most memorable sports events of our times; if you want to read, for the first time or the tenth, Stan's acerbic, irreverent, one-of-a-kind take on it all, this is a book you'll read, reread, and gift to the sports lovers in your life. Transcending sports, this collection, destined to become a classic, is for anyone who savors the magic of deliciously insightful writing. Stan was known for his "zingers." Here are just a few, to get you started.

Owls Find a Knockout Punch—Kefalos and Williams

Philadelphia Daily News
December 24, 1964
[After Temple's Jim Williams scored 30 points in a rousing win, Penn coach Jack McCloskey] looked like a guy who had wrestled a case of TNT and lost.

Good Humor Man Helps

Philadelphia Daily News
May 6, 1965
Jim Bunning has a mind like a bank vault, cold and efficient. Johnny Callison sulks around like someone in constant mourning. Richie Allen enjoys fun, but words like "boy" set his teeth on edge. Then there's the manager, who is usually as grim as three-day-old raisin pudding.

Short Swing, a Full Life

Philadelphia Daily News
May 25, 1966
Doug Sanders swings a golf club like a man trying to kill a rattlesnake with a garden hoe.

No Wonder Bunning Enjoys Tipping "The Hat"

Philadelphia Daily News
August 26, 1966
Jim Bunning has a wife and nine kids, which sounds like 10 good reasons for getting keyed-up for every start he makes.

Spitz: Scared Shiftless or Just a Puppet?

Philadelphia Daily News
September 6, 1972
Mark Spitz is as shallow as a pie plate. Mark Spitz is as deep and as loveable as a saucer filled with vinegar. Mark Spitz has a chance to make it big in the movies if they bring back Charlie McCarthy films and he can tote along swim coach Sherm Chavoor to play the Edgar Bergen role. Has anyone ever written the script for an X-rated puppet show?

Frazier to Smoke Foreman?

Philadelphia Daily News
April 28, 1976
George Foreman has a heart like a lion and a head like a cantaloupe.

Bob Lemon: The Yanks' Quiet Man

Philadelphia Daily News
October 17, 1978
He sits there in the dugout like he's carved out of Ivory soap. Wears wire rim glasses that perch on an incredible nose, all red and crinkly like a spoiled persimmon.

Tose One Who's Not Selling

Philadelphia Daily News
July 16, 1981

Leonard Tose loves the heat in the kitchen. Thrives on it. Gets a psychic tan from it. Hotter it gets, the better he likes it. Bring on the bankers and the bluenoses and the boobirds. Bring on the divorce attorneys. Bring on the tough-talking truck drivers. Leonard Tose has a vocabulary that will melt their transmissions.

Matuszek Hangs On to Job, Sanity

Philadelphia Daily News
April 23, 1984

Len Matuszek hit .282 this spring, led the club in doubles with 10. Drove in 14 runs. Nobody drove in more. That's like climbing Mount Everest with a piano on your back. Wearing roller skates. With a frayed rope. "It was unlike any spring I've ever gone through before," Matuszek said, after a training camp only Abbott and Costello could have loved.

Betting Must Step into Big Time

Philadelphia Daily News
May 28, 1985

If [overly optimistic Garden State Park chairman Bob] Brennan had been captain of the Titanic, he would have broken out the vodka and told the passengers to use the iceberg for ice cubes.

Jaworski Can Run, but He Couldn't Slide

Philadelphia Daily News
September 29, 1986

Rams flushed Ron Jaworski out of the pocket and linebacker Jim Laughlin jolted him hard enough to bust the quarterback's shoulder pads and scramble his neurons.

"I've gotta learn how to slide," Jaworski said sheepishly, 40 minutes after the Eagles stunned the Rams, 34–20.

Jaworski did look like a student in the Jeff Stone School of Sliding and Vinyl Upholstering, tumbling awkwardly into Laughlin's path.

Winners giggle and losers grumble. But that is the second time in three weeks Jaworski has wobbled to the sideline with guys guiding him by the armpits, a worrisome thing that will lead you to sing the blues in the night.

Phillie Mignon Just a Veale Cutlet

Philadelphia Daily News
May 9, 1989
The Phillies face Sandy Koufax tonight. They warmed up for Koufax by facing Pittsburgh's Bob Veale on a cloudy, gray afternoon. It's like warming up to wrestle alligators by playing water polo with sharks.

Last Dance: Ryan Brings Down Curtain after Evans Puts On a Show

Philadelphia Daily News
October 23, 1989
Dick Clark called. He gave the game a 69, terrible lyrics, but you could dance to it, and he wondered if Byron Evans would be available for the next "American Bandstand" special. Evans intercepted a pass late in the third quarter and he felt so good about it, he put on his dancing shoes and did 12 seconds' worth of hully-gully like a guy walking barefoot over hot coals. What in the name of Fred Astaire is going on here?

Try to Think of the Bright Side

Philadelphia Daily News
December 16, 1991
It's over.
    You don't have to wait for the fat lady to warble. It's over.
    Oh, sure, if the Saints faint and lose two in a row . . . and the 49ers lose next week . . . and the Eagles beat Washington, the Eagles can wriggle into the playoffs.
    And if the special teams play the way they played yesterday, the Eagles couldn't beat Martha Washington. They couldn't beat Charles Barkley's grandmother, even if she's double-teamed.
    It's over.

Phils Success Has Been Catching

Philadelphia Daily News
May 24, 1995
Gene Harris, the [Phils] setup man, is as somber as a one-car funeral.

What These Games Are All About

Philadelphia Daily News
July 25, 1995
Izzy, the official Olympic mascot, has an egg-shaped upper body, spindly legs, a fuzzy tongue, a red nose and deep black circles around his eyes. Sort of like John Kruk with a brutal hangover.

Murray's Deli Sports a Familiar Feel

Philadelphia Daily News
February 12, 1999
It is not true that Michael Barkann, Pennsylvania Sportscaster of the Year, takes his lunch intravenously. At Murray's Delicatessen in Bala Cynwyd, he orders a New York–style pastrami sandwich, spreading out of two slices of rye bread. New York–style means the waitress never smiles.

Conklin Makes a Good Impression

Philadelphia Daily News
April 2, 1999
The *Daily News* accountants will be pleased. I took Reggie White, Rich Kotite, Ray Rhodes, Bill Campbell, Johnny Mathis and Bill Clinton to lunch at Potcheen in the Sheraton Rittenhouse Square, and the entire tab was $30.50, plus tip.

Actually, I took sports comedian Joe Conklin to lunch, and he did White, Kotite, Rhodes, Campbell, Mathis, Clinton and a half-dozen other voices during a rollicking meal that was both delicious and reasonably priced.

Last time he checked his list, he had 185 voices on it, "including dead guys." Most of them athletes and coaches, some of them entertainers, some of them politicians. He does a dead-on Clinton, offering nubile interns "a position on my staff" in that raspy southern sincere drawl.

Chef Vola's [Stan's Favorite Atlantic City Restaurant]

Philadelphia Daily News
July 18, 2003
Louise's banana cream pie is still the most fun you can have in Atlantic City with your clothes on.

PART I
Baseball

Introduction

GARRY MADDOX

THIS SECTION ON BASEBALL PRESENTS, for your enjoyment, columns and articles spanning five decades and covering people and events from the unique perspective of Stan Hochman, featuring his views on Jackie Robinson; Hank Aaron; and two of his favorites, Dick Allen and Richie Ashburn—and, of course, his opinions on the 1980 World Series and whether Pete Rose should be in the Hall of Fame.

Stan's sports knowledge and his right-to-the-point delivery of facts captured my attention as I enjoyed an evening of dinner and jazz with him and Gloria or as I sat on the bench in the dugout prior to batting practice.

In the eleven years I played for the Phillies, whenever I arrived at the clubhouse and saw Stan Hochman standing at my locker, I knew he wanted to discuss something edgy. In my playing days, despite what we claimed, we all read the newspapers (no WIP in those days) to see what was being said about the team. The *Daily News* covered sports the best, and Stan was the "must-read."

Stan was the writer who was going to ask you thought-provoking questions: "What is the atmosphere in the clubhouse with the presence of Dick Allen?" Really, Stan? "Will this team finally reach its potential with the addition of Pete Rose as management suggests?" For me to answer double-edged questions requires a tremendous amount of trust in the fairness of the writer, which formed the basis of our relationship outside the game.

Stan always championed the underdog. Just mention a cause to help those who were less fortunate, and he was in. As a board member at the National Adoption Center (now known as the Adoption Center), I saw him give so much time to help kids find families that I thought he was employed there. In sports, it was the athlete over management or the establishment. He identified with minorities struggling to assimilate in the sports world and with athletes who did not live up to expectations—categories that both applied to me.

I felt Stan's genuine sincerity when I read his articles. I am quite sure that readers will enjoy not only this section but the entire collection herein.

A Scorekeeper's Final Inning

Philadelphia Daily News
March 29, 1963

BRADENTON—They got a big tin scoreboard out in left centerfield down here. And they got an old guy who sits in front of it, on a bench. He's got binoculars and he watches the umpire gesture ball or strike. And he's got a transistor radio jammed in his shirt pocket just to make sure.

He sits between the words "ball" and "strike" and he reaches over and sticks the right number on a yellow peg after every pitch. When the hitter makes out, he has to get up and walk a couple of feet and hang the right number next to the word "out."

Only next year, he won't be doing it.

Charley Finley, who is gonna masquerade his players in green-and-gold costumes this year, and who once had pastel-colored sheep grazing in his bullpens, wants an electronic scoreboard. Milwaukee had this rickety playground last year. So the city council of Bradenton eagerly approved a three-year contract with the A's the other day and one of their stipulations was the installation of an electric scoreboard.

You think anyone said, "Hey, wait-a-minute. What about that nice old guy who hangs up the numbers now? What's gonna happen to him?"

Heard about It on Radio

Nah, they just went ahead and passed the deal, and the old guy had to hear about it second hand, on the transistor radio he keeps crammed in his pocket.

Peter Crean didn't look like a man who had just been rendered obsolete. He was busy stripping his tin scoreboard of the legend of the Phillies' 9–2 victory the other day.

He was wearing one of those caps you buy for 90 cents in Kresge's. His face was bristled, and his lips were parched from the sun.

"Yeah," he said. "Nobody's said nuthin' to me yet. I hoid it on the radio. I'm not worried. I'll get another job, parking cars or ushering. They'll find something for me."

Where would Walter Reuther be if everyone yielded this gracefully to automation? But you've got to understand Crean. He thrives on baseball, and he'd sell peanuts just to be around a ballpark.

"I'm from Brooklyn," he said, plucking the zeroes off the pegs and stacking them neatly. "I live and die for baseball. When Ebbets Field opened, I was second on line. At six in the morning.

"I left the house around four, and walked all the way from Greenpernt. And all I had was a nickel to go home on a trolley.

"I was a policeman for 20 years. Then I retired. But I was only 48, and I had no Social Security. On the way, I worked in defense plants as a security officer.

"I'm an old semipro ballplayer. Played with the Bushwicks, even before they went to Dexter Park. Anyway, when I got to be 65 I came down here."

Six-Year Veteran

"I bought a second-hand trailer and moved into the trailer park. I just wanted to be near the ballfield. I'd come out all the time.

"Six years ago, somebody said, 'Hey, Pete. They're looking for someone to keep score.' That's how I got the job. Heck, I was paying my way in. This way I got to see the game free, and I even got paid for it."

In spring training, the pitchers thunder past him in the outfield in disorderly sprints. Then they saunter back to the starting point.

"It's not so bad when they're runnin,'" Crean said. "But when they walk back, I can miss a pitch. I got the radio, but sometimes the guy will be talking and talking about something else, and then he'll say, 'Now, let's get back to the ball game."

"The Braves weren't a very friendly bunch. This team is a lot friendlier, a better bunch of guys."

Next year, Crean will be in the parking lot, shuffling in the dust. OR in the aisles, guiding people to their seats. He is 71, and in his way he symbolizes what spring training is all about, a sad-funny pageant crammed with careers that are ending and careers that are just beginning.

Sartorial Sleuthing

Philadelphia Daily News
April 25, 1967

FRANK ROBINSON has spindly legs. He must be embarrassed by them, because he sometimes stuffs them into three pairs of sweat socks. He can't be too embarrassed by them, though, because he then puts on colored stockings with the stirrups so high he looks like a grizzly bear perched on two icicles.

This sartorial quirk did not keep him from leading the American League in everything, including excitement. You'd think they'd let him hit with a rose clinched between his teeth if he so desired.

But the rules say "all players on a team shall wear uniforms identical in color, trim and style." And a memo has been posted limiting the height of those stirrup socks to six inches in front and six-and-a-half in back. Robinson's socks soar 9½ inches in front and 12 in back, a daring bit of tailoring that even Liz Taylor can appreciate.

A man armed with a ruler and a quest for fair play decided to do some research among the Phillies. The socks ranged from Andy Seminick's snug two-inches above the shoe-top to Rich Allen's approximately nine inches.

"In the old days," sniffed Seminick, "nobody fooled with their socks. You were lucky to get a pair that matched."

These days, the Phillies issue red stockings that rise 4½ inches above their shoe. The laundry, the shape of a man's ankles, and wear-and-tear account for the small individual differences.

Gene (4) Mauch thought enforcing a limit was a good idea. "Some guys are abusing the thing, making themselves look bad," he said. "I can't imagine why a guy would want to wear his socks high."

Second Thoughts on Superstition

Just then, Allen sauntered by, with so much of his white socks showing, a man could get snow-blindness staring at them. Mauch had some second thoughts on superstition.

"Bill White wore his old uniform in the '64 World Series," Mauch remembered. "He'd driven in 75 runs the second half of the season and he wasn't about to change."

"The new uniform was tight," White (4½) recalled. "Look, what difference does it make how high you wear your socks. You hit and catch. The reason the game takes so long to play is that there are so many rules to shorten it."

Ruben (4) Gomez: "I put the socks wherever they land. What's this game coming to? Soon, they'll tell us we have to wear mini-skirts."

Phil (4) Linz: "I think it was Mickey Mantle who started the whole thing. His legs are so big, he slit his socks and wore them high."

Bob (6) Uecker: "Who gives a rap? What about football players? Some wear tape right up to their thighs. Some guys wear more grease than other guys."

Pepper Martin Worst Dressed

Allen danced away when the man approached with his ruler. "You're gonna write me right out of them," he squawked. "These are the socks I've worn since I came up. It's like buying a horse or a car. If you're satisfied, you don't change around.

"It's like my locker. They tried to give me a new one in '65. I had to go right back in that hole. . . . I've had it for three years and I want to stay there."

So Allen continues to dress in the cramped space next to the tin closet where the players keep their valuables. And he continues to wear his socks about nine inches over his shoes. And the first guy to complain will have to fight Mauch.

The night of the investigation, the Phillies were playing the Cubs. Leo (2½) Durocher was properly enraged by the issue. "Who gives a bleep?" he demanded. "If a guy thinks he can hit with his foot, let him leave the bat on the bench.

"Pepper Martin was the worst dressed player of all time, but he could play. He never wore sweat socks or sweat shirt or a jock. His shoes were so bad, he'd have to call time and pour the sand out. But he could play."

A man looked around the clubhouse. The Cubs have two traditions. One is wearing their stirrup socks smack on their shoe-tops. The other is finishing in the second division. Case closed.

Baseball's Best Ever

Philadelphia Daily News
April 9, 1974

HENRY AARON stands alone.

They have been playing this lovely summer sport for 106 years, and Henry Aaron, who developed those lethal wrists lugging ice in Mobile, Ala., is the best player to ever play the game.

He hit a home run off Al Downing last night. Against the wind. Through a murky rain. It soared over the fence in left-center at the 385-foot mark.

Home run number 715. Alone at last. Past the ghost of Babe Ruth, past the memory of anybody who ever played the game. Bigger guys. Stronger guys, swifter guys. But nobody who could do all the things Henry Aaron could do, and do them year after year after year.

"The record, held by Mr. Ruth for 39 years," Aaron said afterwards, "has put me in a position. . . . [F]or years I was somewhat slighted by awards and things presented to other ballplayers."

The words were tumbling out, the sentences fragmented by emotion. "I've played all those games, been out there when I haven't felt good," he said. "But I can't say I'm the best.

"I consider myself one of the best. Joe DiMaggio, he was one of the greatest ballplayers who ever played. Willie Mays, he was one of the greatest. Jackie Robinson, he was one of the greatest. They all fit in the same category.

"I wouldn't say Henry Aaron is gonna be fourth. I'd say Henry Aaron would be first or second."

He can rate the players he has seen in a fantastic 20-year career in the big leagues. The old-timers are ghosts, described by people who believe in ghosts. He did not study the history of the game, because for too long the history of the game was white-on-white.

He contented himself with dreaming other dreams, developing his skills, swinging a mop handle at bottle caps. But when the chance came, Aaron seized it with both his talented hands. He did not squander his skills, he did not chip away at his concentration with frivolous distractions. He went out there, day after day, year after year.

"Twenty years," teammate Dave Johnson sighed. "Against the travel, against the specialized way it's played, with relievers who give you a variety of unhittable pitches.

Do it against relievers who get paid $50,000 to come in for guys like Tom Seaver. And do it with such ease, and with very little fanfare."

Fanfare. They have not devised trumpets that can play loud enough to chorus his praises. Or drums to thump. Or flags to unfurl.

The Commissioner of this strange sport was not even on hand to see it happen. Something about a dinner in Cleveland. Eat your heart out, Bowie Kuhn. You missed the kind of baseball drama that may never happen again.

"Let me just say this," Aaron said, in a post-game press conference. "I know there's been a lot of things written about my performance as far as Cincinnati is concerned.

"Have never went out on a ballfield and not given my level best, regardless of the situation. I played in Cincinnati, two out of three like I was supposed to play.

"He (Clay Kirby) made some very good pitches on me and could have gotten anybody out. And contrary to reports that said I was a disgrace and didn't give my level best, I don't know how to play the game any other way.

"I wanted to hit the home run here . . . and if God didn't see fit for me to hit it at home, well. . . ."

God didn't make it easy. There were pre-game ceremonies that seemed choreographed by sixth-graders that went on forever. Then those lumpy dark skies erupted and it rained.

Downing walked Aaron on five pitches his first time up, accompanied by a thunder of boos. The next time up, in the fourth inning, with a runner on first, Downing threw a ball outside.

Then, he tried to come in with a fast ball he intended to be knee-high. It came in much higher and Aaron lashed that bat through the mist and the ball leaped away.

It seemed to go softly through the rainy night in Georgia, like a balloon, but the mind plays tricks when the heart is beating in your ears.

Bill Buckner, the Dodgers leftfielder, scrambled up the fence like a kid trying to sneak into a game. The ball soared eight feet over his head, over the fence, and into the joyous grasp of relief pitcher Tom House.

"I felt all along if I got a strike to hit I could hit it out," Aaron said. "I was guessing. The first time up he threw me all fast balls. The second time I thought he'd start me out with fast balls. He hung that one.

"I'm relaxed now, a tremendous weight off my back."

There is no telling what he will do now. He is 40 years old, the oldest player in the game. There are more records within reach, and the arithmetic that will convince the scoffers of his place in the game.

For now, we have the toast offered by Atlanta manager Eddie Mathews after the game. Mathews may be at his best with bubbly in his hands:

"To the greatest guy," Mathews said, "and the best ballplayer that ever played the game."

Start the Parade without Me

Philadelphia Daily News
October 11, 1980

SINCE 1972, in his eight years with California and one year with Houston, Nolan Ryan had a record of 112 wins, three losses and five no-decisions in games in which he took the lead into the eighth inning.

That's 112–3.

You've got a better chance of stealing the diamond out of Roberto Duran's earring than you have of beating Houston when Nolan Ryan's got you three runs down in the eighth inning. The Phillies did it Sunday.

"Those last two weeks," Dallas Green growled yesterday, "we had some intense, grind-it-out baseball games with extreme peaks and valleys.

"A team not as tough could have quit on a couple of occasions.

"Nolan Ryan gets you down, 5–2, in the eighth inning, it could have been a disaster. But we didn't quit."

Why is it OK for managers to sermonize after victories? Why are they allowed to brag about how the team didn't quit when it's unlawful for writers, after losses, to suggest that indeed, a team did quit?

———

WHY MUST WE assign glowing intangibles to winning teams? Character? Courage? Discipline? Togetherness?

Those five games with Houston were wonderful, crammed with drama, littered with bizarre events. But the baseball purist had to puke, watching them, listening to that wimpy trio on ABC-TV.

There was more than skill demonstrated. The playoff pressures warped performances out of shape.

Houston lost its best pitcher at mid-season and its best hitter in mid-playoff. The Astros didn't quit.

It wasn't character that created the rally that blotched Ryan's brilliant late-inning record. It was a flare by Larry Bowa, a hard grounder by Bob Boone that clanked off Ryan's glove.

Give Boone points for playing hurt. He was hobbling on one leg and he thumped to first base, blocking out the pain.

Greg Gross beat out a lovely bunt. That's grace under pressure, that's technique, that's terrific.

And then Pete Rose grinned back at Ryan and fretted him through a 3–2 count and walked. Nothing that happened after that qualified anyone for knighthood or sainthood. Spare me sermons about character and columns about courage. . . . [W]e're talking about professional athletes who are paid to play well.

———

AND, AFTER 30 YEARS, the 1980 Phillies have played well enough to win a pennant.

So thousands of people cram an airport to catch a blurry glimpse of returning hung-over heroes. And the Pulitzer Prize–winning morning paper buries the Nobel Peace Prize story below the fold. And I will write 4,500 words on the World Series.

It sells papers. I know that.

People would rather read about Greg Luzinski than Iraq and Iran. It helps them forget high taxes and lousy schools and crime and grime. Sports is the opiate of people. Bowie Kuhn said that. Or Pete Dexter. I have trouble telling those guys apart.

The Phillies don't personify the city any more than that toothless bunch of Canadians did a few years back. The city celebrated because the Flyers played relentless, belligerent hockey. And they celebrate the Phillies winning a pennant because they came from behind, during the season, during the playoffs, and the citizens can relate to that. Hey, some guys play better in September and in October. But that has more to do with muscle fiber than moral fiber.

———

SPARE ME the search for the deeper meaning of what the Phillies have accomplished. A bunch of pampered overpaid athlete-entertainers put aside their petty grumblings for five weeks and played some intense, alert baseball.

Give Dallas Green credit for screaming that message all summer. But be aware that it was easier for Green to do it, because he's got a better, guaranteed job with the organization. He was the right man for this bunch and he tongue-lashed them right into a World Series. The players resent that image, they resent the critical press, they resent the short-tempered fans. They've got enough resentment stored up to melt Alaska. And they showed it by brushing by the hero-starved fans who trudged to the airport to greet them.

The guys who best understand the game, Tug McGraw and Pete

Rose, had the most fun in the playoffs. They will have the most fun in the World Series. They are not afraid to show emotion, not afraid to laugh in public, to do cartwheels in public.

It is a joy to watch Rose clatter home, rumbling into the catcher. It is a pleasure to watch McGraw dance that screwball past one more grim hitter.

I have been covering this team only since 1959, so I was spared the gloom of the mid-'50s. But I have chronicled Tony Curry and Roberto Pena and B.G. Smith and Billy Smith and Charley Smith and Ron Stone . . . and I covered a 23-game losing streak . . . and I covered the collapse in '64 and the playoff nightmares in '77 and '78.

What the Phillies have done this year is nice, because it's been so long since they won a pennant, and because there are some older, hard-grinding guys on the team who may not have more chances to play in a World Series.

But next weekend is Parents' Weekend at Yale and I have not seen my daughter in seven weeks. And that is where I am going to be.

And if the Phillies win, as I expect them to, go ahead, start the parade without me.

That's Incredible—That's Baseball

Philadelphia Daily News
October 23, 1980

SO IT WASN'T WILLIE MAYS scampering under Vic Wertz's fly ball, catching it over one shoulder, cradling it like a baby.

So it wasn't Sandy Amoros scuttling into the left-field corner at sun-dappled Yankee Stadium. So it wasn't Billy Martin scooting under an infield pop nobody else wanted . . . or Bobby Richardson lancing a line drive by Willie McCovey.

The foul pop squirted out of Bob Boone's glove like a slick bar of YMCA soap and Pete Rose was there to snag it.

Snagged it before it hit the front edge of a dugout crammed with pop-eyed players and narrow-eyed cops and mean-eyed police dogs.

And if that's the memorable play to etch the 1980 World Series into the national consciousness, so be it.

Boone gimped after that pop foul on a leg that had never really mended after off-season surgery. On a foot that was swollen and blotchy from a playoff collision.

———

ROSE IS 39, ancient for a baseball player, unheard of for a guy who played every nerve-gnawing game of the regular season plus 11 quick-aging post-season episodes.

The Stanford graduate and the high school dropout converging on a ninth-inning foul pop. And somehow, some way, turning it into an out. While the goofy, marionette of a pitcher waggled to cover home plate, just like the book says you should.

That, friends, is baseball.

That, sports fans, is why baseball is the greatest game in the whole half-vast world of fun and games. Round ball, round bat, making the possibilities infinite.

And no clock to run out on a team rallying from what seemed like hopeless, hapless defeat.

The Stanford graduate and the high school dropout and the crazy relief pitcher and the hyper shortstop and the cool third baseman proved it one more time . . . the joyous drama that is the summer game.

The Phillies turned all those double plays and the Royals couldn't even get a routine forceout at second base. And that is part of the reason the Phillies won the championship.

————

BUT MAYBE they won it when Larry Bowa stole second base in the first game of the tournament, his team trailing, 4–0. Maybe that risky play was a bugler's call to charge . . . that, indeed, the Phillies would be playing aggressive, emotional baseball. The kind of aggressive, emotional baseball that enabled them to win 21 of their last 28 on the road, to keep scrambling off the canvas with nine guys standing over them, counting.

And maybe they won it when Dallas Green grumbled downstairs with his gravel voice and his gravel disposition.

And maybe they won it years and years ago, when John Quinn got fed up with Rick Wise's modest demands for a raise and swapped Wise to the Cardinals for Steve Carlton.

Carlton has had some gallant seasons for the Phillies, but none like this one. Game after game, throwing pitches that splintered bats and broke hearts. He won both his World Series starts and he was magnificent Tuesday night, blitzing into the eighth inning with a four-hitter before the fatigue of 331 innings blind-sided him.

It would be nice to know how he felt about his remarkable season, about the incredible playoffs, about the first baseball championship this city has ever known.

————

HE CONTINUES to hoard his thoughts. He is beginning to resemble an aborigine tribesman who will not be photographed lest you steal his soul in the camera's black box.

He must feel something. If that isn't emotion twitching across his handsome face when he pitches, then someone should check him for Bell's Palsy. He showed up at the parade in a white shirt and tie, quixotic to the end. And if Carlton chooses to bury his emotions deep inside, there is always Tug McGraw, patting his chest after a fluttery moment, pounding his thigh, punching holes in the noisy night sky, striving for records in the standing broad jump.

And then there is Mike Schmidt, who has learned from bitter experience that an overload of adrenalin will jerk his head around like whiplash and turn his palms too damp to grip the bat.

So Schmidt tries to look cool, hoping he can fool his adrenal glands, thus keeping his chin tucked in and his palms dry.

It works. Lord, how it works. The man hit 48 homers and made Gold Glove plays in the field. Has there ever been anyone who ever played this wonderful game with that much power and that gifted a glove? Now the world knows. And more important, maybe Mike Schmidt knows too, just how good he really is.

And for all the splendid things that Bowa and Manny Trillo did in the middle, and for all the key hits Bake McBride rapped and all the balls Garry Maddox caught and for all the intangibles Rose brought to the tournament, the Phillies would not have won it without the extra guys.

———

FRED SHERO ONCE SAID that if you don't use your bench, ultimately it will kill you. Dallas Green used his bench. Used it that last week of the season despite Bowa's harangue. Got Del Unser enough action to thaw out his stroke. And when Green summoned Unser in the World Series, he summoned a sharp, confident pinch-hitter.

Give Green credit for using the youngsters like Bob Walk and Marty Bystro in situations they could handle. Give him credit for squelching that infamous almost-trade of Lonnie Smith for Billy Smith.

Give Paul Owens praise for the trades he did make, for bringing back Dick Ruthven, for swapping John Stearns for McGraw, for rescuing Unser from a free-agent scrap heap. Green kept them involved, kept them motivated. And used them when all those games clattered into extra innings.

"You win 'em late," Schmidt pointed out, "and that means it's guys coming off the bench who are doing it. Pinch-hitters, relief pitchers."

Don't blame them if they cherish the moment, roll the taste of it around like fine burgundy. There is no way all 25 of them will be back to defend the championship.

That's baseball, too.

———

THE PHILLIES have a decision to make on McGraw, who would prefer to stay put, rather than test the cash-green waters of free agency.

Do they trade one of their moody trio of outfielders? Who goes to Texas in exchange for Sparky Lyle? Sign Larry Christenson or lose him to free agency?

Can the guys who do return survive another summer of Green's whip-cracking, finger-pointing monologues? But all that can wait.

"Savor this," Schmidt advised the JFK Stadium mob yesterday.

It is something to savor, even if the only thing you remember is the ball squirting out of Boone's glove and into Rose's grasp. Beauty is in the eyes of the beholder. John Keats would have loved baseball.

Garry Maddox Still Wears White Hat

Philadelphia Daily News
February 4, 1986

DO YOU REMEMBER when the good guys wore white hats? Rode white horses. Never drew unless the other guy drew first.

Said "Howdy ma'am" to ladies, and stopped runaway stagecoaches by leaping between a pair of frothing, sweaty, wild-eyed horses, and somehow yanking them to a halt.

The bad guys wore black hats and their holsters slung low, and drank whiskey out of a shot glass in one arrogant gulp.

Then Dave Garroway invented television, with help from Milton Berle, Jack Paar and Ed Murrow, and we found out more than we really wanted to know about our politicians, preachers and pitchers.

Are there more kids yearning to grow up like Mick Jagger than like Mickey Mantle now? And who abused his body more?

Where did the University of Minnesota recruit its basketball team? From a police lineup? What's that Jack Armstrong, the All-American boy, is sprinkling on his breakfast of champions?

The Philadelphia sports writers honored a genuine good guy with a brand new humanitarian award last night, outfielder Garry Maddox.

The Phillies cajoled Maddox into signing a 1986 contract, then went shopping at the winter meetings and bought not one, but two more centerfielders.

Maddox's new contract has a drug-testing clause in it, because the Phillies wanted it there.

"When it comes down to a contract or no contract, what can you do?" Maddox said the other day.

Reality triumphed over reason. Maddox believes in the Constitution, that Americans are innocent until proven guilty, that he is guaranteed freedom from illegal search and seizure.

He feels he has bargained away his basic civil rights and it pains him. And the pain he feels illustrates just how jumbled is the issue of drug abuse in sports.

Me, I've always been a law and order guy. Test 'em randomly, offer help to those with a problem.

Bench second offenders for two months. Ban third offenders for life.

And if those are tougher penalties than a plumber or a piano mover faces, so be it. You don't find plumbers or piano movers on bubble gum cards.

Maddox argues softly against that vigilante fervor. Lynch mobs trouble him, no matter how noble their intentions. Putting a price tag on liberty distresses him.

"Using cocaine is illegal," he said. "Testing without cause is illegal, too. So you want us to accept one illegal act to fight another illegal act? I have trouble with that."

Does he have trouble with Baltimore's scheme, the players volunteering to accept drug testing?

"It's something for the players association to deal with as a unit," Maddox said. "Not individual teams, not individual players. You do that, and you get 900 different policies.

"A player who doesn't approve of the idea in Cleveland gets traded to Baltimore, then what?

"The thing that concerns me most is a test that comes up with a false positive. That guy's life can be ruined.

"Sure, people say that that sort of thing may happen, but that the end result is important, fighting drugs. Well, if you're the one guy whose life is ruined, you don't see it that way.

"They talk about confidentiality. Don't you think those guys with the New England Patriots thought they had a promise of confidentiality from the owner, from the coach?"

The New England episode, and revealing the names of the users who sought help, put a dent in the battle against drug abuse in sports. It didn't do much good for the cause of investigative journalism, either, but that's another story.

The Orioles insist that management will not be privy to the test results, that the program will be handled by a medical team.

I argue that you need testing, because part of the drug problem is that the user doesn't believe he has a problem, because his thinking is warped by the chemicals.

"What he needs most is forgiveness," Maddox argued.

"The statistics show that cocaine use was concentrated in the 25-and-up age bracket. Now, it's mainly in the 18-to-25 bracket.

"Some guys are coming into the game with problems. And if you looked at the numbers, they are probably the same in baseball as in the rest of society."

OK, OK, but how many doctors, lawyers or Indian chiefs are on bubble gum cards or the backs of cereal boxes?

The average player makes $300,000, the below-average player makes $200,000. Can't we demand a higher standard of behavior from our athletes, to protect the integrity of the games they play, and more important, to be role models for the kids who adore them?

"As a player," Maddox said, "you feel a responsibility to be a role model. There are those of us who can handle it.

"But a lot of players are coming from environments where they need role models themselves. They need someone to look up to. It's not fair to put everyone in that role model category.

"What do you do with the players who can't handle it?

"Study the sport itself. Players are under a lot of pressure. And some try drugs and alcohol because of that pressure.

"I'm not sure that kids today are interested in anything more than what the players do as players.

"When they pick up a paper and see that this guy is a drug user I don't think that they say they're going to do as he does."

The Patriots got to the Super Bowl with what the team psychiatrist called a "negligible problem." Did the other players resent their habits? Did they know?

Maddox played alongside Lonnie Smith one summer. Didn't Smith's erratic baserunning, his spastic stumbles, give him away?

"I didn't have a clue," Maddox said. "You have to know what to look for. I didn't know how to look for it in a baseball environment.

"When I come to the ballpark I'm not looking around to see who's sniffling, and who has a cold."

He will be more vigilant with his sons, Garry and Derrick. And with Lauren, his new baby daughter.

"The boys are like everyone else," Maddox said. "They know the names of the players. They go with the trends. Right now, it's 'The Refrigerator.' They know who he is. But they don't have anyone they idolize and say that's who they want to be like.

"Maybe it is different for them. They play a lot of sports. They don't sit around and watch a lot.

"They've learned a certain set of values. They know what I expect from them. If they like a player and it turns out he has used drugs, I hope they still might respect his ability on the field."

Maddox is a good role model for his own kids, and that is really all we can ask of him. If every player was as sensitive, as dedicated, then perhaps they wouldn't cave in to the pressures of the game.

Saturday he watched one son play indoor soccer, then the other boy play basketball. In between, he cooed gently to Lauren.

Friday he'd visited Children's Hospital, along with Tom Foley and Darren Daulton. Von Hayes and Don Carman spent time at The Child Guidance Clinic, where Maddox has become emotionally involved in the process of patching shattered young lives.

The hospital visit, especially the time spent in the oncology ward, was draining.

"It's really hard to go there, especially when you have kids of your own," he said. "I got to talking to one of the mothers and she said that most of the youngsters we were seeing had cancer.

"After that, the whole thing took on a different perspective.

"I saw one child, maybe about 4 years old, looking real peaceful while asleep.

"And in the next bed there was a child, awake, and you could see the pain. You think about all that."

Maddox makes you think about that, and about justice and civil rights and forgiveness and understanding. And he makes you yearn for a simpler time, when you could tell the good guys by the color of their hats.

Jackie: The First

Philadelphia Daily News
April 14, 1987

BRANCH RICKEY put a gnarled, ex-catcher's hand over the telephone mouthpiece.

"Herb Pennock is calling from Philadelphia," Rickey whispered to Harold Parrott, traveling secretary for the Brooklyn Dodgers. "I want you to hear this."

Parrott lifted an extension phone gingerly, put it to his ear. Years later, in his book, "The Lords of Baseball," he recalled the startling conversation of the two general managers.

". . . [J]ust can't bring the nigger here with the rest of your team, Branch," Pennock said. "We're just not ready for that sort of thing yet. We won't be able to take the field against your Brooklyn team if that boy Robinson is in uniform."

"Very well, Herbert," Rickey said. "And if we must claim the game, 9–0 (on a forfeit), we will do just that, I assure you."

Philadelphia, the City of Brotherly Love, not ready to watch a black man play baseball alongside white teammates? Philadelphia, Cradle of Independence, shackling a man's life, strangling his liberty, denying him unobstructed pursuit of happiness because of the color of his skin?

Jack Roosevelt Robinson broke in against the Braves on April 15, 1947 at Ebbets Field. One small, swift, pigeon-toed step for Robinson, one giant step for mankind.

The Dodgers brought Robinson to Philadelphia. He came, he saw, he conquered. The Dodgers won the pennant, Robinson hit .297, was voted Rookie of the Year.

He would paddle a flimsy canoe, alone, against the snarling, white-water menace of bigotry, through the brackish swamps of prejudice.

This is the story of that courageous, lonely, dangerous journey— and its aftermath—retold by those who played with and against Jackie Robinson through interviews conducted from coast to coast by the *Daily News*. It coincides with Major League Baseball's decision to celebrate the anniversary of Robinson's first season, which began 40 years ago tomorrow.

If some cynics sneered at 40 as a contrived number for a celebration, that cynicism vanished in the storm that followed Al Campanis's babbling commentary on national television about blacks lacking "the necessities" to manage a big-league baseball team.

Campanis? The general manager of the Dodgers, the team that shattered the color line by signing Robinson?

Forty years isn't much in the life span of a glacier. Baseball is still dominated by Neanderthals. Campanis, a man of hardened attitudes, retreats pitifully, and the celebration goes on.

Campanis becomes a shambling milepost that tells us how much of the road remains to be traveled, 40 years after Robinson made history, facing Johnny Sain in Brooklyn on April 15, 1947.

Robinson was shunned by some of his rednecked teammates that first year. He was harassed viciously by men he played against. His team was turned away by the Ben Franklin Hotel on that first road trip to Philadelphia.

Philadelphia has a black mayor now, a black superintendent of schools. Only the color of money decides where a person stays while visiting.

If you don't know that Jack Roosevelt Robinson, and the way he played the game, helped make that possible, then you don't understand the history of baseball or the history of this nation.

"Martin Luther King told me that Jack was his inspiration," said Willa Mae Robinson Walker, Jack's sister, who lives a hard-scrabble existence in Pasadena, Calif.

"Martin Luther King had his dream, but he didn't know how to start it. And then he became aware of Jack, in baseball. And he said, 'This is what I want to do, in other areas.'

"And the black minister from South Africa, Bishop (Desmond) Tutu. I went to dinner with him. And he told me that Jack was his inspiration.

"He told me he had seen a copy of Ebony magazine in a dentist's office and read about Jack and what he endured. And he said that if Jack could go through what he did, others could follow."

———

WHO WAS JACK ROBINSON? How did he come to be the first black major leaguer? How did he endure the indignities dumped in his path, the baseballs thrown at his head, the spikes slashing at his groin, the insults aimed at his heart?

Who helped him along the way? Who hurt him? How did he keep from caving in under the burden of carrying the hopes and dreams of black Americans?

And how did this tough, proud, aggressive man who once had been court-martialed for refusing to sit in the back of a bus on a military base cope with baseball's plantation mentality, turned away in Philadelphia, jeered and jostled in the Cradle of Liberty?

Parrott found another hotel for the team, the Warwick. What he could not find was a place to hide from the savage stream of venom Phillies manager Ben Chapman unleashed that night.

Like so many episodes in this story, the details vary with the viewpoint of the witness, mainly north or south of the Mason-Dixon line.

"Ben was a vocal guy," said pitcher Ralph Branca, who was educated at New York University. "He called him 'black boy' and talked about tossing watermelons on the field, about black cats."

"Ben would ride guys pretty good," said Harry Walker, from Leeds, Ala. "He'd have rode his mother pretty good if she was on the other team.

"In New York, he'd get after Jewish players. I played with the Cardinals before I got traded to Philly. I knew Ben. He was half-Indian and he'd get on Indians. Anything to win a game."

Robinson's signing had been greeted coldly by a handful of Dodgers. There had been talk of a petition, circulated by Dixie Walker, Harry's brother, supposedly with the support of Alabaman Bobby Bragan and Eddie Stanky, an Alabaman by marriage.

"Chapman was giving Robinson a going-over, just like he gave everybody a going-over," is the way Stanky remembered that first trip to Philadelphia. "Called him 'shoeshine boy' and some other stuff.

"Finally, I said, 'Why don't you pick on somebody who could fight back?'

"I remember that year. It was a pleasure being in the same ballclub as Robinson. He was a great baserunner, had great instincts, a great competitor.

"My first at-bat in the big leagues, I got hit in the head. Chicago, Rip Sewell pitching. He was saying, 'Hello, welcome to the National League.'

"They did the same thing to Jackie. And he did not say a word.

"I wasn't against Jackie. I grew up, played soccer, in Philadelphia. One of my best friends was a teammate named Moon Mullins. He played right wing. I was educated with blacks."

Bragan, who now works for the Texas Rangers, does not deny antagonistic feelings when Robinson signed.

"There was never a petition," Bragan said. "There never was any organized meeting to sign a petition. Some people objected. However slight, however great.

"The only one to put it in writing was Dixie Walker. Me, being from Birmingham, I had a hard time with it. Mr. Rickey called me in, asked me if I'd rather be traded or stay.

"I said I'd rather be traded. Because of telling the truth about how I felt, we became fast friends.

"See, I was born and raised in Birmingham. My daddy had a crew of blacks who worked for him in the concrete business.

"I remember as a kid, how they always came to the back door. When you're born and raised in that kind of atmosphere, you just have a different feeling.

"My experience with Jack paid dividends for me when I started managing and I had Maury Wills and Tommy Davis. And later on, Roberto Clemente and Henry Aaron.

"And when Mr. Rickey died, Jackie and I sat next to each other, in the same pew of that church.

"Sure, I remember Chapman needling Jackie. I remember him getting on Pee Wee Reese, too, saying for Pee Wee to get up and give Jackie his seat because Pee Wee had befriended him."

Reese is still called "captain" by his surviving "Boys of Summer" teammates. Shortstop, captain, sweet Kentucky babe, baffling his family and Louisville friends by playing alongside a black man, handling it with grace and dignity.

"I was not trying to be the Great White Father," Reese said. "I had lost three years in the service. I just wanted to play ball.

"I was on a ship, coming back to the States when I heard the Dodgers had signed a black player. Didn't think much of it. And then the radio man told me he was a shortstop. That got my attention.

"The needling I got didn't bother me. Some of it was in jest. Lots of times, though, the truth is told in jest. Guys asking me, 'What is he, your roommate?'

"Through it all I just tried to put myself in his shoes. I knew damn good and well I couldn't have done it. I couldn't have gone to an all-black league and done it.

"I'm not that much of a deep thinker. I just thought how rough it's got to be for this guy. Here he was, trying to make it in the big leagues, taking all that crap they threw at him, plus trying to make it not only for Jackie Robinson, but for the whole black race."

There is one mysterious element in the Robinson-Chapman story. Walter Winchell, the syndicated gossip columnist, turned on Chapman, sprinkling his columns with shots at the manager.

His job in danger, Chapman begged Parrott for a favor, asking Robinson to pose for a picture, shaking hands.

Robinson readily agreed, even volunteered to meet Chapman halfway, behind the batting cage.

Another version of the story has Rickey ordering Robinson to pose with Chapman. The files contain a photo of the two men sharing a distant grip on a bat, but only Robinson is smiling. Perhaps he knew in his heart that the charade was in vain. Chapman got fired anyway.

"I don't remember Stanky challenging the Phillies," Reese said. "But I do remember something that happened in Tampa down the road. I threw the ball real hard to Jackie and he flinched.

"Chapman hollered, 'Hey, don't throw it so hard, little Jackie might hurt his hand.'

"Jack walked in front of me, over to where Chapman was coaching third. He said, 'Mr. Chapman, you've been on my butt for two years and I had to take it. If you ever get on me again, we're going to straighten it out after the game.'

"Chapman realized he could start a riot, so he zipped it up."

There had been other challenges for Robinson that first year. Dismal treatment in spring training, separate and unequal housing in St. Louis, too many meals eaten on the bus while his teammates dined in some segregated roadside restaurant.

The .297 looks like .397 against that backdrop of bigotry.

How could Rickey have known that the incredibly versatile athlete from Southern California could play so well in the cauldron that had been created?

Somehow Rickey knew. When he decided the time was right for what has been called "The Great Experiment," there were other, better-known players in the Negro leagues, including pitcher Satchel Paige and catcher Josh Gibson.

Rickey chose the 26-year-old Robinson, for his youth, his baseball skills, his intelligence, his backbone, his personal habits, his understanding of the role of a pioneer.

Someone reminded Rickey of Robinson's court-martial and acquittal. "Good," Rickey said, "a man of ideals, a battler."

First, Rickey created the camouflage of forming a black team, the Brown Dodgers, ostensibly to play at Ebbets Field while the big leaguers were on the road.

Then he assigned scouts Wid Matthews, George Sisler and Clyde Sukeforth to cover the existing teams, including the Kansas City Monarchs, where Robinson was playing shortstop.

"I had never seen Robinson play," Sukeforth recalled. "I was sent to Chicago to see the Monarchs. Mr. Rickey told me to pay particular attention to Robinson and to his arm. I introduced myself, asked him if he'd make a few throws from the hole.

"He said that he'd be happy to show his arm, but he'd fallen on his shoulder and wasn't in the lineup.

"I thought this might be a good time to bring him to Brooklyn. I asked him to meet me at the Toledo ballpark and we'd travel together by train.

"He appeared right on time. I had two berths on the train. In the morning, I woke up and he was already up and dressed.

"I asked him if he wanted some breakfast and he said he'd wait and eat with the boys (the porters). He felt that even though he was traveling through New York State, he wasn't going to act any different.

"The next day, he met me at 215 Montague St., the Dodgers' offices. I took him in and introduced him to Mr. Rickey. He took it from there.

"I felt like interrupting a few times, to tell him I had not seen Robinson throw, but I was so caught up in what Mr. Rickey was doing, that I never said it.

"Mr. Rickey drew him a good picture. He said, 'If somebody slides into you and calls you a black so-and-so and you'd come up swinging, you'd be justified, but it might set the cause back 20 years.'

"It was late afternoon when it ended. There was no other business that day."

———

IT WAS AUG. 28, 1945, and the historic dialogue began with an innocuous question, Rickey asking Robinson, "Have you got a girl?"

Only then did Rickey tell Robinson he was thinking of signing him for the Dodgers' organization and not the Brown Dodgers.

Then Rickey turned actor, inventing bitter scenes, creating ugly dialogue, painting cruel pictures of what might happen, on and off the field.

There were obscenities that did not come easily to the deeply religious Rickey, persistent poking at Robinson with the thorny stick of intolerance, testing, testing.

"Don't you want a player with guts enough to fight back?" Robinson pleaded at one point.

"I want a player with guts enough not to fight back," Rickey shouted.

And then, after one more passionate warning, a swing of Rickey's right fist, barely grazing Robinson's startled face. Followed by a mocking chorus, "What would you do, what would you do?"

"Mr. Rickey," Robinson said grimly, "I've got two cheeks. Is that it?"

The Big Fall: Survivors of '64

Philadelphia Daily News
July 14, 1989

THE 1964 PHILLIES are a jigsaw puzzle that has been sitting in a musty closet too long. The edges are warped, the colors faded. And, if you clear a space on a hardwood floor and try to assemble it once again, damn, there are some pieces missing.

The 1964 season, that's the one catcher Gus Triandos called "the year of the blue snow." For 150 games it was all lollipops and roses.

World Series tickets were printed; carpenters hammered away at Connie Mack Stadium building an auxiliary press box; a summer tense with racial unrest had mellowed into an autumn ripe with pride.

And then the blue snow turned to gray slush. The Phillies, 6½ in front with 12 to play, lost 10 in a row. The losses clattered to the pavement like marbles from a broken bag. A championship season curdled into a sour entry in baseball's history book, the most dramatic late-season collapse by a front-runner.

The lollipops stuck to the back-seat upholstery, the roses wilted and turned muddy brown.

There have been retrospectives before, in 1974, in 1984. Other attempts to put the puzzle together, to make sense of it.

On Aug. 19, the manager and players will gather again in Philadelphia for the Equitable Old-Timers' Game and a 25-year reunion, swapping memories brittle with age.

Maybe it is time to put a match to the nightmare, the way you do with a paid-in-full mortgage? Maybe it is time to quit digging in the graveyard of that 10-game losing streak?

Maybe it is time to put the puzzle pieces back in the box and tie it with a gaudy ribbon.

Maybe it is time to forgive without forgetting, to applaud the way they played to swagger 6½ in front with 12 left, and ignore the mystery of that 10-game losing streak.

It forever will remain a mystery. The key witnesses, 25 years later, supply vague clues, contradictory testimony, evidence tainted by ego.

First baseman Frank Thomas could not remember hacking off the cast on his busted right thumb to start in the fifth game of that losing streak. He did, going 0-for-4.

Jack Baldschun thought he'd pitched in none of the 10 games, maybe one. He pitched in seven, mostly in middle relief.

Rick Wise, 19 at the time, couldn't believe he'd been used in three of the 10 losses, in mop-up roles.

Psychologists have an explanation for this, the selective memory that enables us to blot out trauma and go on with the rest of our lives.

Thus, what remains an unforgettable chapter in baseball folklore, a scabrous blotch on this franchise's history, a scar on this city's psyche, no longer can be autopsied with accuracy.

It seemed to make more sense to find the players, discover how the wounds have healed, how they have handled a turbulent quarter-century.

Who are they, where are they, what are they doing? I narrowed the search to manager Gene Mauch and 10 players, a significant number. The players were chosen on the basis of charisma, contrast, geography and a flicker of instinct.

I covered that team for the *Daily News*, kept a diary, planned to write a book just as soon as the parade down Broad Street screeched to a halt. I would not be calling as a stranger.

The methodology might be "Boys of Summer," but the results were strikingly different.

Oh, sure, there are shattered marriages and shredded dreams. There are squandered fortunes and broken promises.

But the clear majority of the men interviewed were upbeat, happy in their work, content in their marriage, healthy and bright-eyed and kindhearted.

They recalled 1964 through a personal prism, shaped and colored by their feelings for the game, for the manager, and by what happened in the years that followed.

There were huge surprises. Pitcher Dennis Bennett, footloose and frivolous in '64, is married, with eight kids, starting a risky, new business venture.

Pitcher Jim Bunning, somber as a coroner in '64, got elected to Congress by kissing babies and knocking on the doors of strangers.

Wise, a pitching coach in Houston's farm system, wears a unique ring on his right hand, a ring he bought himself to commemorate his first major league victory. He held onto the ring while forced to sell off so many other possessions to satisfy the tax collector.

Shortstop Ruben Amaro is starting over, new marriage, infant son, managing a rookie league team for Detroit.

And Mauch, sleek and tanned at 63, playing 36 holes a day in Rancho Mirage, Calif., thirsting for one more grab at the brass ring if there's a team out there that thinks he's the absolute right guy to win a championship.

The project, a labor of love, was shadowed by what has become of pitcher Chris Short, in a helpless coma now, victimized by an aneurysm.

Shorty. "Style." His nickname shortened from "Stylish," which is what pitcher Dick Farrell hung on him the first time Chris made a road trip with his spare clothing on a tangle of wire hangers slung over one shoulder.

Short, a key figure in a story I had never heard until now, a raucous spinoff from an exhibition game the Phillies played in Eugene, Ore., in late May that year.

"Shorty put his arm through the window of this Chinese restaurant," catcher Clay Dalrymple recalled.

"I'd already left the place. But here came Shorty and (pitcher) Ed Roebuck, banging out of there with a Chinaman in close pursuit, who may have been carrying a knife. Or a cleaver.

"Roebuck said, 'Run, Catch, run.' So I ran, even though I'm not sure why.

"Ran up this alley. I could hear the guy running, too. He was chasing Roebuck, and Eddie swerved to avoid him and twisted his ankle."

"I was standing across the street," Bennett said. "I was with my parents, who had come up from Yreka, Calif., to watch the game.

"I see our guys crashing out the window and I see Dalrymple hiding in the trash cans in the alley.

"I walk across the street, try to smooth things out. The guy wants to call the police, wants something done about his window.

"I tell the guy I'll pay for it. He says he wants $280. It looked like an $80 window, but I paid him the $280 and he quieted down.

"The thing is, Roebuck really hurt his ankle. So, the next day, he went to the ballpark early, and then limped back in and said he'd twisted it while running."

The injury did not hamper Roebuck's pitching, because the blue snow was still falling. A week later he faced nine hitters, got eight of them to hit weak ground balls.

"He was hurt," Dalrymple insisted. "He just wouldn't let on. Who knows? Maybe it made his sinker sink more."

Dalrymple has returned to his roots, Chico, Calif., squatting in his vegetable garden when he's not on the road for a food service firm.

He drives a VW Rabbit with 178,000 miles on it and seven rock divots in the windshield.

I visited him as part of a trip across America that began in Kissimee, Fla. (Wise), and included Klamath Falls, Ore. (Bennett), with other stops in Palm Springs, Calif. (Mauch), and Green Bay, Wis. (Baldschun).

I talked with Bunning in his congressional office, talked to second baseman Tony Taylor, now the Phillies' first base coach, at the ballpark. Visited with shortstop Bobby Wine, Atlanta's dugout coach, in Norristown when the Braves were in town, with rightfielder Johnny Callison in Glenside, pitcher Art Mahaffey in West Chester.

Had to settle for a long telephone conversation with Amaro in Miami.

Amaro, Baldschun, Bennett, Bunning, Callison, Dalrymple, Mahaffey, Taylor, Wine, Wise and Mauch will be profiled in this series. All but Bunning plan to attend the Old-Timers' Game.

It was fun. Frustrating, but fun.

Nothing illustrates the impossible task of digging out the reasons for the collapse more than recalling the episode in St. Louis.

The Phillies had lost eight in a row and had plummeted into third place, their huge lead melted like a snow cone in hell.

Bennett remembers warming up, creakily before the game, alongside Ray Culp. Sept. 29, 1964.

"My arm hurt so much," Bennett said, sitting in a tavern where he runs the all-day poker game, "I'd rub red-hot analgesic balm on my side. That way, I wouldn't feel the pain in my shoulder.

"Ray was throwing good. Gene Mauch came down to watch us for about five minutes. He looked at me and said, 'You're it.'"

Culp remembers warming up alongside Bennett.

"I never thought I was throwing as well as Bennett," Culp said by telephone from Austin, Texas, where he sells real estate.

"If I would have pitched, I wouldn't have gotten anybody out. I hadn't pitched in so long. My arm had been as big as a football, my elbow swollen."

Mauch looks at it from another perspective, sitting on his patio overlooking the plush Springs Country Club.

"Ray Culp had a bad back," Mauch said, after one of those ominous pauses that became his conversational trademark. "And only Ray Culp and I knew about it.

"Bennett? We needed someone to negate Bill White and Tim McCarver."

Another eyewitness, another angle. Jim Bunning, pitcher turned politician, tilted back in his swivel chair and tucked his hands behind his neck.

"Bennett was the starter," Bunning said. "I watched him warm up. I think I went to (pitching coach) Al Widmar and I said, 'Al, he can't throw the ball to home plate.'

"And he couldn't."

Bennett did not survive the second inning. The Phillies lost that night, and the next night.

Ten losses in a row, golden pennant dreams turned to dust, the dust sifting through rigid, sweaty fingers.

Culp has six kids, ranging in age from 25 to 3. He won't be coming to Philadelphia for the Old-Timers' game. Previous plans, time with the kids is precious, summer league baseball involvement . . .

"Disappointing," is the way he recalled 1964. "I wasn't much help.

"The injury I had, I finally got taken care of with surgery at the end of the '71 season. Actually, I went into baseball with a bad arm."

Actually, the Phillies signed Culp out of his Texas high school. The story that was written and rewritten until it had the aura of truth was that Culp hurt a weary arm learning to throw a breaking ball taught by minor league instructor Ben Tincup.

"Ben was a great guy," Culp said. "I got repercussions from blaming him, but, heck, I was 17 at the time.

"I tore something in back of my shoulder before I ever threw a pitch in pro ball.

"You know how cold it gets in the Appalachian League? Happened on a cold, nasty evening. Ben really helped me. I ended up having a pretty good breaking ball.

"I'd pitched a heckuva lot of ball in high school. Pitched every game our high school team played.

"By the time June rolled around, I'd pitched a full season. State championship tournament, I pitched Friday night and Saturday afternoon.

"I pitched the doubleheader that got us to the state tournament.

"If I could go back, and nobody is allowed to go back, I would not sign that summer.

"That's what caused the injury, the fact that I had a tired arm. It was a mistake to talk about how Ben had worked with me the night it happened.

"In '64 I couldn't straighten out the elbow for a while. I started that game against the Mets (Aug. 15) and I had that big lead (6–0) and had to leave the game in the second inning.

"Didn't pitch for, what, around 30 days. That night in St. Louis was the first time I'd thrown in quite some time.

"I proved later, if you gave me the ball, I'd pitch. I don't hang my head at all. I had arm problems and lived with them.

"If I had pitched in '64 (when he was injured), I wouldn't have gotten anybody out. And my family would have had a tough time eating.

"I won 120 (actually 122) and lost less than that. I pitched a lot of innings with not good stuff. The thing that's true is that I never threw the ball with the same stuff I had in high school."

So Culp was hurt and Bennett's arm was aching. Mauch wouldn't start Wise, a teenager. The manager had lost confidence in Baldschun in the closer role, which is why we saw so much of Bobby Locke and Morrie Steevens and Bobby Shantz.

And why he started Bunning and Short with two days' rest.

It all might have ended differently if Thomas hadn't busted his thumb diving back into second base against the Dodgers in early September.

"They were a half-game in front when I joined 'em," said Thomas, who is retired and living in a Pittsburgh suburb. "And I got 'em to 6½ in front.

"So, yeah, I'd say the injury cost 'em the pennant."

The numbers would justify the bragging. The Phillies got Thomas from the Mets and he drove in 26 runs in the 33 games he played before shattering the thumb.

"The doctors wouldn't go along with me," Thomas said. "I told 'em not to tell anybody, just let me go to the ballpark, give me a Novocain shot and let me play.

"I told 'em I had all winter to heal, but they wouldn't go along with me.

"It happened when Maury Wills put the pickoff play on. I dove back, my right hand went underneath the bag and hit the pin. Like a boxer's break.

"It happened in the second inning. I ended up getting two more hits (actually one more hit) after that. With a broken thumb.

"Went home that night, asked the bellboy to get me a big lard bucket and I filled it with ice.

"Kept my hand in ice all night. Woke up in the morning, the ice had melted and my hand was swollen.

"During the streak I did a radio show (with WFIL's Phil Sheridan) every morning. We'd go over the ballgame. I'd just keep saying, something's gotta break, one little play here, one little play there was beating us.

"I never thought they'd fold like that. One guy can carry a ballclub, but I didn't think one guy could make that much of a difference to lose 10 ballgames in a row."

The next year Thomas was released the day after he fought with third baseman Richie Allen. Allen might miss the reunion to appear at a card show in California. They have made peace with each other.

"I happened to be in Buffalo for an old-timers' game last year and saw Allen's name on the list," Thomas said.

"I was wondering what his reaction was gonna be. When I saw him coming in, I was on my way out to the field. I extended my hand to him.

"He said, 'No, we're brothers' and he gave me a big hug.

"I never hold a grudge. I don't look back in anger. I just felt when the incident happened, if you're gonna punish one fellow, you've got to punish the other fellow.

"Gene Mauch called me upstairs and said I'd been put on irrevocable waivers. He said that somebody was gonna take me.

"I told him that if he was doing it because of the incident I thought it was unfair to me.

"His answer was, 'You're 35 and he's 23.' And that was the extent of the conversation."

Thomas isn't the only one who thinks his injury cost the Phillies the pennant. Others think Mauch panicked, using Bunning and Short so often.

Others can't help wondering about Mauch's tranquil posture throughout the losing streak.

Perhaps there were other, otherworldly forces at work. How else can you explain the business of the contrived rainout?

The Phillies postponed a scheduled game with the Dodgers Aug. 3 because it had rained in South Jersey that afternoon.

By game time it was clear and mild, but the Phillies had avoided facing Sandy Koufax, who had pitched a no-hitter against them earlier in the year and had whipped them eight times in a row.

The game was rescheduled for Sept. 8, during the Jewish holidays. Koufax would not pitch.

And that makeup game, that was the game in which Frank Thomas broke his thumb, diving back into second base.

Don't Play Ball

Philadelphia Daily News
October 19, 1989

SAN FRANCISCO—Avery Brundage ordered the Olympic Games to resume with the blood splotches still thick and wet in front of the Israeli dormitory.

We must not give in to terrorism.

The National Football League teams played two days after John F. Kennedy was assassinated.

The president loved sports and would have understood.

The NCAA played its championship fandango in Philadelphia several hours after Ronald Reagan was wounded by a madman's bullet.

Hey, he was only wounded and he did play "the Gipper" once and he did broadcast ballgames when he was younger.

We are a nation of children, addicted to our games, and it wounds us deeply if they are postponed or canceled by war, death, pestilence, hunger.

What happens, though, when the Four Horsemen are outlined against a blue-gray October sky and two cities are ravaged by an earthquake?

Two cities involved in a World Series. Two cities vying for an ugly, gray trophy with the Bay Bridge as its centerpiece.

Has anyone in Major League Baseball taken a look at the Bay Bridge? It is crumpled, huge concrete slabs from the upper deck splattered against the lower deck.

People were left dangling in their cars when that happened.

People died when Interstate 880 buckled.

People burned to death in fires that roared from toppled homes in the marina.

"I don't think cancellation is at all necessary or appropriate," baseball commissioner Fay Vincent said yesterday.

Necessary? Finding homes for the homeless, that's necessary. Burying the dead, that's necessary. Healing the wounded, that's necessary.

Getting enough blood, grappling for survivors in the rubble, discouraging looting with police presence, that's necessary.

Finishing a World Series interrupted by a tragic earthquake is not necessary. Not today, not tomorrow, not next Tuesday.

"We don't want to conduct baseball while the hunt for victims is going on and the community is in the initial stage of recovery," Vincent said.

Is a week sufficient time? To bury the dead? To heal the wounded? To grope out of the dark tunnel of shock that grips the area?

Give Vincent credit. He made a swift decision to postpone the Series until next Tuesday, he made what seems to be a reasonable decision.

Moving the games to another site would have been outrageous, trivializing what has happened here.

Attempting to resume the games without an audience would have been too daring.

Playing today in a haunted ballpark would have been macabre.

Vincent showed up at the press conference in a white, button-down shirt open at the collar. This was no time for neckties, for etiquette, for pomp.

Be assured that Bart Giamatti would have been wearing a striped tie and a dark, blue blazer and the words would have tumbled from his lips with eloquence, with passion.

Vincent was properly somber, crisply brief. He said all the right things, that the World Series is a blip on the radar screen of tragedy that grips San Francisco and Oakland, that baseball would contribute to the relief fund, that he would not think of playing without adequate police presence at the ballpark and a final, documented report guaranteeing a safe ballpark.

So why do I think they are doing the wrong thing for all the wrong reasons?

The game will survive without playing this World Series to its conclusion.

Put it in the record books as 2–0 Oakland, with an asterisk.

ABC-TV will not go belly-up if it doesn't get all those car and tire and sneaker ads aired. Bo knows.

I keep thinking about something I heard on the afternoon telecast of a Toronto-Oakland playoff game.

Bob Costas and Tony Kubek were teasing each other, like a couple married too long.

And someone handed Kubek a note that said the temperatures would plummet to 30 degrees in Chicago that night for the Cubs-Giants game.

"The gods of baseball," Costas said, trying valiantly to lower his voice. "Everyone knows Wrigley Field is meant for day baseball. . . ."

Let the record show that it was 53 at game time that night, and that the plate umpire wore a short-sleeved shirt.

But the anger wouldn't go away. Baseball has gods?

How godlike can they be if the game is based on a cattle auction, the best and beefiest young players going to the worst teams?

Where were baseball's gods when the owners were treating the players like indentured servants?

What is this mythology about the game that inspires artists and poets and college professors to overlook everything that is devious and dirty about the game?

Who says it's a metaphor for America? And if it is, America is in deep trouble.

I wonder about those born-again zealots who tied a banner signifying a biblical verse to that helpless guinea hen in Game 2.

And I wonder how Giants owner Bob Lurie and general manager Al Rosen feel about attending a ballgame on Yom Kippur, the holiest day of the Jewish calendar.

And I wonder about the Giants players who prayed for fog and wind and swirling dust for Game 3 and got more than they wanted in a 6.9 earthquake.

There are no gods ruling baseball, punishing the wicked, rewarding the just.

And if, by some chance, they do exist, why challenge them by luring 62,000 people back into an earthquake-battered ballpark?

The fans who were there on Tuesday were the real heroes. They reacted calmly, filed out gently, drove away cautiously.

But the clocks are frozen at 5:04. The sunlight was glinting off the thick, green grass, the air was brittle with anticipation, the mood intoxicating.

Suppose, just suppose, another aftershock comes grumbling through the ballyard in the seventh inning, douses the lights, snuffs out the music, what then?

Can you ask the fans to be heroic one more time? Or do you risk the tragedy that comes with panic, the stampede through suddenly too-narrow gates?

I had gotten Game 3 tickets for Dr. David Leof, a psychoanalyst, a fan, a warm and wonderful teddy bear of a man.

"When it happened," he said, "it threw me against the railing. I thought I was having a cerebral hemorrhage.

"I thought I was dying. And then, when I could move one leg and then the other, I suddenly didn't give a damn about the earthquake."

Yesterday, Leof was available for his patients at his Fillmore Street home, built in 1904.

"I canceled my appointments for Tuesday and Thursday," Leof confessed, "and my clients must hate me, this man they trust their souls to, canceling sessions to watch a baseball game.

"But I am a mishoogana (crazy person) when it comes to the Giants.

"I would not want them moving the games to some neutral site. To take it out of a community that is shocked, anxious, grieving, that would be wrong.

"These people have gone through tragedy. You see the sense of community at work.

"There are two teams they have been cheering for, their dreams realized to have them meet in a World Series. It would be a double indignity to send the games to some neutral site.

"Whether it's appropriate to play so soon gets complicated. It's a natural disaster, not caused by terrorists or the lunatic fringe.

"You have to pull the community together and go on. Maybe they can dedicate it to the people who lost their lives, somehow make it a community celebration.

"What complicates it is the aspect of a subway series. Do you build community spirit by polarizing two sports teams against one another?

"Because it's a subway series and one team must lose, maybe it's a good idea to just forget about it, put it in the books as 2–0.

"And, as crazy as I am about the Giants, I could not root against Dave Stewart when the Oakland community has lost 200 people in a highway collapse.

"The World Series has lost interest for me."

Leof has more important things to do, holding frazzled nerves together, patching wounded psyches.

Traffic was gridlocked on Lombard Street. A florist handed roses to the weary drivers.

"Give thanks," he said, "to the higher authority of your choice."

Give thanks that that maligned ballpark shrugged off nature's harshest blow, and that the fans were brave and well-mannered.

And don't go back inside again anytime soon.

Tears Mix with Love for Bart

Philadelphia Daily News
November 16, 1989

NEW YORK—Priscilla Baskerville, of the Metropolitan Opera, sang Bart's favorite hymn, "Amazing Grace."

Bruce Froemming sat there, in Carnegie Hall, surrounded by strangers, and sobbed.

Yes, that Bruce Froemming, little guy who umpires big-league baseball games with a voice as shrill as a factory whistle, with a scowl as grim as Alcatraz. Sobbed.

"I lost it," Froemming confessed later, after the celebration honoring A. Bartlett Giamatti, the baseball commissioner who died too soon this summer.

The Yale Glee Club sang from the upper balcony like a choir of heavenly angels.

Marcus Giamatti, Bart's oldest son, spoke with fervor of Bart's love for the game, "the last pure place where Americans can dream . . . the last great arena, the last green arena . . . where everybody can learn the lessons of life."

Roger Angell, the poet laureate of the game, spoke proudly of Giamatti's insights; Milwaukee Brewers executive Bud Selig talked of Giamatti's legacy of love; and Claire Smith, the fine Hartford columnist, recited a warm and wonderful counterpoint to the gloomy historians who have painted the 1989 season with such thick, black strokes, citing the emergence of Ken Griffey Jr., Nolan Ryan's 5,000th strikeout, Jim Abbott's remarkable rookie season, the rebirth of the Orioles. . . .

Fay Vincent, the new commissioner, tried to find single words to describe his old friend, trying honesty, belief in process, freedom, and settling finally on civility.

His voice shattered near the end of his tribute to his noble friend, and then he gave us all one fearful moment by turning too soon from the podium and collapsing on stage.

Moments later, the color had sifted back into his face and he waved off the audience's concern, with a sheepish smile.

In all, a powerful, moving celebration of Giamatti, the teacher who wanted America to heed the symmetry of baseball, the message of baseball, the lessons of baseball, the joy of baseball.

He was an idealist and proud of it. He knew his vision of the game was of a paradise lost. But he was willing to wear his heart on his sleeve in the quest to regain that paradise.

The umpires understood. Which is why two dozen of them gathered at the Metropolitan Club afterward, to share memories of Giamatti, that bearded scholar who spoke in exotic phrases, delivered in an unfamiliar cadence, that somehow hummed with love.

Richie Phillips, head of the umpires' association, and the force behind the luncheon gathering, announced the founding of Bart Giamatti internships for Yale athletes who will work summers in the struggling city of New Haven, Conn.

Giamatti loved Yale, loved athletics, loved New Haven. The umpires have made the right call.

Dr. Bobby Brown, the American League president, spoke of Giamatti's warmth.

"He loved all people," Brown said. "He could talk to the president of the United States one minute and the next minute to the guy delivering the laundry.

"And he would have something interesting to say to each of them. And he would make the guy driving the laundry truck feel as important as the president.

"He exuded passion and compassion for his fellow man. He was so bright, yet so common."

Brown's brief comments triggered memories of my last meeting with Giamatti, one-on-one in his office, during the time Pete Rose was using the court system to delay the inevitable.

My daughter, Anndee, had written about Giamatti as a reporter for the Yale *Daily News*.

And when I prodded him about that unfortunate letter to that Ohio judge in behalf of Paul Janszen, he smiled and sighed, and said, "Now I know where Anndee got her questioning style."

It was a harpsichord moment, and he pretended not to watch me quiver with pride, busying himself with the ashes from still another cigarette.

He would have been proud of his son's memorable speech yesterday, sequined with humor, ablaze with love.

"Never argue with the umpire," young Giamatti boomed, recalling a backyard clinic in hitting, copying Bart's window-rattling baritone.

"Try to understand him. Remember, he has a rough job to do. He keeps and protects the laws of the game."

Froemming had scratched some notes on the back of an envelope during lunch, knowing he would be called upon to speak.

"You talk about love," Froemming said. "He gave love to everybody.

"He'd walk into our clubhouse and he'd talk to the clubhouse man, making him feel special.

"'And how are you, sir?' he'd ask him. 'Are these fellows treating you right?'

"Bart respected and loved us. It was something we've never had from anybody in the game before.

"His son talked about Bart as a teacher and he was that. Communication was never better between the umpires and the commissioner's office.

"And now he's gone. I miss Bart. I loved Bart."

Froemming is a tough, fiery guy, a good umpire. He thinks Giamatti wanted the umpires to know he cared about them because he was a law-and-order kind of guy.

He applauded Giamatti's desire to make the ballpark a calmer, safer place. And he understood Giamatti's willingness to swim against the permissive tide that is eroding our society.

"I want what's right," Froemming said. "That's the way I run my games. That's the way I run my life.

"We had an umpire whose son got involved with drugs. We could see it coming and I tried to talk to the guy about it.

"He said, 'Hey, everybody does it.'

"I can't stand that talk, peer pressure, everybody does it. That's absolute bleep.

"That's a weak cop-out, a cane, a crutch. All that permissiveness, that's the problem with our society."

The hymn, the eloquent speeches, the memories, had left Froemming gloomy. Others recalled episodes to chase the sadness.

"The All-Star Game in Oakland," writer Hal Bock said. "That was the year all those home runs were flying out of ballparks.

"Press conference in that huge hall behind home plate, first question from a radio guy in the back of the room.

"'Are the baseballs juiced?' the guy hollers.

"Giamatti never blinks. 'No more than I am, sir,' he said."

Ted Sizemore, ex-ballplayer, now an executive with Rawlings, told of the time he was summoned to New York by Giamatti.

Hurried to his office and found him there with umpire supervisor Ed Vargo and a man with an electric saw.

A suspicious bat had been confiscated from a player's locker and Giamatti wanted Sizemore to explain corking and how to detect it.

The carpenter sawed where Sizemore directed, and sure enough, the bat was corked.

Sizemore recalled Giamatti saying, "The general public doesn't have a lot of respect for the average big-leaguer's intelligence, but I am truly impressed by this much ingenuity."

Impressed and angry. You can be sure he did something about it, just as he did something about the sandpaper in Kevin Gross's glove and the pine tar in Jay Howell's mitt and the rule-shattering gambling of Pete Rose.

A. Bartlett Giamatti loved hustle and headfirst slides and crashing into catchers and dirty uniforms. But he loved good character even more.

And that was the name of yesterday's game.

Cepeda Deserving of Plaque in Hall

Philadelphia Daily News
July 9, 1993

THE KIDS WRIGGLED in the metal bleachers, but not out of boredom. The kids wriggled in the metal bleachers at 5th and Allegheny because the metal bleachers were hot enough to fry bacon.

It was 101 in the shade, and the kids wriggled inside their Puerto Rican Rookie League T-shirts, but the only sound you heard when Orlando Cepeda talked to them was the sizzle of skin against the metal bleachers at 5th and Allegheny.

"Why waste life, dealing with losers?" Cepeda challenged them. "Be with a winner.

"Life is based on effort. Nothing comes easy.

"I made a mistake. A huge mistake. It would be easy for me to say I didn't do it. I did it.

"I went to jail. For marijuana. I was dealing with the wrong people.

"I let the Puerto Rican people down. My mother suffered. All of my relatives suffered. I'm here today, when I could be in my air-conditioned room, telling you the danger of dealing with the wrong people."

Blunt, simple, in language they could understand. They listened, sitting raptly on those metal bleachers because Councilman Angel Ortiz had told them that Cepeda, along with Roberto Clemente, was one of the two greatest Puerto Rican players in history.

And they listened, because they could see his eyes glisten behind those aviator glasses, and they could hear the sincerity ripple through his words.

Cepeda made a mistake, a huge mistake. In 1975. For 160 pounds of marijuana. Did 10 months in jail, did two months at a halfway house in North Philly. There used to be a ballpark there.

He is on the Hall of Fame ballot next year for the 15th and final time. Are the writers who vote unforgiving? We know, from past experience, they can be unaware, uninformed, uninspired.

He will need 75 percent of the votes cast this winter. If he fails, there will be five years in limbo because a harsher, more conservative veterans committee studies his numbers, sniffs at that cloud.

He hit .300 or more in nine seasons, which is eight more times than Reggie Jackson, who will be inducted this year.

His lifetime average is .297. He hit 379 homers. Of all the eligible players who averaged .295 with 300 homers, he is the only one not in the Hall of Fame.

Guideline 4 has kept him out, the paragraph that comes with the ballot each year and talks about character, integrity and contributions to the game.

"Character, what does that mean?" Cepeda asked at Veterans Stadium, while the Giants hammered the Phillies.

The Giants are taking Cepeda on the road this season, a whistle-stop tour of America's ballparks, hoping that voters will get to meet the man and be convinced of his righteousness and thus his worthiness of being elected to the Hall of Fame.

Cepeda had gone from the ballfield at 5th and Allegheny to a Buddhist Center near Roosevelt Boulevard and now he was speaking of Buddhism and the way it has reshaped his life.

"It has changed me, 150 percent," he said. "It is the best thing that has happened to me.

"It has taught me to share. Sharing, that's best for you, for others.

"Today, those kids, those innocent faces. That is the best thing I do. Talk to them, tell them to stick together, to give back (to the community)."

Cepeda works with Sports Fans Against Substance Abuse, visits inner-city schools, participates in the Athletes Against AIDS program.

Does that sound like a man of character, of integrity?

"The Hall of Fame," he said, "that's very important to me. That is the ultimate for any baseball player.

"And I could use it to help other people. I could tell people, because you make a mistake, your life is not shot.

"You get into the Hall of Fame, the label changes, you get to go places, you have the stage, the platform."

He could humbly duck the question, but that is not his style. Why deceive and then regret not telling the truth?

"I've been through hell," he confessed. "I came close to taking my life.

"Out of jail, living in Los Angeles, no money, no name, no escape. You have fame, you have money, you think you're bigger than life.

"Some people make a mistake and nobody knows about it. In my case, I did it. I don't know why.

"Sometimes a human being needs to wake up. That woke me up. Through that, I have become a better person.

"I have been very lucky. I have gotten as many as 250 votes one year. But, now, it is out of my hands.

"I want to get there. It would be the biggest thing in my life. For me, for my family, for my country.

"You ask me how they should judge? I always felt they should judge based on what you do on the field.

"I think I did enough on the field.

"But the mistake I made, they always bring that up. I guess I have to live with it. I'm not afraid to talk about it.

"That is my message, that you can overcome anything. I've paid my dues, I've suffered the consequences."

When are the scales balanced? If the writers reject Cepeda once more, are they telling the kids who might be paying attention that in the voting game, you get only one strike and you're out?

It is a tough call. It is one thing to ask a baseball writer to decide hit or error, it is another to ask him to make moral judgments on a man he's never met, and in too many cases, has never seen play.

Cepeda was a splendid player, with power, with speed, with a lust for the game.

One kid in the scorching bleachers asked him how old he was.

"I'm 55, going on 35," he hedged, laughing.

His knees are 66, arthritic, creaky. But the rest of him is youthful, exuberant. He still loves jazz, good food, good friends.

You had to be there, in California, when he batted against Sandy Koufax in those stormy Giants-Dodgers games.

And you had to be there, 5th and Allegheny, 101 in the shade, when Orlando Cepeda talked to those kids about doing the right thing.

He likes what he sees now when he looks in the mirror. He would like it even more if in January he looks in the mirror and sees a Hall of Famer.

Do They Really Want to Tell It to the Judge?

Philadelphia Daily News
March 31, 1995

BEAUTIFUL, HUH? Baseball's fate to be decided by a 40-year-old woman who doesn't know Phil Rizzuto from mushroom risotto.

Couldn't happen to a nastier bunch of guys.

This morning, in Manhattan's U.S. District Court, judge Sonia Sotomayor will listen to arguments on whether to grant an injunction requested by the National Labor Relations Board, on the grounds that the owners did not bargain fairly with the players.

"I know nothing about this," she said, when the case landed in her court, "except what the common layperson reads in the *New York Times*."

If that innocent statement doesn't get things settled before Sunday's scheduled Mets-Marlins opener, nothing will.

What the common layperson reads in the *Times,* bless its solemn, gray pages, makes the owners look like a greedy, bumbling bunch of boobs and the players resemble the purest, noblest legion since "Up With People."

Can you imagine the testimony when Sotomayor tries to get a handle on this 232-day-old strike? Go ahead, imagine.

Judge: Just how many teams are there in the major leagues?

Owner: Your honor, there are 28 teams, plus the two new, expansion franchises that paid $130 million apiece to be part of the grand, old game.

Judge: Doesn't sound like an industry in trouble to me. How many of those 28 teams lost money last year?

Owner: Uh, your honor, uh, the accountants have not come up with a final analysis, what with the tax deadline approaching, and so on.

Judge: There's an H & R Block on the corner. Use it during lunch break. Meanwhile, how many players are on each team, and how much do they earn?

Player: There are 25 players on each team, your honor. The average salary is $1.2 million and the minimum wage is $109,000.

Judge: (Whistles) I thought the minimum wage was $5.25 an hour. The vital issue before me is whether the owners bargained fairly, and whether there was an impasse before the owners changed the work rules unilaterally. So how long have the negotiations been going on?

Owner: Since December 1992, your honor, but the players didn't come to the table for a long time.

Player: That was when the owners said a salary cap was etched in stone, your honor. It's un-American to put a lid on how much a skilled entertainer can earn, whether it's David Letterman or David Cone.

Judge: Who's David Cone? I know who David Letterman is, and I know the network pays him based on how many viewers tune in and how many sponsors are willing to buy commercial time. How are baseball salaries determined?

Player: Well, the player's agent negotiates with the team's general manager. If they can't agree, the player goes to arbitration. He submits a figure, the team submits a figure, and the arbitrator, usually some economics professor from Northwestern, picks one of the numbers, based on what other .260-hitting second basemen are making, usually around $2 million.

Owner: We'd like to get rid of that system, your honor, because we think it's unstable, unfair and un-American.

Judge: And if the player doesn't like the decision, is he free to go elsewhere, the way Letterman switched networks?

Owner: Uh, no, your honor, not until he's been in the major leagues for four years. At least that's our proposal for free agency. Then, he's free to sign with the highest bidder.

Player: Objection. Under the owners' proposal, if a team spends more than $44 million on players, it gets taxed 50 percent of every dollar over that. And that would discourage wonderful owners like George Steinbrenner from bidding on free agents.

Judge: Where would that tax money go?

Owner: It would go to help the small-market teams, the ones that don't have radio-TV contracts like Steinbrenner's. They couldn't just keep it. They would have to meet a minimum payroll number, so salaries would stay high.

Judge: Why not establish a free market and have everybody be a free agent every year?

Player: Noooo, your honor.

Judge: Well, then, why not share all the television and radio money? And give the visiting teams a bigger share of the gate?

Owner: That sounds like socialism, your honor. What would be the incentive to win a championship if every owner got an equal piece of the pie?

Judge: Well, I can see where it would be tough for Minnesota and Montreal to compete with New York and Los Angeles under the old system.

Player: Well, to tell the truth, your honor, Minnesota has been in more World Series lately than the Yankees. And Montreal, with the smallest payroll, had the best record when we hit the bricks.

Judge: So, let's see if I've got this straight. Owners want to draw fans and they want to have a winning team. Which explains why they are willing to pay some barely literate hooligan $6 million to hit a baseball.

The owners want the players to keep them from squandering their money that way, so they've asked them to go along with the tax on payrolls over $44 million.

Have the so-called impoverished owners shown signs of fiscal responsibility during the work stoppage?

Owner: Well, your honor, Seattle did sign Jay Buhner to a $15.5 million deal, but he's a fine player who has never been arrested for arson. And the Phillies signed Gregg Jefferies to a $20 million deal to play leftfield, a position he has never played before, so you can't compare him to other leftfielders.

Judge: Gregg Jefferies? Isn't he the whining wimp who wrote an open letter complaining about his Mets teammates? I remember reading it in the *Times*.

If I grant the injunction and the players go back to work, do the owners intend to lock them out, knowing they'd be liable for huge damages?

Owner: We would hope you won't grant the injunction. We're not sure what we'll do if you do. It is hard to get 21 owners to agree on anything. It was hard to get the owners to agree on how the replacement teams would be stocked.

Judge: Replacement teams, what are they?

Player: A bunch of scabs, your honor.

Owner: Objection. The replacement players are butchers, bakers, candlestick makers. We're prepared to field their dreams.

Judge: Boring movie. I can't believe Newt Gingrich wanted to lock all of you in a room to watch it. Me, I think you all sound like Forrest Gump. Remember, stupid is as stupid does.

Summer in the City

Philadelphia Daily News
April 9, 1997

I GREW UP POOR and unworldly in the East New York section of Brooklyn. All white, mostly Jewish neighborhood. Splendid playground three blocks away with handball courts and paddle-tennis courts and a basketball court with concrete benches where you sat, waiting your turn to take on winners.

Maybe because we were so poor and I was so unworldly, it's hard to remember what Brooklyn was like 50 years ago when Jackie Robinson shattered the color line.

I do remember that radio comics got laughs out of the mere mention of Brooklyn in those days, and outsiders thought we all pronounced it "thoid base" and "woik" and "boid. " The team was nicknamed "Dem Bums" and Willard Mullin made a living doing cartoons of a seedy character with ragged clothes and a dormant cigar butt moaning, "Wait 'til next year."

Me, I was a Giants fan. My friends were tolerant. Itzie was a Giants fan, too, because catcher Harry Danning was Jewish, and if he wasn't sure about pitcher Hal Schumacher, he was willing to give him the benefit of the doubt.

There wasn't that much to do in Brooklyn besides the Dodgers and maybe the Bushwicks, who played teams like the House of David, bearded guys. Fights at Sunnyside Gardens and later on at the Eastern Parkway Arena.

Ebbets Field was a great place to watch a ballgame, the fans so close to the action, Hilda Chester hanging over the leftfield wall clanging her cowbell and Shorty Larrieux leading the Dodgers "Sym-Phony" through the aisles during the seventh-inning stretch. The Abe Stark billboard in right-center reading, "Hit Sign, Win Suit." Homers that soared into Bedford Avenue. Predominantly white crowd. Brooklyn's blacks saved their baseball dollars for trips to the Polo Grounds, the Elite Giants against the Homestead Grays or the Pittsburgh Crawfords.

The Dodgers were lovable losers in the '40s. I was tempted to root for them when they signed NYU's Ralph Branca. But I loved Mel Ott and the Giants, even before Sid Gordon moved into the neighborhood.

We'd wait for Gordon after games at the Polo Grounds and ride home with him on the New Lots Avenue subway line, making awkward small talk.

Once, Itzie goaded me into showing him the deck of baseball cards I'd drawn in India ink on gray shirt cardboard. And he signed the one that showed him swinging the bat.

I was the only kid on the block who went to college. I was a junior at NYU, the Bronx campus, in '47. I read as many sports pages as I could and I marveled at Dan Parker in the *Mirror*, courageously taking on the Mob for its stranglehold on boxing.

But I can't recall any earnest crusade in the *Times* or the *Journal-American* or the *Herald-Tribune* or the *World-Telegram* for integrating baseball. Television was in its infancy. Talk radio hadn't been invented yet.

The rednecked reaction of some big-leaguers got skimpy play when Robinson was promoted to the Dodgers. I do remember Leonard, the African-American steward at the Student Union building, beaming at the news.

He talked to us, me and Kenny Lee, a devout Yankees fan, about Josh Gibson and Satchel Paige and how he was worried because he wasn't sure Robinson was the best of the black players he had seen and he wasn't sure Robinson had the gumption to stand up to the abuse he was bound to take.

He said that Robinson ran funny, pigeon-toed, but that maybe he was tough enough because he'd played football in college and he'd been in the Army at a time when it wasn't comfortable for blacks in the Army.

And then it happened, Opening Day against the Braves, Robinson playing first base. No protest marches, no celebratory parades. Plenty of empty seats in the ballyard, plenty of African-American faces in the stands.

And a bunch of us, on the corner that night, arguing only about whether Jackie Robinson could play, whether he could make it in the big leagues, whether Dixie Walker was so dumb he couldn't recognize that this guy could unhinge a pitcher with his speed, too dumb to accept Robinson as a teammate.

What did we know about bigotry, growing up poor and unworldly in Brooklyn 50 years ago?

Joe, It Wasn't as Easy as It Looked

Philadelphia Daily News
March 10, 1999

JOE DIMAGGIO made it look easy, gliding across the prairie that is centerfield at Yankee Stadium. It wasn't easy. It wasn't easy because it was Yankee Stadium, because it was New York, with nine newspapers then, because of the pin stripes on the uniform, as confining as prison bars if you're shy and intense.

Joe DiMaggio was shy and intense. He just made it look easy.

DiMaggio hoarded his privacy. Yet he married a showgirl named Dorothy Arnold first, and then years later, Marilyn Monroe, a sex goddess.

DiMaggio cared about the history of the game, the traditions. Yet he wore those garish Oakland uniforms when he went to work for Charlie Finley.

We will never learn what went sour in that marriage to Monroe because DiMaggio never collaborated on an authorized biography, nor did he cooperate with film projects. Just as we will never learn how he managed to smother the jitters raging inside him to make it look so easy, gliding across the prairie that is centerfield at Yankee Stadium.

All we have from that marriage of two very famous people is rumor and innuendo and the anecdote about Monroe cheered by the troops in Korea on a USO tour, telling DiMaggio, "You can't imagine what it was like."

And DiMaggio answering bluntly, "Oh, yes I can."

We do know that when Monroe died, under mysterious circumstances, it was DiMaggio who choreographed the funeral. And it was DiMaggio who sent roses to the gravesite three times a week for 20 years.

It is sad and it is comforting too, that DiMaggio shunned offers to share his secrets. He had earned his privacy, earned it by playing in 10 World Series, earned it by hitting .325 in his 13 seasons, earned it by driving in 1,537 runs, earned it by hitting safely in 56 consecutive games in 1941.

Was he ever envious of the millions the modern players are making? If he was, he could take solace from charging $3,995 for an autographed bat. Signed only 1,941 of them. Not one less, not one more. Signed them all in an elegant handwriting.

He was content to be introduced last at old-timers' games, and to insist that he be introduced as "America's greatest living ballplayer."

Was that a shot at the crotchety baseball writers who did not vote for him in his first two years of eligibility to the Hall of Fame?

Let others poke around trying to establish and explain his icon status. Ernest Hemingway tried. In a novel called "The Old Man and the Sea." Has a Cuban fisherman say, "I would like to take the great DiMaggio fishing. They say his father was a fisherman. Maybe he was as poor as we are and would understand."

Years later, Paul Simon wrote a song that was used in the movie "The Graduate." Had a plaintive line in it, "Where have you gone, Joe DiMaggio, a nation turns its lonely eyes to you."

DiMaggio didn't understand it. Wary, he thought it might be derogatory.

And now, a nation turns its lonely, sad eyes in his direction. Sports columnists tried to pry beneath that tortoise shell. Red Smith's last column ended with a reference to the Yankee Clipper. Smith wrote about "a longish period when my rapport with some who were less than great made me nervous.

"Maybe I was stuck on bad ballplayers. I told myself not to worry. Someday there would be another Joe DiMaggio."

It will be amazing if another DiMaggio surfaced. Bernie Williams had to have $12.5 million a year to keep working that same harsh prairie that is centerfield in Yankee Stadium. And Bernie Williams is no Joe DiMaggio.

It will be 10 times harder to make it look easy, 20 times harder to deal with the media mob, 30 times harder to fend off the agents swarming with endorsement deals.

It would be nice if no one ever hit safely in 57 games. Not even Doug Glanville, who would handle the media yammering with dignity, and read all he could about DiMaggio. Glanville is a rare flamingo in the alligator swamp that is baseball today.

Pete Rose came close and coped humorously with the spotlight. Turned nasty when it ended, though, grumbling about the pitches Gene Garber threw to snuff out the streak after 44 games in 1978.

In contrast, DiMaggio said, "Ken Keltner [Cleveland's third baseman] was a little tough on me tonight." And then he borrowed $18 from shortstop Phil Rizzuto while walking back to the hotel from the ballpark. Vanished inside a tavern, to relax, alone.

DiMaggio was a loner. Does that explain why he was a folk hero into his 80s? Did Americans cherish his aloofness, regarding it as a quiet counterpoint to today's noisy athletes?

Did he represent the American Dream, a high school dropout, son of a fisherman, who went on to greatness on the ballfield, and a marriage, however brief, to the sexiest woman on the planet?

Maybe it was those awkward yet convincing commercials for the Mr. Coffee gadget? Maybe Americans sensed that here was a guy who pumped his own gas, shined his own shoes, kept his thoughts to himself? Maybe the zealous fans knew that DiMaggio had to haggle for a raise the year after he led the league with 46 homers and batted .346.

He lived in Florida, and when HBO produced a documentary that included some warts, DiMaggio made a rare TV appearance during a World Series broadcast. To set the record straight?

I will always remember sitting in the dugout with DiMaggio before an old-timers' game in Washington. He was being polite if not expansive. And when the inevitable line about his graceful outfielding came up, he said firmly, "They made it sound like it was easy. It wasn't. It was hard."

He had taken himself out of one of his final games. And maybe that's why he was a folk hero into his 80s. Taken himself out when he couldn't run down a pop fly he used to catch in stride, without a deep breath.

And when he announced his retirement, he said simply, "I'm not Joe DiMaggio anymore."

The rest of us never knew what DiMaggio was really like. But DiMaggio knew. And that's all that counted.

Mantle Documentary Hits a Home Run

Philadelphia Daily News
July 11, 2005

MICKEY MANTLE drank too much. Slept too little. Lived for today because he thought he only had a fistful of tomorrows. All that booze destroyed his liver. When the doctors were rummaging around inside him, transplanting a new one, they found a cluster of aggressive cancer cells they had no cure for.

If he lived recklessly, he was determined to die gracefully.

Mantle, pale and gaunt, looked into the television lens and rasped, "I would like to say to the kids out there, to take a good look. You talk about a role model. . . . [D]on't be like me!

"God gave me a body, ability to play baseball. . . . [I]t was just wasted. I was given so much. I blew it."

It's all there, triumph and tragedy, in HBO's terrific documentary, "Mantle," which debuts on Wednesday. The handsome, boyish face, sagging into lumpiness, and then a dry, parchment look.

"You could see his whole life in his face," someone says.

Maybe "I blew it" doesn't rank right up there with Lou Gehrig's "I consider myself the luckiest man on the face of the earth," but it ought to be celebrated for its honesty, its earthiness. It's an eloquent message to kids, who too often are seduced by the sizzle while ignoring the substance of an athlete's life.

Mantle played for the New-new York-york Yankees-yankees, and perhaps the architects will find a way to duplicate that distinctive Yankee Stadium echo in the new ballyard they're going to build in the Bronx.

Played 18 seasons, went to the World Series 12 times. Hit 536 homers, was voted Most Valuable Player three times.

Came up from Joplin, Mo., as a teenager and was handed No. 6. The Yankees save the single-digit numbers for guys with a special aura, special talent. Babe Ruth was No. 3, Gehrig 4, Joe DiMaggio 5.

Awed by the big city, overmatched by big-league pitching, Mantle struggled. Demoted to Kansas City, the slump persisted, his confidence sagged. His dad, Mutt, drove up to see him, jolting him out of his despair, threatening to put him to work in the zinc mines back home in Commerce, Okla.

The scolding worked. Mantle started hitting, was recalled.

This time, wearing No. 7, he prospered, even though DiMaggio, playing his final season in centerfield, went half of Mantle's rookie year, 1951, without talking to the kid. And then DiMaggio hollered "I got it" on a fly ball to right-center and Mantle pulled up awkwardly and tore the cartilage in his right knee stepping in a drainage hole.

His father wound up in the New York hospital bed alongside Mantle, dying of Hodgkin's disease, which had claimed two of Mickey's uncles at 35. Mickey was sure he was going to die young.

"And that fear," Billy Crystal says in the film, "drove him to despair, drove him to the bottle, to, 'Who gives a bleep. . . . I'm a dead man.'"

All of which led to legendary binges, to nightclub brawls and late-night crawls. Teammate Whitey Ford, bless his heart, refuses to rake through the ashes of those stories. "They've all been told 100 times," Ford says bluntly. "And I have nothing to add to it."

It's not that the Mantle family is squeamish about the carousing. Two of his four sons talk openly about what it was like, growing up as drinking buddies of their famous father, because that was the only way he thought he could bond with the boys.

"I was living with five active alcoholics," sighs Mantle's widow, Merlyn. "I was a crazy lady. I had four kids and Mick."

Mantle quit before the '69 season, saying bluntly, "I can't play anymore." Not surprisingly, Mantle was unprepared for life after baseball. He took an Atlantic City casino job and was banned from baseball for a while. One son, Billy, died at 36 of a heart attack. Another son, Danny, checked into the Betty Ford Clinic after 17 years of alcohol abuse. Mantle decided to try sobriety.

Bob Costas, who idolized Mantle, interviewed him after Mantle had gotten more encouraging letters than any previous patient at the clinic.

"I hope people, at the end," he told Costas, "will say, 'He turned out all right. . . . I'm proud I named my son Mickey.'"

Merlyn wrote and told him how much he meant to her "all those years." He spent his final, frail days campaigning for organ-donor awareness. He died in August, 10 years ago, a very old 63. He turned out all right. People were proud they had named their son Mickey.

The Reel Richie: A Baseball Life Worth Reliving

Philadelphia Daily News
April 3, 2008

RICHIE ASHBURN has been gone from the Phillies broadcast booth for 10 seasons and the ballclub is still scrambling to replace him. Not that they haven't tried. They've brought in a fistful (OK, a handful) of new guys, and some of them even got along with the holdovers.

What would Whitey have said about the fourth-inning shuffle? "Hard to believe, Harry." The seventh-inning handoff? "Boys, we may have to put a revolving door on the booth." The guy doing color, wearing a Phillies warmup jacket, in the stands while the game is in progress? "Oh, brother!!!"

Ashburn used to needle Garry Maddox, wondering how Maddox felt being "the second-best centerfielder in Phillies history."

And if Garry had asked coyly, "Who's the best?" Whitey would have said softly, "You're lookin' at him brother." Can you imagine the one-liners he'd rattle off, between puffs on that mahogany pipe, about starting a season with 11 pitchers and just as many broadcasters?

It's all there, the wit and wisdom of Ashburn, captured lovingly by Dan Stephenson, in a feature-length film called "Richie Ashburn: A Baseball Life." It debuts April 14 as part of the Philadelphia Film Festival, and will be available on DVD April 22.

Ashburn genuinely hated pitchers, and that comes through loud and clear. "They cheat," Whitey says. "They spit on the ball. They cut the ball. They're not a group with very good character. Never trust a pitcher. I wouldn't want my daughter to marry a pitcher."

The only other aspect of baseball he hated more than hurlers was having one bunt with one out and a man on first and third. "You're saying to the opposition," Ashburn snarled, "'Here, let me hand you the second out.'"

He loved the fans, and the fans loved him back. They loved his honesty, his passion for the game. They loved his irreverence. They loved the give-and-take rapport with Harry Kalas, two guys having fun broadcasting a game that ought to be fun.

That infamous game that started at 1:26 A.M.? Whitey starts it out by needling Kalas about doing his best work at that hour of the day, "the shank of the evening."

Plus, he had the taproom cred, because he had played here, with distinction. They knew what they had even when some songwriter wrote a ballad about Willie, Mickey and The Duke. Yo, Ashburn led the league in hitting twice, rapped out more hits in the 1950s than anybody, more than Mays, Mantle, Snider. Centerfield at Connie Mack Stadium, that's where triples went to die.

And that's what makes the film special, home movies of Ashburn, as a kid, growing up in Tilden, Neb. Signs with the Phillies for a $3,500 bonus and they send him to Utica, where manager Eddie Sawyer converts him from catcher to centerfielder despite the impassioned squawks of Richie's dad, Neil.

The rest is gaudy history, the Phillies ending a miserable decade of ineptitude by winning a pennant on the last day of the 1950 season, Ashburn snuffing a Dodgers rally by throwing out Cal Abrams at the plate. "A routine play," Ashburn said years later, baffled by the fame it brought him.

The Mets plucked him from the Cubs in the expansion draft. He hit .306 for them and then retired because they lost 120 games and he hated that, even more than he hated pitchers. He liked to tell the story about getting a boat for being named MVP of that woeful team and how the boat sank. It was a metaphor really, for the way losing drowned his enthusiasm for the game, and why he quit after hitting .306.

He pondered politics and then opted for the broadcast booth because you can't kiss babies with a lit cigar in your mouth. He wrote a sharp, opinionated column for the *Bulletin* and then the *Daily News*. And he wondered aloud whether he'd become the first guy to be rejected by the Hall of Fame in three categories, player, announcer, writer.

He got to Cooperstown the same year Michael Jack Schmidt was inducted and the town was awash in a sea of red. Ashburn delivered a straight-from-the-heart acceptance speech, thanked the fans and called it "the greatest day of my life."

The fans, thick as ants on the Cooperstown pasture, cheered loud enough to shimmer the surface of Oswego Lake. It's all there, in the movie, and if you loved Richie Ashburn, you will love seeing it all again.

Even Bumbling Bud Couldn't Rain on This City's Celebration

Philadelphia Daily News
October 31, 2008

BASEBALL IS a beautiful game, as colorful and unpredictable as a butterfly's flight. Alligator tough, too. It has to be, to survive and thrive in spite of the knuckleheads running the sport.

Celebrate the city's first major championship in 25 years today. Celebrate the second championship in Phillies history today, hug strangers, cheer yourself hoarse, strut, swagger, maybe even shed a tear, even if there is no crying in baseball.

And then, after the last shreds of confetti have been swept from the streets, the last beer bottle recycled, the last lamp post climbed, pause, sigh, and thank your lucky stars that a bumbling, fumbling, stumbling commissioner did not snatch this triumph away from this title-parched city.

So many questions to answer, so many answers to question. How could the Las Vegas bookmakers, with calculators for hearts, know what is fair and just in baseball when Bud Selig did not?

If you bet on the Phillies in Game 5 on Monday night, you collected, even though the game was suspended with the score tied at 2–2, bottom of the sixth. In Vegas if the home team is leading after 4½ innings, the game is official for betting purposes. Go past the fifth inning, an inning must be completed or the score reverts back to the last completed inning.

That's common sense. But Selig had decided, in advance, that Game 5 would go the full nine innings if they had to wait until Thanksgiving to complete it. And then, with the winds howling and the rain pelting down and the infield a treacherous swamp, he waited until the Rays sloshed out the tying run, top of the sixth.

And then he suspended the game, without giving the Phillies the chance to bat under the same wretched conditions. And then he threw baseball's weather forecasters under the pontoons, along with the valiant groundskeeper. And, oh, yeah, he somehow forgot to tell Joe Buck and Tim McCarver, doing the game on Fox, about his ruling, designed to protect baseball's tawdry image.

Is this the same commissioner who allowed the entire 1994 World

Series to be canceled? And now he's worried about an awkward ending, a rain-shortened clinching game?

It's nonsense, theater of the absurd. You play World Series games in late October in the east, you're asking for trouble from Mother Nature. Rain, snow, sleet, gloom of night. You ignore competent weather forecasters predicting heavy rain and start the game, that's double jeopardy. You start games at 8:37, that's greedy, that's dumb. Plus, you've wiped out your under-16 audience.

Do you think Fox cares? If you started games earlier, could you still show those putrid but profitable beer commercials? Would you lose some viewers west of the Rockies? Bottom line sets the starting time. The commissioner might not like it, but the owners love the obscene fee Fox pays for the rights and that's the name of that game.

Why was the umpiring so shabby? Because Major League Baseball has a basic agreement with the umpires that a skilled umpire cannot work the World Series 2 years in a row. What sport mandates that its best officials cannot work the showcase games?

Shorten the season, play scheduled doubleheaders on Memorial Day, July 4, Labor Day. Start weekend postseason games in midafternoon. A World Series inning must be completed to count. Otherwise, the score reverts back to the previous inning.

Put up $5,000 a man and play the All-Star Game winner-take-all, and you'll see intensity return to the game. Alternate homefield advantage in the World Series from year to year.

Let the players decide the outcome of the games. That's when you find heroes at the bottom of the lineup, that's when Chase Utley throws a runner out at the plate with a memorable play. That's when Charlie Manuel sticks with a hitless Pat Burrell until he doubles, and then pinch-runs for him and the pinch-runner scores the winning run. That's when you get a World Series to cherish.

That's when Cole Hamels is voted Most Valuable Player and never really whines about the wretched conditions on Monday night. Maybe because his wife once appeared on "Survivor," where they eat scorpions and sleep in trees and build rafts to get across raging rivers.

Whatever. Enjoy the championship feeling. Celebrate, you've waited long enough.

Rose Still Showing His Character

Philadelphia Daily News
September 10, 2010

PETE ROSE wants to know, what kind of a guy was Ty Cobb?

He knows the answer, he just wants you to think about it before you ask him whether he belongs in baseball's Hall of Fame. He knows that there's a fistful of bigots and braggarts in the Hall of Fame, some drunks and skunks, cheaters and wife-beaters.

So he wonders out loud why there isn't room for one more rule-breaking scoundrel who bet on baseball and then denied it for 14 years?

"The Hall of Fame is all about stats," Rose said recently in a long, revealing interview with Graham Bensinger. "I know a lot of guys in the Hall of Fame and they're not a bunch of altar boys. If you think I'm the only guy with a skeleton in his closet, then you're hissing up a rope.

"What kind of guy was Ty Cobb? What kind of guy was Babe Ruth? I can name three or four players in the Hall of Fame who spent time in a penitentiary."

Rose knows Cobb's stats: a .366 lifetime average, 4,189 hits, 2,246 runs and 897 stolen bases. He also knows that Cobb got 222 out of 226 votes in the very first Hall of Fame election, more than Ruth, more than Honus Wagner, more than Walter Johnson.

On Sunday, Rose will step onto the Cincinnati Reds' field to be honored for the 25th anniversary of when he broke Cobb's hit record. It is only the third time he has participated in an MLB event since he was banned in 1989.

"Character was never mentioned, back then," Jim Bunning growled during a recent visit to Citizens Bank Park to honor Roy Halladay for his perfect game. "Pete doesn't belong in the Hall of Fame because he's a convicted felon and there are no convicted felons in the Hall of Fame."

Whoops. Maybe Rose can call Bunning and name those ex-cons for him. (The issue may soon become moot when twice-convicted George Steinbrenner gets enshrined.)

If Pete calls, Bunning can then tell Rose about the current guideline that says voting shall be based on character, integrity and contributions to the game. He might even tell Pete his chances of getting approved by the veterans committee are slim and none and that Slim has just left town.

Pete, apparently, would take his chances.

"My friends know what kind of player I was," Rose said. "My teammates know, my fans know, all my managers know what kind of player I was. I don't need a Hall of Fame plaque to prove that to them."

In case you've been living in Botswana for the last 2 decades, the skeleton in Rose's closet is 10 feet tall and ominous, an indefinite suspension for betting on baseball while managing the Reds.

"I was wrong, I got caught," Rose says. "Most people are like me, 'Get over it!' I didn't break up the Beatles. I didn't shoot JFK."

It may be time for Rose to update that line. He can point out that he didn't torture dogs, he didn't snort cocaine, recite a whole laundry list of crimes he did not commit.

What he did do was shatter Rule 21, thou shalt not bet on baseball. They post it in every clubhouse. Prominently. Rose told Bensinger he did it because he's a competitor and he needed something "extra" when his playing days ended.

Never mind that he could have taken up golf, or backgammon, or ballroom dancing. He chose betting on baseball and he ended 14 years of denial when he confessed in a book. And if people think that's dumb and greedy, he's got news for them.

Rose says he confessed his gambling to Bud Selig a year before the book came out. Mike Schmidt brokered a meeting with the commish and Rose told Selig everything. Says he left the meeting confident he was going to get reinstated, and "then something happened."

Selig, in the twilight of his dim days as commissioner, has given the Reds permission to honor Rose on the anniversary of his breaking Cobb's hit record.

You're not gonna believe this, but Rose couldn't make it on the actual date (tomorrow), because he has a previous commitment at a casino. So much for reconfiguring his life, which is what Bart Giamatti asked him to do.

Ken Burns, who grinds out those long documentaries on baseball, says, "I absolutely believe Pete Rose should be in the Hall of Fame. If you exclude Rose, you have to exclude many other people beginning with Babe Ruth and Ty Cobb and others whose behavior would not stand the test of our current moral standards."

Burns recently suggested that they wait until Rose dies, so that he doesn't get to experience the joy of being inducted. Now that is cold!

What Rose accomplished as a player made him a first-ballot Hall of Famer. He belongs, and not because there are a fistful of scoundrels already enshrined.

Maybe they should scrap the pious guideline about character and integrity because they're not going to evict Cobb or Ruth or Gaylord Perry, who wrote a book bragging about breaking the spitball rules.

It took a while, but Rose confessed. And now he says he's sorry and that the one thing in his life he wishes he could change was betting on baseball. His plaque can become a teaching moment at Cooperstown if it includes the part about gambling and the long suspension.

Oh, and one other statistic that Rose may not know:

When Cobb died, only four, count 'em, four, baseball people showed up at his funeral.

Dick Allen Belongs in Hall of Fame

Philadelphia Daily News
February 15, 2015

DICK ALLEN LED the entire cockeyed world of baseball in OPS-plus for 10 years, from 1964 to 1973. His number was 165, higher than Henry Aaron, higher than Willie McCovey, higher than Frank Robinson, Harmon Killebrew, Willie Stargell, Roberto Clemente and Willie Mays.

Dominate any phase of the game for 10 years, pitching or hitting or slugging, and you oughta be in the Hall of Fame. Allen is not in the Hall of Fame. The other seven guys are.

Philadelphia's City Council, which can't always agree that today is Tuesday, unanimously passed a resolution last week urging the committee that's going to nominate overlooked players who played in the Golden Era, from 1946 to '72, to consider Allen.

The resolution was sponsored by Councilman Jim Kenney. Kenney remembers being taken to the ballpark by his father, remembers seeing Allen scrawl "Boo" in the infield dirt. That would have been 1969, when Allen had heard enough booing, dodged enough missiles playing the outfield with his batting helmet on, to sulk his way out of town.

"He was our Jackie Robinson," Kenney said. "Robinson was under orders to not respond to the taunts. Allen came along a lot later and spoke his mind."

Speaking your mind shouldn't keep you out of the Hall of Fame. Not speaking to the media, that shouldn't keep you out. Not when Steve Carlton and Eddie Murray are in. Not when your OPS-plus is higher than Aaron and Stargell and Mays.

OPS, that's a sabermetric abbreviation for on-base percentage plus slugging. OPS-plus, that factors in the ballpark you played in and the league you played in. Figure that 100 is average, 150 is excellent, 165 is superstar. Case closed.

You can't argue baseball without involving those decimal-point guys and their cockamamie equations and their baffling abbreviations, WAR, WHIP, OPS-plus. Bill James is their godfather, and Bill James once wrote that Allen was so disruptive that he cost his team more games than anyone in the entire cockeyed world of baseball. Said Allen was the second-most controversial player in history, right behind Rogers Hornsby.

Bill James was a snot-nosed, 15-year-old in 1964, when Allen hit .318, scored 125 runs, drove in 91, kept slugging in September when some of his older teammates gagged and spit up a 6½-game lead with 12 to play.

Smacked 29 homers that season, some of them over the Coca-Cola sign atop the roof at Connie Mack Stadium, which is why he also scrawled "Coke" in the infield dirt in '69, the year he sulked his way out of town.

How in the name of Pythagoras did Bill James get to know Allen well enough to figure out an equation that made him so cancerous in the clubhouse that he cost his team so many games? Times tardy, plus times showing up with Heineken on his breath, multiplied by time spent with the grounds crew instead of schmoozing with the media, plus games spent dressing in an equipment room?

"Everyone knows he liked the occasional libation," Mark Carfagno said that day in City Council. Carfagno, whose nickname is Froggy, and who sings Sinatra songs with a band and works the PA system at high school games, talks that way.

He was part of that grounds crew, and he is leading the last-ditch drive to get Allen to Cooperstown, while crediting Dick Allen Jr. as the catalyst. Mainly because they are trying to squeeze an endorsement from the Phillies, and Froggy left the franchise on a contentious note.

Carfagno can recite the numbers from memory, the 351 homers, the 1,119 RBI, the seven All-Star Games, on and on, enough stats to melt a sabermetrician's cold heart.

He has a squadron of people gathering endorsements from former teammates, from stars of that era. He brought a fascinating muddle of Allen fans to City Council that day, a stat guy who played with Allen in Wampum, the former home dugout security guy, a woman who cooked meatballs for Allen and asked him to hit a home run for her and he hit two that day.

Carfagno knows the numbers are strong enough. What he focuses on is buffing Allen's image 50 years down the rocky road. "Remember a kid named Rick Bosetti?" he rasps.

"Got called up, got put into a game as a pinch-runner. Gets picked off. Sits, and then gets used again, pinch-runner. Boom, gets picked off again. Kid comes up the dugout ramp crying his eyes out.

"Dick sees him, wraps his arm around him, takes him in the back, to an equipment room. Sits the kid on a bench and pulls up a chair, and stays there till 2 in the morning, consoling the kid.

"Next day, there's a story in the paper about Dick Allen leaving the ballpark early. Crazy! Dick don't say a word. Don't defend himself. That's the kind of guy he was."

Allen stays aloof, while Froggy and his friends poke around in the ashes of his career, battling lottery odds to get their hero into the Hall of Fame. City Council believes he belongs. So do I.

PART II
Horse Racing

Introduction

HORSE RACING, AT ITS CORE, is a sport for dreamers. The economics are daunting, the races dangerous, the chance for significant success a long shot. Yet the people in it keep coming back dawn after dawn, week after week, year after year.

It was that striving that so appealed to Stan: the story of the unknown trainer with a chance to win the Kentucky Derby, the old jockey trying to recapture glory that was once his, the owner with no background in the sport who somehow came up with a horse that could outrun all the blue bloods.

Stan could tell their stories so brilliantly because he was so curious about their backgrounds, so empathetic when asking questions, so smart in anticipating openings and getting to the essence of his subjects. Gaining trust is critical for any writer, and Stan had the almost unparalleled ability to make interviews into conversations. He was so prepared and knew so much about so many subjects that one thought led to another, and, soon enough, a framework for a story had evolved in which the writing would flow from what he had learned to what he shared with his readers.

It was always the people around the horses who made his stories come to life, but Stan also appreciated the magnificent animals that could run twice as fast as humans. Stan was there for Secretariat and Ruffian in the 1970s. In 1985, when he was covering horse racing exclusively, he grabbed hold of the Spend a Buck story that really began one April Saturday night in Cherry Hill, New Jersey, and would not let go.

Stan especially loved the Triple Crown, and I will always treasure the conversations we shared each spring when all the top three-year-olds arrived in Louisville for the Derby and proceeded to work their way through Baltimore and New York for the Preakness and Belmont Stakes. He wasn't at the big races anymore, but he still followed them with the rare passion that made him such a legendary writer and will live on forever in the stories he told and how he told them.

Turcotte: The Man Who Rides Superhorse

Philadelphia Daily News
June 11, 1973

RON TURCOTTE won the eighth race at Belmont Park Saturday. The horse paid $2.20, the 2–5 Exacta paid $35.20. People who bet the horse cheered. Even people who didn't bet the horse cheered.

Turcotte posed for pictures in the chaos of the winner's circle and did a brief bit on teevee. Then he scurried off, unbuttoning the blue-and-white checkerboard silks while he scurried.

Then Ron Turcotte came back and rode in the ninth race. He rode a four-year-old colt trained by Elliott Burch that hadn't run since March, when he was a distant ninth. This time, the horse finished a winded seventh.

The eighth race was the Belmont Stakes, $125,000 added, third jewel in the Triple Crown. Secretariat won by 31 lengths, in record time (2:24), ninth horse in history to win the Kentucky Derby, Preakness and Belmont, the first since 1948.

It was a magnificent performance that mauled the senses, the copper colored horse reaching out with those powerful strides right to the end, Turcotte glancing disdainfully over his left shoulder, surveying the rubble of the field.

It called for champagne and kisses and flowers and yips of delight and hugs and laughter. But Ron Turcotte was too busy changing into the grey-and-yellow silks he wore in the ninth race, mile-and-a-sixteenth on the grass, for three-year-olds and upward which had not won three races other than maiden or claiming.

Ron Turcotte was trying to tell us something. About horse racing. About life. Words come home to Turcotte. He is one of 13 kids, raised in the Canadian forests, a tough wiry little lumberjack before finding his way to the racetrack.

"There was no way I'd skip the ninth race" Turcotte explained afterwards in the hollow jockey's quarters. "The man (Burch) expected me to ride. . . . [T]hat's why he put me on the horse. . . . [T]here's responsibility involved. Besides, the man has put me on some real good horses through the years."

A guy catches the winning touchdown pass in the Super Bowl he doesn't rush right out to play a night game for the Pittstown Firebirds.

But racing is different. For every day you sniff the roses, there are 50 days where the aroma is something vastly different.

"I don't feel I'm better than anyone," Turcotte tried to explain, while guys prodded him in search of superlatives. "I've been lucky to get on that kind of horse. Anybody could have rode this horse and done the same thing."

Maybe, maybe not. But nobody had done what Turcotte had done for 25 years and people wanted to know how it felt. "Like a dream," Turcotte said.

A dream? Was it a dream Turcotte dared dream when he was an apprentice jock? "No," he said sharply. "I don't think ahead like that.

"I feel this way, you don't get too high on anything . . . and you don't get too low when something goes wrong, to where you want to drop everything and quit. I take every day, day by day.

"I've had my ups and downs. I've been taken off good horses. Same way as other riders been taken off good horses."

In the nerve-frazzling world of the racetrack, a jockey is subject to the whims of the owners and trainers ready to pin too much blame on the rider when the horse loses and dole out too little credit when the horse wins.

Turcotte accepts that as a fact of racing life. "The horse was on his own," he said, summing up the incredible race Secretariat had run.

"We went for the lead. . . . [T]hat's as good a place as any," he said. "The other horse (Sham) was alongside me. He (Lafitte Pincay) had a good hold. I had a good hold.

"What surprised me was the other horse was finished so early. We didn't go five-eighths and he disappeared."

The only race left was against the clock. How did it feel to be 30 in front in the stretch?

"Com-FORT-able," Turcotte said, reverting to the Canadian pronunciation. "But he might bobble. . . . [A]nything can happen. . . . [Y]ou can't relax.

"Me, I'm usually relaxed. I don't ride tense. If you do, the horse feels it too."

It was an hour after the race and the writers were still jiggling with excitement. Turcotte displayed all the emotion of a teevee repairman. It is the kind of icy temperament owners and trainers look for in riders.

"I glanced over at the teletimer," Turcotte said, "and I saw how fast we'd gone six furlongs, so I had rode him the last 10 jumps, going after the record."

Secretariat, the super horse, destroyed the record. Turcotte, the relaxed rider, had been able to read the little neon teletimer lights, going by at 40 miles an hour with 69,000 people screeching at him.

Turcotte allowed us just one peek inside that armor he has built around his emotions. "Sure, I was nervous this week," he confessed. How did it show, someone asked swiftly?

"My heart beat sometimes," he said without a semblance of a smile. That's what the man said. Not "my heart beat faster sometimes" or "my heart skipped a beat sometimes."

Maybe that's the way you have to be to ride a Triple Crown winner, stoic, nerveless, humble. On Saturday, Secretariat was magnificent. The jockey didn't do a bad job either.

Ruffian Takes Tragic Last Stride

Philadelphia Daily News
July 7, 1975

RUFFIAN ALWAYS LEADS. You could look it up. All those "ones" in the Racing Form. One, one, one, one. Ten races, 10 ones in the charts. Always on the lead after a quarter of a mile. Always.

This time, Foolish Pleasure broke on top. Just the two of them, spurting out of the starting gate, a half-mile away, tiny toy-like figures at that distance, stirring little puffs of sand.

Foolish Pleasure in front? That is not the way the colt had run in the past. Braulio Baeza urged him on. Baeza, the solemn jockey with posture like a "one," and the face like an inscrutable mask.

Baeza, who detested Frank Whiteley, the trainer of Ruffian. Had he somehow transmitted that hatred to the horse beneath him? Was he going to find out just how much spirit Ruffian owned in the first quarter of a mile, test her, push her, prod her, look her in the eye and measure the size of her heart?

They came hurtling down that straightaway together, perilously close. Ruffian surged even with the colt and rushed ahead. She always led. The charts said so. Something deep inside that huge black filly said so.

And then it happened. "I heard a snap," jockey Jacinto Vasquez would say afterwards. "It sounded just like when you break a stick.

"I had about a length (lead) at that point. The other horse was on my horse's rump. She was running very comfortable. I had a lot of hold. My instructions were to go as fast as I had to.

"She didn't give no warning. Lucky I had a lot of hold or I could have gone down."

Baeza knew at once. "My horse was running the way I wanted him to at that point," he said afterwards. "I hears something snap and I knew what happened."

The Great Match Race was over. Over before it had gone a half-mile. What was going to be a golden day for racing turned the color and texture of ashes.

Ruffian, undefeated in 10 races, maybe the finest filly ever, lurched to her right, thumping into the colt. Two more drunken steps. Then Vasquez dismounted.

Foolish Pleasure sped on. Baeza shot a glance past his left shoulder.

The colt rushed on, the adrenalin raging inside him. "Geez," jockey Angel Cordero said, in awe, "he went six furlongs in 1:08 by his-SELF."

Six furlongs in 1:08 3–5, and then the lonely gallop to the finish line, completing the mile and a quarter in 2:02 4–5 to hesitant cheers. The crowd of 50,764 peered toward the backstretch, where a bulky green horse ambulance chugged towards the injured filly.

This is not what CBS-TV had in mind when it contrived the Great Match Race. All that dough, most of the $350,000 purse, with another $50,000 to the owners of Master Derby. NOT to run. All that battle of the sexes hoopla, even though the filly was bigger, sturdier than the colt.

Foolish Pleasure was not unbeaten. He had won only one of the Triple Crown races. It was not a match made in racing heaven, but a duel set up in some Madison Avenue hell.

They got the proper backdrop. Clouds the color of puce, according to their commentator. Jagged bolts of lightning. Air thick with mist, ominous, foreboding.

They took Ruffian back to barn 34, led her off the ambulance, and propped her up while they swabbed the blood away and changed the transparent inflatable plastic cast.

She seemed to whimper helplessly. Mrs. Stuart A. Janney, wife of the filly's owner, patted her head gently. Tears clouded her eyes. She crumpled a program in her restless hands.

"She shattered both sesamoids in her right leg," Dr. Manuel Gilman, the examining vet said. "She'll be saved if at all possible."

How did it happen? "Just a bad step she took," Dr. Gilman explained, his arms bloodied. "Nobody can explain it."

A bad step. At 37 miles an hour. Crash 1,125 pounds on an ankle as flimsy as your wrist . . . [and] if it is turned the wrong way, it will shatter. The sound, says the rider, is like a stick breaking.

Why? Maybe Ruffian hurt herself hurtling down the long straightaway, an untested portion of the racing strip? The other alternative was to start the race on the clubhouse turn and Whitely had squelched that.

Maybe they hardened the racing strip too much, grinding it to Indianapolis firmness to ensure fast time? Who knows? Match races were designed to decide who had the best horse, me-against-you, winner-take-all.

That was before television sank its vampire fangs into sports. There are gaps to be filled on Sunday afternoons. Rig up a girl-versus-boy race and make the pot too sweet to resist. And if it turns out to be Evel Knievel versus Snake River Canyon, that's show biz.

Racing biz is not like show biz. Even if CBS did run that dopey segment of old movies as a teaser to the Great Match Race, Mickey Rooney, Pat O'Brien, Shirley Temple and Barry Fitzgerald burring all over Seabiscuit. Ugh.

"Every time you saddle one, you hope they come back in one piece," said Leroy Jolley, the trainer of Foolish Pleasure. He had a victory that was drum hollow.

"With horses that run this hard it's a risk you run. They throw all they have into it. And if it kills them, it kills them. You're always sick when you see something like this happen.

"It could have just as easily happened to me. It has in the past. I feel my horse could have beaten her anyway, and I'll always feel that way. It's a tough game and you don't play it in short pants."

In short pants. Or with empty pockets. Or with your heart on your sleeve. Horses are fragile. The best ones will give you everything they have. And sometimes, when they reach for everything they have, they take a bad step and shatter those fragile ankle bones.

"They'll have to be awful lucky to save her life," said Vasquez at twilight. "But they (the vets) can do great things. She's a very smart filly and she'll cooperate."

Smart and swift and courageous. Maybe too determined for her own good. She could not endure having another horse in front of her at the quarter-pole, so she dug in harder and took that tragic false step.

The Great Match Race did not break her heart. Just her right front leg. But horses cannot fathom that excruciating pain. They cannot support themselves on three legs.

They had to destroy Ruffian last night. It is not a game for people in short pants. But the little boy in all of us cries at the sad death of this great big horse.

This Horse Has a Shadow of a Chance

Philadelphia Daily News
November 7, 1984

DENNIS DIAZ sold his Florida insurance agency, and he needed something to do with his time and his money, so he bought some race horses.

Heard about a guy in Paris, Ky., with some horses for sale. Saw this herd of skittish thoroughbreds thrashing around in the pasture and picked out a lovable runt named Spend a Buck, because he liked the slick way the colt ducked out of harm's way behind the bigger, stronger yearlings.

Paid $12,500 for him. Never got to meet the previous owner, who was off dodging a posse of creditors and perhaps the sheriff, too. Turned the little colt over to Cam Gambolati, who had been training horses for a couple of months.

Spend a Buck got bigger and bigger and Gambolati's dreams started reaching for the sky. Sort of like the magic seeds in "Jack and the Beanstalk."

"This," Gambolati said eagerly, "is a real Cinderella story."

Cinderella? Did Cinderella have to pay $120,000 for her ticket to the royal ball? That's what it's costing Diaz to make Spend a Buck eligible for a mile race on Saturday for 2-year-old colts, a race worth $1 million.

Was Cinderella afraid of her own shadow? Or only the wicked stepmother's shadow? Spend a Buck spooks when he sees certain shadows.

The frisky habit hasn't kept Spend a Buck from earning $559,985 so far, but it makes big races an adventure.

"I am now trying to find the biggest shadow roll I can buy," Gambolati said, referring to the fuzzy strip they strap above a horse's nose to keep him from being startled by shadows.

"First time he ever did it in a race, was at River Downs. He was 10 (lengths) in front. First time he'd gone around two turns.

"Got to the spot where the starting gate tire tracks had left their marks and he jumped. Won by 15, anyway.

"Took him to Chicago for the Arlington Futurity and Pat Day worked him for me one morning. The sun was at a certain angle, created a shadow, and he dumped Day.

"The Futurity, that day was gray and cloudy, so I didn't think he needed a shadow roll. Then we took him to Meadowlands for the Young America. That's night racing, so I didn't think there'd be a problem.

"But he took the lead in the stretch, was drawing off, and just past the sixteenth pole he saw where the gate had been and he jumped. Straight up.

"He couldn't get himself back together and he got beat less than a length by Script Ohio. I take the blame. (Jockey) Angel Cordero said he'd have won, but you hate to change equipment when a horse is winning."

Gambolati had planned to keep the horse in the East, perhaps run in the Remsen at Aqueduct. And then, the dagger of bad luck struck down two of the leading 2-year-old colts.

Smile, a Florida blur, developed bone chips in one knee. And Saratoga Six, a California comet, shattered a leg in a workout.

"I was trying to get hold of Cordero," Gambolati said, "and he was trying to reach me to tell me Saratoga Six broke down. Within two hours and 47 phone calls we decided to come out here."

Gambolati is 35, looks 25 and sometimes thinks 55. He waited until Spend a Buck had handled the plane flight to Hollywood Park before putting up the first $40,000 of Diaz's money. The other $80,000 was due this morning.

"I think it's a bad gamble, putting up 120 to win 450 (thousand)," Gambolati said bluntly. "But money is no object to Dennis. I came up with the idea, but he said, 'Let's go!'

"The colt has already won $560,000, so it wasn't out of our pockets. And, hey, this race is a mile, out of the chute, so there'll be no gate marks.

"I always thought he'd like a hard race track. He's got the action to handle it. Worked him Saturday morning. Went five-eighths, and the first quarter in 25 seconds.

"First time in his life. Every other time, he goes 22, with his neck bowed. He went in 59⅕, with the last quarter in 23⅕.

"That's it. He's got to learn to relax early. He's just so competitive. But here, mile race, long stretch, he's got a shot."

He will have to find a way to beat Chief's Crown, who came west in hopes of tangling with Saratoga Six. Script Ohio is in the race. And so is Image of Greatness, a George Steinbrenner colt who sizzled by nine in a 6-furlong maiden race at Santa Anita. Won in 1:08⅖, probably a world's record for a maiden race that didn't involve gazelles.

"This is a total Cinderella story," Gambolati said, his eagerness bubbling through his words like champagne. "I've been on my own, what, 10 months. You've got an owner been in it a year and a half. You've got a horse like this.

"When Dennis got started, he bought four fillies from Norm St. Leon, who was retiring. Two were broodmares. He gave me two fillies to train.

"One filly caught the virus and died. A real nice filly. I thought, 'I've got two fillies, one can't run, the other one can, and she's the one that has to die.' But, that's the racing business.

"Now, everything's happened so quick, it hasn't dawned on me. I don't want to sit down and think about it.

"The only thing is, nobody has ever given this horse any respect. When Chief's Crown didn't run in the Young America a guy wrote that the field wasn't much.

"Hey, this is the leading 2-year-old money winner and nobody gives him any respect. Maybe, it's because of me and Dennis. But they ran the mile and sixteenth in 1:45 at Meadowlands, and that's 3/5ths quicker than Swale ran it last year.

"If you're looking for a horse, a true, honest, good horse, who knows how to win, this is it.

"We've just got to get him out of that jumping habit. In this race, nobody is going to win easy. It's too tough a race.

"He'll have to run his eyeballs off. But I'd like him to be in front down the lane. It would have to be a better horse to go by this horse."

The racing establishment doesn't want to know from Cinderella stories. It wants the expensive horses to win. It wants splendor and it wants sunshine.

Gambolati wouldn't care if the day came up dark as midnight. No sun, no shadows. And besides, Cinderella does some of her best work after midnight.

At the Races: Right Up Shoemaker's Alley

Philadelphia Daily News
May 5, 1986

LOUISVILLE, KENTUCKY—He had roses in his lap and tears in his eyes and scuff marks on his left boot, the kind of ominous smudges the inner rail makes when you scrape against it going 45 miles an hour with a 1,000-pound racehorse under you.

His horse had been battered at the start and herded back to last place. He had come from 30 lengths back, plunging through the narrowest of gaps in the homestretch, rumbling through the cramped alley that separates darkness and daylight.

Willie Shoemaker had won his fourth Kentucky Derby Saturday at age 54 on a colt named Ferdinand with a glorious ride that was a dazzling mix of patience, daring and skill.

"This was better than the rest," Shoemaker said, "because I'm in the twilight of my career."

Better than the first Derby victory, back in 1955?

"I was too young then," Shoemaker said bluntly. "I didn't know the difference."

For one golden afternoon, with 123,000 screaming witnesses, with millions more watching on world-wide television, Shoemaker's twilight was emblazoned with rainbow colors.

He is older now. He knows the difference now. He always has known his way around this lopsided race track, even if he misjudged the finish line once on Gallant Man.

And he knows the shortest path to the finish line when there are four horses careening in front of him, and a slender gap nearer the rail.

Even at 54, it does not take him long to decide, so he aimed Ferdinand into the dark alley at the eighth pole and came out the other side unscathed. Then he commenced to lash his horse lefthanded and he spurted away from the screeching traffic jam behind him to win by 2¼ lengths.

The safer path was going wide, around the wall of horses churning dust. The riskier route was inside. How long do you think it took Shoemaker to decide?

"One, two, three, boom," he said.

He estimated the elapsed time at "three seconds," but the euphoria had warped his memory, his sense of distance. It was more like a second and a half, three strides, long enough to go through the sliver of daylight and darken it for Pat Day on Rampage, who might have won it all, if he had gotten there first.

"I could have gone to the outside," Shoemaker said bluntly, "but why go around three or four horses when you can save ground to the inside?"

And why risk life and 54-year-old limbs to ride cantankerous horses when you've got a gorgeous wife and a young daughter at home, and enough money in the bank, and a 12-handicap in golf that is deceptive?

"Nah, I don't worry about him being too old," said Charlie Whittingham, who trains Ferdinand. "You play golf with him, you better not bet against him if you're a hacker."

A whole lot of people bet against him Saturday, which is why Ferdinand went off at 17–1. Ferdinand was 1-for-4 this year and had wobbled home 7 lengths back of Snow Chief in the Santa Anita Derby.

The jockey was 54 and hadn't won the Derby in 21 years. The trainer was 73 and never had won the Derby. The breeder, Howard Keck, was 71, and never even had entered a horse in the Derby because he has billions of dollars and the patience that goes with that kind of bankroll.

Whittingham tried to tell people that his colt hadn't liked the "greasy" surface at Santa Anita that day, that his horse was improving, that he had said 26 years ago he would not be back to Churchill Downs unless he had a horse good enough to win the Derby.

Shoemaker is 4–11 and weighs 96, so you get 30 pounds of lead in your saddle when you hire him to ride a Derby horse. You also get 30 years of experience and 30 pounds of heart.

"Nobody," Whittingham said of Shoemaker, "can be as good at 54 as they once were. But he's got those great hands that let him do so much with a horse.

"He can do things that not even the best cowboy who ever rode a horse could do. He won't panic. He won't get you in trouble."

Saturday's race was cowboy-rough. Ferdinand had the inside post and when the gates clanged open, Shoemaker was in instant trouble. Wise Times thumped Mogambo. Mogambo thrashed Ferdinand and they thundered through the stretch the first time, with Shoemaker snug as paint along the rail.

"I didn't panic and I didn't try to rush him too soon," Shoemaker recalled. "I said, 'Well, I'm here. . . . [T]here's nothing I can do about it. I'll just take my time and gradually move him through the field.'"

Ferdinand began moving through the field down the backstretch. On the far turn, the front-runners gasped. Favored Snow Chief's gauge flickered at empty and Rampage had to swerve to avoid him. The English horse, Bold Arrangement, surged to join Broad Brush and Badger Land on the lead.

"It was pretty tight," Shoemaker said blandly. "But when you've got enough horse you can get through."

Enough horse, enough heart.

Bold Arrangement held on to be second, three-quarters of a length ahead of Broad Brush, the quixotic Maryland horse.

Behind them were strewn 13 others, some with legitimate excuses that will provide vigorous conversation between now and the Preakness, two weeks hence.

The time was mediocre, 2:02⅘, slowest in the last 12 years. The last half was a turtlish 53 seconds, the last quarter a lumbering 25⅘.

The first two finishers were the only horses in the field of 16 running without medication (Bute or Lasix).

The ever-popular, complex Dosage formula that analyzes pedigree held up again. Favored Snow Chief didn't have the proper bloodlines to win at a mile and a quarter, Ferdinand did.

Day mourned his bad luck. Alex Solis, who may have moved too soon on Snow Chief, said his horse got tired. Jorge Velasquez, on Badger Land, said he "nearly got killed" in the bumper-car start.

The other jocks had excuses. Shoemaker had the roses in his lap and the tears in his eyes and his fourth Derby triumph, his sweetest.

Nobody's won more than five and Johnny Longden rode until he was 59, so there may be enough time.

"I can't think about next year," Shoemaker said. "I ride day to day."

Shoemaker knows that twilight turns to darkness in an instant. One, two, three . . . boom.

Slots Could Taint Great Sport of Horse Racing

Philadelphia Daily News
December 31, 2002

HURRY UP and build it. They will come.

Hurry up and build that race track in Chester, Pa. I don't care whether they're gonna race thoroughbreds or harness horses or Appaloosa ponies, mile track, half-mile bullring, wood chips, dirt, Bermuda grass or AstroTurf.

I don't care whether the license goes to some mysterious zillionaire in Lebanon, or some local real estate wizards or a syndicate of area horse owners and trainers. Just hurry up and build the thing, so the governor can stick slot machines in the adjoining building.

The governor, that's Ed Rendell, one of my favorite people. His campaign included a pie-in-the-sky proposal for slot machines at six Pennsylvania race tracks. Said how they'd generate $500 million a year in revenue and how that would buy a lot of prescription medicine for a lot of very old people who live in the state.

You're aiming for $500 million a year, those slots would have to be churning 24 hours a day, 7 days a week. They'd have to be geared to skimpy payoffs and an occasional bell-ringing, light-blinking jackpot.

Slots at the trots? Yo, it beats the alternative by a country mile. Aren't you weary of inhaling fumes from those casino buses lugging Pennsylvanians to Atlantic City to play the slots and lose their Social Security checks downtheshore? Rendell, he's weary of counting Pennsylvania license plates in the parking lot at Mountaineer Park in West Virginia, where they have slots.

West Virginia, isn't that where a rich construction guy bought the winning Powerball ticket last week? That's America's game. Ray Charles says so. Warbles about "America's game, the one and only Powerball" in those television commercials that run every 24 minutes or so.

Who pays for Ray Charles, for the backup singers, for the television time? The suckers who play the 120-million-to-1 Powerball game, that's who. Who pays the nickel out of every dollar bet to the convenience store that sells lottery tickets? The players.

Who pays the $100,000 bounty the owner of the C & L Super Serve in Hurricane, W.Va., collected for punching the winning ticket? The players, that's who. And how come it was ballyhooed as a $315 million jackpot and the rich construction guy who won it collected only $113.4 million after taxes?

He thanked God for the computer picking the winning numbers in the $100 batch of tickets he bought. Said he was writing out checks for 10 percent of his winnings to three parsons in the Church of God. Said he would try to hire back most of the workers he had to lay off before Christmas because the weather had gone bad and business had suffered.

You think God had anything to do with a rich construction guy with a good heart winning the jackpot? Ask your preacher next Sunday, see whether it doesn't start a lively debate. Ask the preacher at the church near the C & L Super Serve, who put a sign out front warning that Americans were spending more on gambling than on groceries.

Whoa, this is the sports section, and this column is about a proposed race track in Chester, one of those bleak cities that lost heavy industry and now is hurting for better schools, more jobs and affordable housing.

"Delaware generated $80 million with just 1,500 slots," Rendell said during a chance encounter at WIP. "They're going to 3,000. We're thinking about 6,000 at Pennsylvania tracks."

And how many names would be added to the welfare rolls? How many gambling addicts created? How many marriages shattered, families disrupted?

"If you think that social ills are inevitable," Rendell countered, "look at it this way, all those people from Pittsburgh who go to Mountaineer Park to gamble, they can't get treatment for addiction, because those programs are only available to residents of West Virginia.

"We will designate a portion of the revenue to gambling-addiction therapy. People love to gamble. They are going to gamble. The only ones who will really be hurt by this are the bus companies."

That is horse manure, and the governor knows it. But our society is in deep trouble, its priorities warped. And Pennsylvanians are riding those buses to Atlantic City and driving to Delaware Park or Dover Downs to yank those slot-machine handles, dreaming pitiful jackpot dreams, squandering those taxable dollars out of state.

He feels he must tap into that gambling urge to help the elderly who can't afford prescription drugs. He must figure out a way to attract dedicated teachers to decrepit schools and their overstuffed classrooms.

While he was mayor, he talked about a special lottery to cover the city's contribution to two new ballparks. Even daydreamed about riverboat gambling.

Me, I'm caught in the crossfire. I hate the lottery, think it's a tax on the poor to help the elderly. I hate the scam of getting 500-to-1 if you hit the three-digit Daily Number when the proper odds are 1,000-to-1. Hate paying Ray Charles to sing about "America's game." Hate the social costs, the misery that follows in the wake of legalized gambling like screeching seagulls around a garbage scow.

I love racing. I love the spectacle. I cherish the challenge of handicapping a race, trying to visualize how it will be run, which horse will cross the finish line first. You're competing against the other players, not against some harsh, immutable house odds.

Off-track betting, simulcasting races from other tracks, gives the bettor a chance to pick a winner every 5 or 6 minutes. However, it also bankrupts the reckless player quicker than you can say Pete Rose.

When more and more states legalized lotteries, racing had to do something to counteract those huge rollover jackpots. So they devised the Pick Six concept, in which you had to pick the winners of six consecutive races. It helped, then it attracted the rats, which explains those three former Drexel frat brothers conspiring to rip off the Breeders' Cup Pick Six.

Luckily, greed and stupidity tripped them up, and they will do time for the crime. Maybe Rendell, who loves sports, will consider the equivalent of the British soccer pools, a football parlay card in which a gambler must pick every NFL winner against the point spread on a 15-game Sunday.

Meanwhile, build the race track in Chester. Make sure a piece of the slot-machine action goes to the purses, which will mean better horses competing for more money, bigger fields, making it tougher to pick the winner, and bigger payoffs if you can.

Seabiscuit: A Horse from the Wrong Side of the Track

Philadelphia Daily News
July 22, 2003

IT'S A TRUE STORY! There was a horse named Seabiscuit. Raced in the late 1930s, when America was staggering out of the rubble of the Great Depression.

Little horse, stubby, mud-colored. Decent, but not dazzling bloodlines. Lazy enough and cantankerous enough to lose his first 16 races, even though Hall of Famer Sunny Jim Fitzsimmons was training him. You could have snagged him out of a claiming race for $2,500 at one point.

A California auto dealer named Charles Howard bought him. Howard had come to San Francisco with 21 cents in his pocket. When the earthquake of '06 ravaged Frisco, he transformed three Buicks, his entire inventory, into ambulances, into dynamite-carriers for the firefighters, into money-making chariots. He was rich and restless, still grieving the death of his young son, when he got involved with racing.

He promoted Seabiscuit with an auto dealer's zeal, sending champagne to the pressbox after victories (even after a narrow loss) and campaigning brazenly for a match race with the legendary War Admiral.

His taciturn horse trainer, Tom Smith, had encouraged Howard to buy Seabiscuit, praising the horse's "spirit." Smith was a mysterious cowpoke, cold and silent as an icebox. Had soft hands he used to heal hurting horses, and a soft voice he seldom used around strangers. The writers couldn't unearth his background, so they invented stories about him.

Smith shared nothing with the media, sticking a look-alike horse in Seabiscuit's stall, working the horse in pre-dawn darkness, handcrafting a bell to prepare his horse for the walkup start against the favored War Admiral.

He hired Red Pollard to ride Seabiscuit. Pollard was a brash one-eyed jock, abandoned by his parents as a youngster, with a face full of scars he'd accumulated fighting for meal money, a head full of Dickens and Shakespeare he was happy to share, and enough broken bone X-rays to cause him to glow in the dark.

Laura Hillenbrand wrote a remarkable book about Seabiscuit and the people around him, and how he became America's horse, at a time the nation was desperate for hard-trying heroes. It was crafted like a tapestry, vivid colors, rich in detail, pulsating with passion.

The movie "Seabiscuit," which opens Friday, is based on Hillenbrand's book. What writer-director Gray Ross has done is pour 8 gallons of cioppino into a 59-gallon pot. Some delicious stuff gets left out, some drab stuff gets left in.

Watching the movie is just like being at a racetrack, two minutes of dramatic, compelling action, followed by 23 minutes of waiting around.

Which is why so few people go to the racetrack anymore. Oh, they're still betting fistfuls of dollars, but they're betting by computer or by telephone or shuffling into an Off Track Betting parlor where they can wager on seven different racetracks simultaneously. There are glitzy casinos, and a swamp of lotteries to satisfy America's gambling lust.

It wasn't that way in the late '30s. Seabiscuit drew huge crowds wherever he raced, and he raced everywhere, from Tanforan to Narragansett, lugging high weight, which is why they called those races handicaps. Crowds of people came to see him, the men in suits, the women in broadbrimmed hats, looking for a change of luck, thirsting for excitement.

They crammed into movie theaters, too, seeking a couple of hours of escape from life's dreary box. Hollywood latched onto the formula early. In the 1930s alone, they cranked out 68 films involving horse racing.

Most of them involved a little boy or a little girl enchanted by a horse. In most of them the horse had bleak bloodlines, a wrong-side-of-the-tracks thoroughbred with a mean streak as wide as W.C. Fields. Horse got sick, little boy or little girl nursed him back to health and watched him, tear-stained, win the big race.

Judy Garland and Mickey Rooney worked together for the very first time in a movie called "Thoroughbreds Don't Cry." Rooney played a jockey pressured to throw a race. Garland sang two songs.

Rooney had a juicy role as a down on his luck jockey who tutors the teen-aged, wide-eyed Elizabeth Taylor in the classic "National Velvet."

Shirley Temple was held as ransom for losing racetrack bets in the captivating "Little Miss Marker." Bob Hope, working without Bing Crosby, starred in "The Lemon Drop Kid," a comedy about a racetrack tout mixed up with mobsters.

The Marx Brothers frolicked through "A Day at the Races." Wallace Beery tugged at your heartstrings in "The Champ" with Beery buying a horse for his kid and then boozily gambling it away.

Later, Hollywood would use racetracks as the setting for crime stories, mostly complex robbery plots. Stanley Kubrick's early film, "The Killing," is a grim story of a racetrack heist sabotaged by double-crosses.

Occasionally, filmmakers told the story of a real horse and the real people around him. "Phar Lap" was the best of those, the story of an Australian wonder horse that died in America under mysterious circumstances.

Meanwhile, Seabiscuit was a pioneer in sports marketing. There was a ladies hat with a fishnet veil, wastebaskets, two kinds of oranges. Hotels, laundries, humor magazines used his likeness in their advertising.

In 1949, Hollywood cobbled together "The Story of Seabiscuit" and it was wretched, a clumsy distortion of a wonderful story. It starred Barry Fitzgerald as an Irish trainer who gets to handle Seabiscuit. A grown-up Shirley Temple plays his niece, a nurse, who falls in love with Seabiscuit's jockey.

Maybe not that hokey after all. Pollard, recovering from a shattered leg, romanced and married his nurse, Agnes Conlon. You never get to meet Agnes in the current "Seabiscuit," 200-to-1 over the early flick, which is praising with faint damns.

Gary Thompson will critique the movie Friday for its plot, acting, photography. I looked at it through the eyes of a jaded sports writer, a dedicated horseplayer, a poorer-but-wiser part-owner of a handful of brittle horses.

Ross spends a lot of time justifying the film, with black-and-white scenes of the Great Depression designed to explain Seabiscuit's popularity.

The horse lost 56 times, perhaps the only 56-loss horse honored with a statue at Santa Anita, a best-selling book and two movies. Despite those grim soup-kitchen scenes in the movie, we don't get a clear explanation of why Seabiscuit captivated America and got more newspaper space than Hitler and Franklin Delano Roosevelt.

There are a couple of scenes of Smith giving pre-race instructions to Pollard in the jockey's room, the last place a trainer would choose to discuss strategy. Most of the frantic negotiations and the shattered plans for the match race with War Admiral are missing in the movie. Somehow, the fact that Seabiscuit was $2.20-to-1 and War Admiral was odds-on is overlooked in both the book and movie.

The racing sequences are fascinating, what with helmet-cams giving you a look between the horse's ears as he pounds down the track. Standout jockey Gray Stevens does a first-rate job of portraying the swagger of jockey George Woolf, who got to ride Seabiscuit while Pollard rehabbed from busted limbs. Chris McCarron did a terrific job choreographing the racing sequences.

Hollywood's stringent rules about how hard you can work animals meant that 10 different horses played Seabiscuit. In one vital scene Pollard wins aboard a scruffy horse with a matted winter coat (in California?) awash with sweat. Ugh.

For dramatic effect, Ross has Seabiscuit rallying from way back in the 1940 Santa Anita Handicap. The charts show he was second most of the race and then blitzed past pacesetter Whichcee, winning handily. And why did Ross feel he had to invent a cartoonish racetrack announcer named Tick Tock McGlaughlin, played to the corny husk by William H. Macy? For a sprinkle of humor, tutti-frutti ice cream in the cioppino?

Me, I longed for the color and drama of Joe Hernandez's race calls at Santa Anita, and the raspy eloquence of Clem McCarthy's broadcasts. The chaotic day of the match race, which Seabiscuit won handily, McCarthy was trapped by the mob crammed into Pimlico. He couldn't get to his perch atop the clubhouse to call the race. He scrambled onto the rail near the finish line and called the race from there, with 40 million Americans tuned in.

The frantic scramble doesn't make the movie. It's a good film, worth watching, but I think it falls a furlong short of Hillenbrand's brilliant book. Hey, what did you expect from a print journalist who used to rise at 3:30 to get to the barns at Churchill Downs before dawn the week of the Kentucky Derby, beat the media mob, perhaps coax a nugget from some leathery trainer who appreciated good, old-fashioned hustle?

Citation Dominated in Different Era

Philadelphia Daily News
June 3, 2008

CITATION'S JOCKEY was a guy named Al Snider. Went fishing one day off the Florida coast. Never came back. Gone. Poof. Vanished without a trace.

Jimmy Jones, the Calumet Farm trainer, called Eddie Arcaro. Told him he was putting him on the next Derby winner. Arcaro probably said, "Thank you, sir," because that's the way legendary jockeys talked to legendary trainers back in the day.

It was 1948, and Citation won the Kentucky Derby by 3½ lengths, won the Preakness by 5½. Warmed up for the Belmont by winning the Jersey Derby by 11. And then, 77,700 fans heard four of the most ominous words you can hear at a race track . . . "stumbled at the start!"

June 12, 1948. Citation stumbled at the start, recovered quickly and went on to win the Belmont by eight lengths. I was there that day because I thought Citation was the greatest race horse in the cockeyed world and I wanted to see him win the Triple Crown.

Rode the 7th Avenue Subway to Penn Station. Caught the Long Island Railroad's rickety Belmont Special to the race track. Paid $2 for admission to the grandstand. Peeled two meaningless pages out of the Daily Racing Form and slid them between slats of a seat. That way, the seat was yours for the rest of the day, even when you left to go to the windows or the restroom or the concession stand.

Race-track etiquette. Most of the men wore suits. And hats.

Real hats, Indiana Jones fedoras. And the women wore crisp summer dresses.

So I was down $6.60 before I ever made a bet. And I knew I couldn't bet Citation if they hammered him down to 1-to-5 because that meant betting $20 to win $4 and I had never bet $20 on a race in my life because I couldn't risk the anguish of losing.

Seven horses dared to challenge Citation in the Belmont so you could bet the race win, place or show. No exactas, no trifectas, no 10-cent superfectas, no rolling daily double, no Pick-3, Pick-4 or Pick-6, no over-under, odd-even, eeney meeney miny moe or whatever else they're throwing out there these days to entice the pie-in-the-sky lottery players.

And the more I think about that day, the more I think about how racing has changed over the last 60 years and how gloomy that ledger looks.

They raced on hay, oats and water in New York back then.

No Bute, no Lasix, no once-a-month shots of an anabolic steroid called Winstrol, whether the horse needs it or not.

Citation ran often. And swiftly. The first time Arcaro rode him, he got him beat in the goo at Havre de Grace in something called the Chesapeake Trial by something called Saggy. It wasn't so awful because Saggy loved the mud and he later sired a champ named Carry Back and Arcaro wasn't about to punish his 3-year-old colt with the Triple Crown races on the horizon.

First, Arcaro had to choose between Citation and the Calumet speedball Coaltown. Six years earlier, Greentree Stables had given him the choice of Shut Out or Devil Diver. Arcaro chose Devil Diver and finished sixth in the Derby. Shut Out won.

Jockeys are right there with sports writers when it comes to picking winners. That's one of the few things that hasn't changed.

So Citation won the Derby Trial on Tuesday. And that Saturday, in the chaotic Derby paddock, Arcaro turned to Ben Jones, Jimmy's dad, and asked softly, "Are you sure I'm on the right one?" And Jones said, "You're on the right one."

Pow, faster than you can say Devil Diver, Coaltown sped off to a six-length lead. Citation caught him in that long Churchill Downs stretch and breezed by him. Paid $2.80, the lowest win price in Derby history. When it was over, Arcaro sent part of his earnings to Snider's widow.

Just for the record, Arcaro did not wear advertising on his right leg, the leg the crowd and the camera see. In the winner's circle, he did not swap his helmet for a chocolate brown baseball cap with a trucking company logo. If he had, Ben or Jimmy Jones would have ripped the Calumet's devil's red silks right off his back. Right then, right there.

They didn't allow place or show betting in that Derby. Same thing in the Preakness, where Citation paid $2.20, the minimum.

If you're keeping track, that made the mile-and-a-half Belmont Stakes Citation's fifth race in less than 6 weeks. Won 'em all. Won the next nine. Finished the year winning 19 of 20. Won at every distance from 6 furlongs to 2 miles. (Won that 2-miler on 3 days' rest.)

Won at 10 different race tracks in seven different states. Won on tracks rated fast, sloppy, heavy and good.

All that racing caught up with him, even if nothing else with four legs could. Missed the entire 1949 season with osselet problems. Calumet didn't miss a beat with Coaltown, named horse of that year. Calumet founder Warren Wright died in '50 but not before restating his wish that Citation become the first thoroughbred to earn a million bucks.

So they brought him back as a 5-year-old and he won a 6-furlong sprint at Santa Anita. That made it 16 in a row, a record Cigar equaled but couldn't beat decades later. He won only once more, because he kept hooking Noor, finishing second six times, pushing Noor to world records to beat him.

Nowadays, you win two big races, you've got your million. But he was still short. So they sent him out there as a 6-year-old and his fans winced as he finished third, third and off the board. He lost the Argonaut Handicap and then won the Century and the American, beating his stable-mate, the filly Bewitch. They ran 1–2 in the Hollywood Gold Cup and that did it. Citation had his million, he could retire.

It was 25 years before another horse won the Triple Crown. Secretariat. Won the Belmont from here to Hoboken. Thirty-one lengths. I was there for that one, as a journalist. It took 25 years, but that was the first time I saw a race horse I thought was better than Citation.

California Chrome Throws Breeding on Its Ear

Philadelphia Daily News
June 3, 2014

IT'S THE EARS. It's gotta be the ears.

You're looking for answers to the riddle of California Chrome, how this humbly bred colt, with its geezer trainer and its loud co-owner and its 42-year-old jockey, wearing the ugliest silks in recent memory, has a chance to make horse racing history, go ahead, start with the ears.

Chrome will be odds-on on June 7, in the Belmont. His breeding screams that he can't go a mile-and-a-half against rested rivals. The colt has half-a-ton of skills. Reading his daunting pedigree isn't one of them.

If he wins the Belmont with that silhouette of a jackass on his jockey's back, he will do something that hasn't been done in 36 years, not since Affirmed, win racing's Triple Crown.

His co-owners have caught more than lightning in a bottle. They've caught thunder, a tsunami, hailstones and halibut bones. Chrome's momma is Love the Chase, whose only win was in a maiden claiming race at Golden Gate. Steve Coburn and Perry Martin bought the slow but sincere filly for $8,000. That earned the new owners the harsh nickname, "Dumb Ass Partners." Hence the D-A-P on the blinkers and the donkey on the silks.

Chrome's daddy is Lucky Pulpit, who hasn't sired anything that has won beyond $1\frac{1}{16}$ miles. Stud fee was $2,000 at the time, a bargain-basement price tag. Date took place on a sun-scorched horse farm, 18 miles from nowhere. The foal showed up with four white feet. (More about this later.) They drew his name out of a hat, so we're lucky he's not Stetson 7½.

Coburn started talking Kentucky Derby that day. He is the loud partner and he wears purple shirts and green ties and a cowboy hat that's gotta hold 12 gallons if it holds an ounce. In racing, you bray about the Derby around a new foal and you might as well spit into the wind. (More about this later.)

It is an intoxicating story, this bubbly brew of science and superstition. Dick Jerardi, as he always does, has brought *Daily News* readers the human side, the old-school trainer, Art Sherman; the loud Coburn; the friendly jockey Victor Espinoza.

The breeding fascinates, puzzles, and a search for answers led to Laurie Ross, a sweet, smart woman who has studied pedigrees for over a decade. She has been Horse Racing Nation's pedigree analyst since 2010.

Just for the record, she thought Chrome would "hit the wall" in the mile-and-a-quarter Kentucky Derby. He won easy, did it again in the Preakness at 1-to-2.

"When I look at a pedigree to determine how far a horse may want to run," she said, "I take into account the sire's racing record and winning distances of his progeny. With a new stallion, I look at his sire, dam, damsire and siblings for distance/precocious factors. I do the same with the dam, her siblings and offspring.

"It isn't an exact science. About eight of 10 times the horse will follow the dictates of his pedigree/conformation. Occasionally, one, like California Chrome, will outrun their pedigree.

"Sometimes the large heart factor comes into play. Other times, they could be a throwback, where all of the genes line up in a way that they didn't with the rest of the family."

She is talking large heart as in size, dimensions, not those mystical intangibles sports writers scramble for: determination, courage, toughness. Big heart handles the oxygen more efficiently, bolsters speed and stamina. And that's before we knew about the nasal strips on Chrome's nose.

Short of an ECG, how can we even guess that Chrome might be powered by a large heart? "The easiest way," Ross answered, "is to look at his ears. One unique characteristic is curly ear tips. Look at Secretariat's ears. Another noted for her curly ears is Zenyatta. Last year's Derby winner, Orb, also has the ears. California Chrome's ears look very much like Secretariat's."

Go back too far studying a pedigree and the gene pool is diluted, confusing. "California Chrome's dam has an interesting inbreeding to a mare named Numbered Account," she said. "This mare was a champion 2-year-old filly in 1971. Set a track record for 5 furlongs, equaled one at 9 furlongs.

"Numbered Account is by the great Buckpasser. Her dam was by Swaps. She can also be found in the third and fourth generations. If you have good genes from a superior mare, you want to breed in more of the traits she offers."

Inbred 3 x 3 to Numbered Account, nice! Big heart, curly ear tips, efficient stride, another gear once they turn for home, those four white feet churning. Even nicer! Ah, the four white feet. Ross was not familiar with the childlike rhyme I'd heard around the racetrack: one white foot, buy him; 2 white feet, try him; 3 white feet, be on the sly; 4 white feet, pass him by.

"The only issue with white hooves, not legs," she cautioned, "is that since they lack pigment, they tend to be softer than a black hoof. This opens up a host of problems such as cracks and other injuries."

Whoa! Fifteen seconds later, I had a different rhyme, thanks to Yahoo. One white foot, keep him not a day; 2 white feet, send him far away; 3 white feet, sell him to a friend; 4 white feet, keep him to the end.

The last word goes to Archie Moore, the legendary fighter. Someone asked Moore about the chances of a plodding fighter winning a title. Moore answered, "You can't win the Kentucky Derby with a blue-nosed mule."

Moore was thinking about quick hands, quick feet, a quick mind. That's prize fighting. The Belmont is a horse race. It only looks like a prize fight some years. Bet with your head, not over it.

PART III
Boxing

Introductions

WEATTA FRAZIER COLLINS
AND LARRY MERCHANT

S TAN HOCHMAN WAS THE GREATEST sportswriter of them all—a gem. He was an honest reporter who wrote and spoke the truth. He was the only one my dad truly trusted.

—WFC

S TAN WAS A PART OF MY LIFE THAT WAS GOOD, a part that I left behind me in Philadelphia. He was just all-around good—a good writer, a good reporter, a good commentator, and a good man. His death hit me like a hard left hook.

Although when I hired him in 1959, Stan's first beat for the *Daily News* was baseball, I was drawn to him because of some boxing columns he had written for the *San Bernardino Sun*. They were columns about a very colorful boxer on the West Coast named Art Aragon. I read them and put them in a drawer. I said to myself that I was going to hire him the first chance I got.

I didn't know then that Stan would turn out to be the most quintessentially "pure" writer and reporter I had ever encountered. I remember we were covering the Dodgers in the Coliseum before Dodger Stadium was built. It may have been during a World Series. I was on my sixth paragraph, sweating it out. And Stan had already written a column, a game story, and a sidebar.

Stan always got the story and told it with seemingly effortless grace.

—LM

A Fight to Cherish

Philadelphia Daily News
March 9, 1971

"LET ME GO get my face straightened out. . . . I'm not this ugly," Joe Frazier said. The words came slushing through a chunk of ice he was grinding between his aching teeth, trying to chill the pain in his jaw into submission. There was a lump under his right eye and a lump under his left eye and a lump on his forehead and a crackle of dried blood alongside his left nostril.

Handsome, he wasn't.

"All those things you guys been writing about me," he said, working hard to arrange those lumpy features in a smile, "what you got to say now?"

All those things people had been writing had been the taunting words of Muhammad Ali, that Frazier was too slow, too dull, too heavy-legged, and too homely to be a champion.

And while Frazier was clutching ice to his lumpy face, Ali was hunched in a police car, its siren screaming as it screeched through New York's clogged traffic to a hospital to assay the damage to a jaw that was swollen like a soggy jack-o-lantern.

Had Ali been able to talk, he might have echoed Frazier's words. All those things those guys had been writing about him had been churned into so much confetti in a terrifying-wonderful savage-skillful bitter-sweet kind of fist-fight.

Judges Clash on Scoring

Frazier won. A unanimous decision. But one judge called it 11–4 and the referee had it 8–6–1, their scoring clashing on seven of the 15 rounds. If two skilled observers had agreed to disagree that often about something unfurling in front of them, can you understand now why the easiest sort of criticisms have been repeated about the two fighters until they were accepted as though engraved on stone by some Biblical hand?

It turned out that Joe Frazier was not too slow, too dull, too heavy-legged to be the champion. He was swift enough to pursue Ali throughout most of the savage fight. He was smart enough to bob-and-weave and provide an elusive target to Ali's snake-quick jabs.

He had the legs that enabled him to dart forward for that one crunching left hook in the 15th round that sent Ali careening onto his back.

"He takes some punch," Joe Frazier was to say later. "Oh my God. That shot I hit him with, I went down home and got that one. From out in the country."

It came whistling out of Beaufort like the Suncoast Limited, screeching on invisible tracks, sending sparks into the night. Only the wail of the whistle was missing. And it crashed into Ali's handsome head just like the locomotive it resembled.

"Believe me, he's a good man," Frazier said.

Both Targets of Skeptics

For all the people who had demeaned Frazier as too slow and too mechanical, there were as many who scorned Ali as some kind of faint-hearted narcissist who would curl up and wither if somebody fetched him a clout to his handsome head. They decided he had lost enough of his speed and a fraction of those incredible reflexes and that would make him easy prey for those kidney-rattling hooks that Frazier throws.

Well, Ali spent a lot of time with his feet planted firmly, banging away at Frazier with both hands. And there was that one round they could have fought in a telephone booth, imprisoned in one corner of the ring.

The legend of Muhammad Ali came tumbling down last night in Madison Square Garden with 20,455 witnesses and a fair portion of the theater-going world looking on. Joe Frazier, who learned his trade in the grimy, head-knocking atmosphere of Philly's gyms, provided the push. Not spectacularly, but—rather—in Frazier fashion. Grim, relentless and no quarter given.

Ali, whose handsome face had smiled and taunted its way through the decade, now knows what the other side of the business is all about. Would you believe that after it was all over he couldn't or wouldn't talk. Couldn't is the more probable explanation.

What happened is that Joe Frazier whipped Muhammad Ali in the one way that most people agreed he couldn't, over 15 rounds of magnificent prize fight. Joe did it like a man climbing the mountain, grunting and puffing and struggling but never taking his eyes off the peak. He couldn't put his man away like he said he would, so he methodically took him apart. And in one breathless instant, during the

15th and final round, he sent the left hook soaring home like a demolition ball.

Ali went down thunderstruck. That he got up at all wipes away any doubt what the man has inside him. That he finished the round and the fight is a credit to him, boxing, and Joe's knowledge that he had it won anyway.

Ali wobbled through the final two minutes with the right side of his face beginning to resemble one of those Florida grapefruits. A half hour later he was whisked away to a mid-Manhattan hospital where they were to determine if anything had to be wired back together. Souvenir of that Philadelphia hook again.

Among the things that Ali missed after the fight was the press conference and he skips those as about as often as he loses. So you know the guy was hurting.

"He said for you all not to worry about it, that he'll be back," said Drew Bundini Brown, who filled in for the former champion.

"He couldn't talk very much when he got back to the dressing room," Bundini added, "but he did want to know if he had put up a great fight."

The answer to that is a resounding affirmative. And if it was Ali's Last Hurrah, and you have to wonder if it won't be, then it was a loud one. Frazier earned his victory every inch of the way and the guys and dolls in the $150 seats got their money's worth.

The scoring was peculiar but unanimous. Referee Arthur Mercante had it 8–6–1, giving Joe four of the five final rounds and calling the other even. Judge Artie Aidala had it 9–6, giving Frazier six straight runs from the third through the eighth and Ali two of the final five. Judge Bill Recht saw it 11–4, giving Ali little more than a pat on the head.

The two *Daily News* writers at ringside both scored it 8–6–1.

It was obvious from the moment of the fighters' entrance that the socio-political implications had gripped the crowd almost as firmly as the promise of seeing two guys hit each other on the chin. The ration of cheers and boos for each was rated, roughly, a draw. At times during the night, chants of "Ali-Ali-Ali" swept through the arena only to be answered by "Joe-Joe-Joe" being chorused by the other side. Feelings were strong.

They were in the ring too. You didn't get far into this fight before you began to realize that these guys don't like each other—really. No put on.

Round one began as expected. During the instructions in the middle of the ring, Mercante's speech included approximately 1/3 as many as Ali's, who was talking only to Frazier. Joe laughed.

All through the night the byplay continued. A minute into the fight, Frazier sank his first hook to the body. And Ali turned to the crowd, shaking his head, assuring everybody it was nothing. Unfortunately, he was not available an hour later to edit the impression.

The head-shaking routine became a pattern as the fight wore on, usually following a fierce exchange. Ali broke out the rest of the repertoire, too, at times patting Joe on the cheek, a form of humiliation that is better practiced on someone with a little less steam in the left hook.

Frazier, surprisingly, joined in. In the fifth round, after absorbing a barrage from Ali, Joe dropped his arms and laughed. At the end of the round, as he spun toward his corner he flung his right hand toward the canvas in a motion that could only be interpreted to imply that Ali's best bolt was something short of lightening.

Throw out the psychological warfare and the rest was all heavy artillery. Ali came out fast as had been anticipated and the stuff he was triggering in the first round had KO written on it. He was backing up only occasionally. He was not on his toes and the idea was to end it right there.

Frazier, as he always seems to do, waded through the downpour of jabs and hooks and right hands and began mounting his own toll of damage. There was a big left hook near the end of the third that shook Ali. And Joe hurt him with the first of two solid hooks in the fourth.

At that point the fight seemed to be turning toward Frazier. But it wasn't to be as clear a victory as it appeared.

Ali survived fierce body punishment in the seventh, shook off a terrible hook midway through the ninth round and then reversed the pressure forcing Joe to back up near the end of those three minutes.

Early in the 10th, Frazier appeared to turn toward his corner pleading eye trouble, but he later explained that he actually was talking to referee Mercante, who accidentally had thumbed Joe's eye while breaking the two.

Ali was stunned by another hook in the 11th, and spent the rest of the round stumbling around the ring with Frazier in frantic but unsuccessful pursuit.

"He was on Queer Street there," Bundini Brown was to admit later.

Frazier failed to follow up that advantage during a slow-paced 12th round. The two stood in a neutral corner and bombed away for most of the 13th and Frazier went back to the body in the 14th.

Then 25 seconds into the 15th, he double hooked for one of the few times during the evening. The first struck Ali on the elbow, the second nearly put his head in the mezzanine. Ali went down as if somebody had jerked the ring out from under him. He was up at two however, waited out the eight count, and finished the round—mostly courtesy of Frazier, who was already celebrating. He had to know the knockdown was only a punctuation mark.

"I feel stronger than I did when I went in," Joe told the assembly of writers some 10 minutes later, peering from beneath swollen eyes. He didn't, but he had earned the right to say it anyhow.

"I want him to come to me and apologize for all the things he called me," Frazier added. "He mumbled something after they announced the decision, but I couldn't understand. I didn't make him crawl across the ring like he said he would."

Then Frazier told it like everybody had seen it. "I got to give him credit," Joe said. "He takes some punch. That last shot I hit him with, I reached all the way back home for."

Rematch? "I don't think he'll want one," Frazier said. "And me and Yank (Durham), we got to go home and take it easy for a while. I've been working 10 years for this night."

So had the other guy and what it fetched him was an ugly jaw and a loss a lot of people thought never would come. "God knows I whipped him," Joe said.

God knows he surely did.

Drugs Topple Bitter Gypsy Joe

Philadelphia Daily News
September 22, 1971

GYPSY JOE HARRIS had rings on his fingers and bells on his toes. He wore red velvet trunks when he fought and red silk underwear when he didn't. He had guys trailing in his wake, screeching and wheeling like so many seagulls around a fishing boat.

Yesterday he was wearing lumpy green pajamas and a plastic bracelet. His arms dangled lifelessly in his lap and there was a 14-inch scar on the left one, where he had hacked at it with a knife in a frantic effort to carve away the needle marks.

Gypsy Joe Harris is in the Drug Clinic at St. Luke's Hospital, trying to whip a heroin habit. His face was lumpy and his belly was bloated and his eyes were glazed while he recited his own obituary.

"They killed me without me being dead," Harris said yesterday. "They took away the only thing I had going for me . . . fighting."

The State Athletic Commission took away Gypsy Joe's license on October 11, 1968. He had won 24–25 fights, but he showed up for the 26th one with an inflamed eye. So they sent him to a specialist, and the doctor said the right eye was practically blind. So the commission took away his license, and the life gushed right out of Harris.

"I went to kill myself one morning," he said, the words shuffling out like they were wearing slippers. "I climbed out on the Ben Franklin Bridge. I looked down and I started thinking. I knew when I hit that water I'd start thrashing around. I can swim, see. So, I figured, what's the good?

"I climbed down off that bridge and I walked past the guard and he looked at me kinda funny, but I kept going. I was down, man, really down. I ran into some junkies. I asked 'em for dope. I had no money and they said I was crazy. But I talked them out of some.

"After that, it got to be a $75-a-day thing. Skag, that's what they call it. I whipped it once, quit cold. But a month ago I went back on it. I can beat it any time I want to. I don't have to put no drug in my arm. But I've gotta fight. I've got to do what I want to do."

A Style All His Own

Gypsy Joe Harris could fight. Ho boy, could he fight. Like nobody else. Zigging and zagging and bipping and bopping and bowing and clowning. People loved him, a bald-headed child of nature.

He skipped training lots of times and he boozed pretty good between fights and he showed up at weigh-ins overweight sometimes. And sometimes he didn't show up at weigh-ins at all.

He waltzed past Curtis Cokes in Madison Square Garden, but when it came time to fight Cokes for the title in Texas, they couldn't find Cokes with radar, and the fight never came off. They put him in with Emile Griffith at the Spectrum. Griffith banged him around with left hooks. That night there weren't too many guys trailing in his wake.

He was supposed to fight Manny Gonzalez in 1968, but it kept getting postponed. Then came that pre-fight exam. They snatched away his license and his dreams were dead. Finished at 22, flung back onto the street like some empty Scotch bottle, ready to be shattered into a zillion pieces.

The bitterness rages in him. He lashes out at some invisible conspiracy only he perceives. He rages against bureaucratic bungling and he mutters against corruption. He rambles about his Constitutional rights.

"I'm gonna get me some money," he promised. "Beg, borrow or steal it. And I'm gonna get me a lawyer and I'm gonna sue. Life, liberty and the pursuit of happiness, that's what America stands for, right? Well, they're not letting me pursue my happiness.

"The Supreme Court has already said that you can't protect a man from himself. A friend of mine told me that. Well, that's what they're doing to me. I'll sign a waiver.

"The thing is I ain't gonna die in the ring. I was 24-and-1, not 1-and-24. And all that time I couldn't see out of my right eye. They knew it, and let me fight, and then all of a sudden they took my license away."

Harris has always said that his eye was injured years ago. "October 31, 1957," he said. "Halloween night. Got hit by a brick. Went to Cooper Hospital. Intern operated on me, shoving the eye back into place.

"I was supposed to go back to the clinic, but I never did. My mom had a baby then, and I wanted her to use the money for the kid, so I never went back."

How then did Harris ever pass the pre-fight physicals? It is one of the nagging questions that ducks an answer the way Harris used to duck the other guy's jab.

"The commission doctors knew about my eye," he insisted. "I said that I used to memorize the chart. Well, that's a lie. I just said that because I wanted to protect them, because they had gone along with me. But you look at the old films of the weigh-ins and you'll never see me put my hand over my right eye to read the chart. It never happened.

"In October, 1966, they sent me to a specialist in Rittenhouse Square. He turned in a three or four page report on the things that were wrong with my eye. But, they still didn't stop me from fighting until 1968. How come?"

How come? "I think he was dealt with unfairly because he had become too tough to handle," Bernie Pollack suggested last night at the Spectrum. Pollack is a fringe figure in the Philadelphia scene, a mink farmer and fur dealer with a passion for the fight game. He befriended Harris, invited him to train at his farm near Reading, and wound up staking him to a stack of money.

"I quit giving him money," Pollack said, "because guys told me he was on dope. I can't say that I saw anything direct, but there was one time when he was obsessed with the idea of returning to Philly for one night. I remember him sitting there, rocking furiously.

"They say that he lies but I never knew him to lie about anything connected with fights. He told me he was blind in one eye and I believed him. But one day we were walking in the woods and he said there's an insect climbing on that tree. It was 100 yards away. When we got up close, there was this caterpillar there. It was incredible. Animal vision I called it."

Harris had sought Pollack's friendship during one of those stormy periods when he became disenchanted with the management he was getting from Yancey Durham and Willie Reddish. Durham was in Houston yesterday, scouting a meaningless heavyweight fight, trying to con some meaning into it.

"I'm sorry to hear about Gypsy Joe," he said. "But if he's stupid enough to get involved with drugs, he's got to pay the price. I saw him last Tuesday. He wanted some money for some food. He said he wanted $10. I gave him $7. He said he'd been up all night and had no food."

There are some critics who blame Durham for Harris's bitter fate. He denies the charges in that booming voice that rattles windows and intimidates nagging questioners.

"I tried everything I could do," he said. "I asked him to come live with me. He wouldn't. I had my wife prepare food for him. I offered him

$5 a day for every day he came to the gym. He wanted the money in advance. I'd give him $5, I'd never see him again.

"Remember I had a 50–50 partner in Willie Reddish, so don't go putting all the blame on me. I guess you could say he was doomed from the start. Even if he had become a champion, his time was limited. The streets would have got him.

"As for the commission, I abide by the rules. If he had been blind before that, how would he have passed in Pennsylvania, in New York, in Texas?"

How indeed? "I don't see how he could have only had one eye the way he got around the ring and put all those tricks on you," Joe Frazier wondered aloud. "But they couldn't let a man go out there with one eye, just because he wants to. Lots of times, a man gets knocked down, he wants to get up and keep going but they stop the fight because they don't want a man to get killed."

Frazier had an affinity for Harris, despite the disparity in size and lifestyle. "Yank did all he could for him," he said. "He tried to make him put his money away. But Gypsy said, 'No, he was old enough to take care of his own money.'"

Frazier: The Man Had It All

"The man had talent. He had stamina and he had ability. He could walk off the street, walk into the gym and beat the hell out of you. I'd like to give him a job, but he's got to straighten up first."

Duke Dugent had found some work for Harris, training kids at the 23d PAL gym. It was Dugent who had spotted signs of drug addiction, sent Harris to a doctor and recommended treatment at St. Luke's.

"It's a pathetic case," Dugent said. "He's a helluva fine person. I had him since he was nine. He ran in here one night to get away from some gang trouble. I had him through 78 amateur fights.

"When they took away his license it was like cutting his legs out from under him. He could have been a world's champion. He was like a cat. He was the biggest crowd-pleaser this city ever had."

The cat-quickness was drained out of Harris yesterday. He slumped in the chair, plopping chocolate caramels into his mouth, trying to suck some sweetness back into his system.

Boxing commissioner Frank Wildman spent the day in Harrisburg. Around midnight, he talked about Harris, and the decision to deny him a license.

"We had that report (in 1966)," he recalled. "It said one eye was 100 percent and the other eye was in bad shape. Put yourself in my pants. The vision, plus thinking the only way Gypsy could make a living was with his fists.

"Then, you think you'd be an executioner if you sent him out and he got his head blasted. We know he was a better fighter with one eye than a lot of guys with two. But say he got whacked on the other eye. What then?"

What then? "It wouldn't happen," Harris promised. "I can handle myself. There's guys out there fighting, making big money, and none of 'em can whip me.

"What happened to me is what happens to lots of junkies, musicians, artists, smart people. The same thing happened to them in some other way. They got stopped from doing what they wanted to do.

"Let me fight. It's all I know. I'm no stickup man. I'm no thief. But I tell you this. You won't find me back in here again. But maybe the next time I'll wind up in the penitentiary."

Holmes Stings Ali: An Era Ends with 11th Round TKO

Philadelphia Daily News
October 3, 1980

LAS VEGAS—It was as graceless as a firing squad execution.

Muhammad Ali does not smoke, so they could not offer him a final cigarette. He needed a blindfold when it was finally over, to cover his lumpy, blackened eyes.

Larry Holmes demolished Ali last night in the parking lot of Caesars Palace, riddled him with jabs and hooks, splattered him with combinations. And for all the defense he mounted, Ali might just as well have had his hands tied behind his back, to some rigid stake.

His manager, Herbert Muhammad, wanted it stopped after 10 lopsided rounds. And Angelo Dundee delivered that message to referee Richard Green over the whining protests of Bundini Brown.

Ali sat there on his stool, his arms dangling wearily in his lap, as Green signaled the end of the fight, the end of a career, the end of an era.

***

ALI, the three-time heavyweight champion, came up empty. Completely empty. Parched, powerless and pitifully empty. He was less than a shadow of his former self because he had melted 30 pounds away from his shadow-casting bulk.

Holmes won every minute of every round. The three judges had the unbeaten WBC champion ahead, 10–9, in all 10 rounds, and judge Duane Ford even called the 10th and final round 10–8. That was the saddest round in Ali's long and brilliant career. He drifted along the ropes while Holmes moved with him, throwing an occasional jab, a half-hearted hook.

"A few times there," Holmes confessed afterward, "I didn't want to hit him. But I did what I had to do."

Holmes did what he had to do. He beat up a 38-year-old fighter who looked 48.

Afterward, Ali was too "tired" to come to the post-fight press conference. Holmes showed up, hardly breathing hard enough to flutter a candle. He showed up full of praise for the man he had just demolished. "He gave me a helluva fight," Holmes said. "I really respect and appreciate him."

What fight was Holmes watching? Was he suffering after-effects from a sparring-session thumbing earlier in the week? Some cynics suggested that Ali had tiptoed through a lot of rounds without ever throwing a punch, which is a parody of what heavyweight championship fights are all about.

―――――――

"THOSE WHO SAY it was a farce can go jump in the lake," Holmes countered. "We don't care about them.

"A lot of those who say Ali didn't throw a punch, let them jump in a ring, go through what athletes go through, sitting in a room, no sex, no nothing, worry about . . . 'Is this guy gonna knock my head off?'

"Walk out there and have the guy say, 'I'm gonna kick your butt.' See if you can do that."

Nobody in the media mob of 700 was volunteering to fight Holmes or Ali or anybody else. But Ali did get $8 million for this charade, and that is a lot of money for a trip down nostalgia lane.

The old Ali surfaced in the pre-fight tomfoolery, snarling at Holmes, pretending to run at him. But when the actual fight started, Holmes answered all of Ali's taunts and tricks with punches. And once he saw he had a shell in front of him, Holmes took to clowning, too, wiggling his hips in the fifth round. After the ninth, Holmes tapped Ali on the butt at the bell, a gentle reminder of one last prophecy gone sour. Ali had promised, "His behind will be mine before nine."

Holmes ran his record to 36–0, stretching his knockout string to eight in a row, eclipsing Joe Louis's modern mark of seven consecutive KOs.

―――――――

THERE WERE other reminders of Louis in this shambles. Because Louis came back at 38 and got trampled by Rocky Marciano. But Louis fought gallantly in the early rounds that night. Ali hardly threw a punch for the first four.

"I was hoping he knew something I didn't know," said Gene Kilroy, his business manager. "I thought he'd come out punching. But he couldn't do it." Ali came out chattering and Holmes came out jabbing. A good punch beats a good punch line every time.

Holmes breezed through those first five rounds, and the crowd of

24,780 grumbled. But Ali had done this before, as recently as the first fight with Leon Spinks.

Perhaps he was letting Holmes get weary or overconfident? But the evidence ruled out that theory when Ali left the right hand cocked the few times he had a chance to throw it.

The message simply wasn't traveling through his 38-year-old nerves quickly enough to deliver the blow. "I expected just what he done," said Holmes. "He was trying to throw a sneak right hand and a left hook. I look like I can be hit with a right hand. You throw it, and I'm not there."

––––––––––

A LUMP DEVELOPED under Ali's left eye in the sixth. Ali kept gesturing for Holmes to come forward and Holmes responded with a crushing left hook to Ali's ribs that might have shattered them. Ali reached back in time in the seventh, dancing around the ring. But the choreography lasted only for 90 seconds. The last 90 seconds of the round belonged to Holmes.

Holmes might have caught Ali with a slightly low punch in the eighth, because Ali twisted away in pain. Holmes was measuring him through the ninth. And when Ali's supporters in the crowd started chanting, "Ali, Ali," Holmes marched his flurries to the cadence.

Referee Richard Green wanted to stop it after nine, but Angelo Dundee talked him out of it. After that final pitiful three minutes, Dundee ended the bout, knowing there was no way Ali could pull it out.

So Ali delivered on one miracle out of two. He slashed 30 pounds from his body. But he could not slash two years of rust from his reflexes.

Well, maybe he delivered two miracles out of three. He did get $8 million for the fight. The live gate was a record-breaking $6 million. The fight generated some $30 million in revenue and did wonders for a sagging Las Vegas economy.

Ali weighed 217 for this one. He had not been that light since Zaire and the shocking victory over George Foreman.

––––––––––

HE WAS ABLE to befuddle the slow-witted Foreman. But last night he couldn't think of anything to derail Holmes.

There was tremendous irony in the awkward finish. Ali first won the heavyweight title when Sonny Liston quit in his corner in Miami after six rounds. That night, Dundee had to shove a half-blinded Ali out of his corner to continue to fight when a medical substance leaked into his eyes.

This time it was Dundee who kept Ali in the corner, ending the fight after 10 rounds. According to Nevada rules, it goes down as a TKO in the 11th round. That is some consolation for people who had Round 11 in the office pool. But there was little consolation for the people who paid big money to watch the lop-sided fight.

Heap Big Night: Camacho's Indian Outfit Highlights Wild Evening

Philadelphia Daily News
February 5, 1990

ATLANTIC CITY—Hector Camacho, who doesn't look Siouxish, danced into the ring wearing a feathered headdress, a buckskin monogrammed loincloth, suede boots with bells.

Vinny Pazienza, who bows to no man when it comes to bad taste, wore white trunks highlighted by embroidered red hearts with a Valentine's message that said "Kick A—."

Camacho did just that Saturday night at Convention Hall. Tomahawked Pazienza's face into a bloody mess, war-danced his way to a unanimous, 12-round decision, retained his World Boxing Organization junior welterweight title and left the ring to a throaty chorus of boos, probably from the folks who have never forgiven Sitting Bull for what he did to Gen. Custer.

It took Pazienza a while to get to the post-fight press conference because, between stitchings, a brawl broke out in his dressing room involving a tribe of Duvas and a process server looking for trainer Kevin Rooney, who owes the feds and Trump Plaza a lot of wampum.

And if that wasn't bad enough, the Convention Hall escalator malfunctioned and 12 fans wound up in the hospital.

And if that wasn't bad enough, some pugnacious customer sucker-punched Jack O'Donnell, the president of Trump Plaza, damaging two ribs.

So, where was Hulk Hogan while all this raucous stuff was happening? Oh, you say the Hulkster is getting ready to fight Mike Tyson, for $100 million?

Cool down, Snookster. Tyson is going to get a million bucks to referee a Hogan–Randy "Macho Man" Savage match in Detroit, and after the heavyweight champ whacks out Savage for dirty tactics, then you can start talking Tyson-Hogan, for all the tea in China, for all the coffee in Brazil, for all the corn in Iowa. Especially for all the corn in Iowa.

Camacho was terrific, and that's no Sitting Bull. Pazienza gave it his best shot, which is a forehead to the other guy's Adam's apple.

It was a fight bristling with action, awash in emotion, re-establishing

Camacho as a prime-time player, and has there ever been a 39–0 fighter as maligned?

In other, sanctioned bouts on the card, Pernell Whitaker kept his International Boxing Federation and World Boxing Council light-weight title, doing a 12-round clinic on Freddie Pendleton and winning a unanimous decision.

And Michael Moorer retained his WBO light-heavyweight championship, stopping the elusive Marcellus Allen after nine rounds.

But the really big winner was Trump Plaza, which promoted the fight.

"When you get done," said executive vice president Gary Selesner, "adding up the gate receipts, the pay-per-view income, the casino drop, foreign sales and delay telecast sale, this will be the most successful fight Trump Plaza has ever done.

"On Friday, the increment was $500,000 in casino drop. And Saturday night the increment was $3 million, when we did $5.2 million."

That's a lot of busted blackjack hands, a lot of snake eyes thrown, a lot of double zeroes on the roulette wheel.

Before Saturday night, Trump Plaza was content to recoup its site fee through gate receipts (this one drew 12,134 customers) and the casino profits.

This time, Trump Plaza Sports and Entertainment handled the pay-per-view deal, too.

"This event," said TPS&E vice president Bernie Dillon, "had the highest universe potential. There were 14 million homes with the ability to turn on the event."

If an expected 1½ percent of the homes subscribed at $20, Trump Plaza made a small profit. If 2 percent tuned in (280,000 homes), it meant a hefty profit.

With New England blanketed by snow yesterday, and another showing set for 4 P.M., you can just visualize proper Bostonians saying, "Margaret, wotta you say we watch the Eye-talian kid fight that Metzican who thinks every day's Halloween, hey?"

"Most promoters are happy to break even with a first event," Dillon said modestly. "If everything falls into place, we're looking at a profit of a couple of hundred thousand, and that would make us quite happy."

Somewhere, Bob Arum is sputtering, about pay-per-view expertise, about the vital part promoters play, about loyalty.

Does Trump Plaza's grand experiment mean a dwindling role for the Arums, Don Kings and Dan Duvas of the world?

"Promoters develop fighters," Dillon said. "They look for fighters in the amateurs, in club fights, they invest a lot of money to develop that talent.

"There will always be a place for the promoter. We're simply looking to control our own destiny. We're content to shrink the slice of the pie that goes to the promoter.

"Expertise comes in two ways. You have to have the expertise to know how to pick an event.

"And secondly, from an entertainment standpoint, you have to produce quality events.

"You can't fool the public. Oh, maybe you can fool 'em once, but you can't fool 'em twice."

The Trump folks picked a nifty event, matching two colorful, charismatic guys with big mouths.

And when it was over, Camacho announced that he wanted Dan Duva to promote his future fights, after he got through punching out what's left of Aaron Pryor's lights.

Duva wouldn't touch that one with a 10-foot hypodermic needle. And commissioner Larry Hazzard rolled his eyes in a "no way" look when asked if he'd approve a license for Pryor, a persistent drug abuser.

Word is that some backward state, such as Pennsylvania, might play host to that one.

"When he fights me," Pryor slurred Saturday night, "he'll be fighting a man."

Camacho's timetable calls for Pryor, followed by another waltz with Ray Mancini, followed by a blockbuster date with the Julio Cesar Chavez–Meldrick Taylor survivor.

"For that one," said Kathy Duva, "Dan would stand on his head."

As classy as he was in the ring, that's how crude and rude Camacho was when the fight was over.

Mingled with all the wrestling clatter was a kernel of truth about the lack of current crowd pleasers.

"This is a new year, a new decade," Camacho bragged. "Ray Leonard can't get no sweeter. Mike Tyson's too short. I'm Mr. Excitement."

It ain't bragging if you do it, said Muhammad Ali. Camacho did it to Pazienza.

Mancini was part of the pay-per-view telecast team.

"He said what he was gonna do and he went out and did it," Mancini said begrudgingly.

In the ravaged land of boxing, a guy doing a flamenco dance in an imitation leather loincloth can be king.

And that's the name of that game, slightly revised by the folks at Trump Plaza.

Low Blow: Douglas Doesn't Deserve to Lose Title

Philadelphia Daily News
February 12, 1990

MIAMI—It's over.

The fat lady has sung her tonsils off, even if there are no fat ladies in Japan.

James "Buster" Douglas beat Mike Tyson from here to Yokohama, and if anybody tries to snatch the championship belt back on some flimsy technicality, they ought to smear the guy with honey and nail him to a red anthill.

Douglas won the title despite an incompetent referee and two inept judges and a promoter who was rooting passionately for Tyson in front of a crowd that sat there, inscrutably silent.

If they swipe Douglas's title it would make the Brinks job look like small change. If they snatched the belt back it would give cruel and unusual punishment a bad name.

Everyone knows the trouble Douglas has seen.

That's the way HBO works. They book a Tyson title defense, they must fill the hour somehow.

So they send Larry Merchant and a film crew out to interview the challenger, up close and personal, make him famous for 15 minutes before Tyson leaves the guy rumpled on the canvas like soiled laundry in 90 seconds or so.

It was easy with Douglas. Hard on Douglas, easy on the scene-setters.

Douglas has seen more tsuris than Tevye in "Fiddler on the Roof," and that's been running for 27 years.

Douglas's life story makes Rocky I, II, III and IV look like Disney flicks.

You look in the dictionary and next to "pathos" you find Douglas's picture.

His father, Dynamite Douglas, a gutsy fighter, walked away from him because he felt Buster wasn't dedicated enough, tough enough.

One of Buster's three brothers died of an accidental self-inflicted gunshot wound.

His mom died of a stroke the day before Buster was scheduled to leave for Tokyo.

His wife left him.

The mother of his 11-year-old son has been diagnosed with leukemia.

The guys closest to Douglas walk around with pocket calculators, counting their blessings.

And then, against all odds, Douglas beat up a guy impersonating Tyson, knocked him senseless in the 10th round.

And then, before the champagne could dry on his 'do, before the fourth "Thank you, Lord" could be amended, all sorts of hell broke loose.

A pure and simple case of promoter Don King kicking a man when he's up.

King, you see, had plans for Tyson, beginning with a June 18 date against Evander Holyfield.

In case you missed it, the blond guy at ringside who looked like he had swallowed some bad sushi was Donald Trump. Tyson-Holyfield was set for Trump Plaza. They even had the logo for the fight. They were gonna call it "The Big One."

Stick two heavyweights in a ring and sometimes the best-laid plans of the richest men in the world get scrambled.

The Japanese Boxing Commission is protesting the outcome. That means the World Boxing Council executive council will meet in New York sometime next week, holding public hearings on the outcome of the fight.

First, they ought to place judges Ken Morita and Masakazu Uchida under house arrest. Lock 'em in a dark room and make 'em watch Gerry Cooney videotapes for 72 hours.

Morita had Tyson leading, 87–86, and Uchida had it 86–86 when Douglas turned out the lights on Tyson.

I gave Douglas the first five rounds, awarded the sixth to Tyson, the seventh to Douglas.

I gave Tyson a 10–8 edge in the eighth round when he reached down to the cellar for that wrecking ball uppercut that decked Douglas.

Thus I had Douglas leading, 87–83, when it ended with a referee named Octavio Meyran embracing Tyson solicitously.

Meyran since has confessed to a pitiful error, saying he was late in picking up the count of the knockdown timekeeper.

Indeed, perhaps Meyran was a second, or even two seconds, late starting his count, but a weary and battered Tyson was late trudging to a neutral corner.

Douglas's head never hit the canvas. And he took most of the count, while on one knee, gazing intently at Meyran.

Who was Douglas supposed to listen to? The timekeeper? The ring card girl? Ivana Trump?

Douglas got up between 8 and 9. The bell clanged moments later.

Afterward, Douglas insisted he was not hurt, just surprised, toppled while off-balance and a trifle careless. The way he fought the ninth round would indicate Douglas is telling the truth.

Douglas earned that belt, hammering a lethargic, confused Tyson, beating him to the punch and tying him in clumsy knots in close.

Douglas honored the memory of his mother, showed enough courage and fortitude to please his father, provided a lasting memory for his son, and he gave underdogs everywhere fresh hope.

Vegas wouldn't touch the fight with a 10-foot chopstick. No price on the outcome, but you could bet over-and-under on the fight lasting four rounds.

Douglas beating Tyson might be the most remarkable upset in boxing history. Cassius Marcellus Clay thumping Sonny Liston into abject surrender as a 7–1 underdog was shocking, but Liston was old and distracted and the finish had the aroma of dead dolphin.

This one has a stench, too, because of the judges' cards. If, somehow, Tyson had wobbled through the last three rounds, might he have stolen a decision he didn't deserve?

There are some other questions to be answered. How many options did King squeeze out of Douglas's camp in return for giving him the title shot?

Does Holyfield get first shot at the new champ? Or must he wait while Douglas picks someone softer for his first defense?

Does Tyson fire the guys who worked his corner in whispery confusion Saturday night? Does he abandon the lifestyle that sent him into the ring pudgy and unprepared?

When he comes back, if he comes back, he comes back as the challenger. The heavyweight champion of the world is James "Buster" Douglas, and those who would dispute that are scoundrels who would trample truth and justice.

Artistic License

Philadelphia Daily News
March 7, 1990

GEORGE WASHINGTON DUKE, the sinister fight promoter in "Rocky V," has this sports writer in his pocket.

So, when Tommy "Machine" Gunn easily whips Union Cane to win the vacant heavyweight championship and the post-fight press conference unravels into snarling chaos, the sports writer on the take asks the toughest, nastiest questions because Duke wants to goad Gunn into fighting the battered, broke Rocky Balboa.

Which tells you everything you need to know about what Sylvester Stallone thinks of sports writers.

Rocky is busted because while he was in the Soviet Union, his accountant and lawyer ripped him off, which tells you what Stallone thinks of accountants and lawyers.

In "Rocky V," a Philadelphia lawyer named Jimmy Binns plays a Philadelphia lawyer named Jimmy Binns.

Uh huh, the same Jimmy Binns who led the legal scrum to keep the Rocky statue, that ugly hunk of hardware, in front of the Art Museum, where it blotches the loveliest view our tattered city has to offer.

Does life imitate art or what?

Put the statue on Jimmy Binns's front lawn, even if you have to move a jockey with the ring in his hand. Or a pink flamingo.

"Leprechauns," Binns said, laughing. "Irish guys have leprechauns."

Or put it on the downside of the Penrose Avenue bridge, so that visitors coming into town from the airport are distracted from that slag heap of rust and the mountain of flattened cars that is now their first memorable sight.

Stick it near the Italian market, where Rocky ran. Or outside the slaughterhouse, where he pounded sides of beef to toughen his hands.

Yo, it doesn't even belong near the Spectrum, because Stallone used the Los Angeles Sports Arena to film the fight scenes in the original "Rocky."

Ship it to Camden if the Sixers and Flyers move across the river. Camden has a feel for underdogs.

I don't wanna argue whether it's art or junk or commercial or racist or a symbol for underdogs.

I'm a paid-up member of the Art Museum, and I still don't understand the charm of Andy Warhol's soup cans. And LeRoy Neiman's smeary sports cartoons make my list of the most overrated things in America.

When the Art Museum had that Jasper Johns exhibit, I went, prepared to scoff, because Norman Braman had paid $4.2 million for one of Johns's paintings, and most of the others looked like elaborate smart-aleck rebus puzzles.

But the one Braman owns was big and exciting and colorful and crammed with fascinating imagery. And that's what art is all about.

Stallone says he's helped popularize the museum and done wonders for attendance. Which is garbage, because most of the people who run up the steps don't go inside the museum.

Don't get me wrong. I admire Stallone.

Here's a guy whose acting skill runs the emotional gamut from A to B, who coulda been a bum in the streets, but persevered against all odds to go the distance, to become rich and famous.

He did popularize that view from the top of the Art Museum steps. And he does help the city's sagging economy when he films "Rocky V" here. And he does give Stu Bykofsky a muscled-up target to snipe at.

And he did give the mayor a rare chance to talk art and literature with someone his intellectual match.

I just wish he didn't have this skewed vision of what Philadelphia sports writers are all about, depicting them as rude, crude, corruptible. And dull.

How do I know?

Because I'm in "Rocky V," playing one of those rude, crude, unimaginative writers.

I wasn't going to write about my experiences until the movie came out. But I changed my mind when Stallone tried to renege on his promise to tote that dreadful statue off the museum steps as soon as he finished filming in Philadelphia.

Funny thing is, Binns helped get me the part. Binns sat there, puzzled, through rehearsals, while they tried 11 professional actors, and none was nasty enough, belligerent enough.

"So I told them," Binns explained, "why don't you get the real thing? And I gave them the names of sports writers to call."

They called, asked us to show up at a photo studio on Orianna Street to be "taped."

The *Daily News*'s Elmer Smith and the *Inquirer*'s mild-mannered Bob Seltzer were there, too, apparently auditioning for the part.

We ignored the script to free-wheel our way through the scene, merrily insulting the fighter, his victim and boxing in general.

That night, Diane, the casting person, called. I had a part. Show up at Convention Center at 6:30 the next morning.

Showed up at 6:15. Channel 10's Al Meltzer was already there. So was a catering truck dispensing juice, coffee, croissants and cereals.

There were dressing rooms assigned (they misspelled Hochman, Meltzer and Seltzer, getting only Smith right). And a hasty visit to the makeup trailer.

The four of us, plus two guys from Jersey who make a living doing bit parts in movies, were gathered for a run-through by the director, John Avildsen.

We took turns reciting lines like "C'mon Duke, Cane's a paper champion. Everyone knows that."

And then Avildsen pointed at each of us, assigning a number. I was "three," which meant two nasty comments, not questions.

That's not my style, but I decided to pattern my approach after the acerbic Mike Marley, the *New York Post* boxing writer, and his Spanish Inquisition style.

Avildsen saw the real writers struggling with the dialogue and said, "If you're not comfortable with the lines, go ahead and change them to the way you'd say them."

So, when George Washington Duke says that Union Cane was the recognized champ, I was supposed to yelp, "We know the rating system can be manipulated. . . . [B]ottom line is, Tommy Gunn beat a second-rate fighter with a glass jaw."

I changed it to, "Tommy Gunn beat a second-rate fighter with so much glass in his jaw he tinkled when he walked."

Avildsen chuckled, the other actors grinned, and rehearsals commenced.

It took us 18 takes to get it right, mostly because the actor playing Duke kept botching his lines.

Tommy Morrison, the fighter who plays Gunn, was terrific, properly defensive, sincerely annoyed by the yapping writers.

We broke for lunch, roast chicken or vegetarian lasagne, artichoke hearts, marinated mushrooms, cheesecake and chocolate pudding.

Never mind that Stu Nahan put sliced olives on his chocolate pudding, the lunch break was fascinating.

Binns talked about the trouble finding a fighter to play Cane.

"I suggested Evander Holyfield," Binns said, "but he said he ain't losing to anyone in Hollywood or anywhere else.

"Frank Bruno, he was doing mime in England. Mike Dokes wasn't tall enough. Razor Ruddock had a fight scheduled. Bonecrusher Smith didn't make it past the screen test.

"And then they found Mike Williams, who is built like a brick outhouse and very good in the part."

We regrouped, with the cameras facing the media mob this time. Stallone suddenly appeared in a black, leather coat.

Almost immediately, he began to rewrite his script. And when I delivered my line about so much glass in his jaw that he tinkled, I glanced over in time to see Stallone give a waggled sign of displeasure to Avildsen.

Five minutes later, Avildsen asked me to change the line to, "so much glass in his jaw he oughta be a chandelier."

Did I mention that there was this statuesque redhead in the first row?

Well, Stallone decides to give Nahan one more sarcastic line about who Tommy was gonna fight next, the redhead in the front row: "I hear she comes cheap."

Everyone, actors, writers, crew, went "oooooh." The redhead must have winced, too.

Stallone took up a parade rest stance in front of her and said, "Hey, babe, that's show biz. Next movie, maybe you'll get to play a nun."

Twelve takes and we nailed it. Finished at 4:55.

Gunn, properly goaded, raps on Rocky's door, challenges him to fight. They brawl in the streets.

Originally, Rocky was going to die, but they thought that'd be a bummer, so they changed the script.

Good choice. Rocky's got this teenage son, and five years from now, we could have "Rocky VI" with the kid giving up a promising career as a sculptor, risking those gifted hands to become a fighter despite Rocky's anguished pleas.

They could polish up the Rocky statue one more time and trundle it up the parkway to that other museum.

Stick it on the front lawn, near the guy with his chin in his hand, his brow furrowed in thought.

Who knows, it might increase attendance at the Rodin Museum. By then, Rocky will be too old to climb steps.

The Only One to Blame Is the One Going to Jail

Philadelphia Daily News
February 11, 1992

MIKE TYSON is going to the slammer. Guilty on one count of rape, two counts of criminal deviate conduct.

A meteoric career that began behind bars will end behind bars, one more American tragedy.

So, who's to blame?

Mike Tyson is to blame. And he faces a maximum of 60 years to think about it, to accept responsibility. Accepting responsibility, that's a vanishing trait, which is the real American tragedy.

Bill Cayton, still Tyson's manager of record, will blame promoter Don King, for not keeping a tighter rein on the former heavyweight champion.

King will blame racism, because he always does.

Sexists will blame Robin Givens, married briefly and tempestuously to Tyson, for doing him wrong.

Liberals will blame cultural deprivation, because Tyson grew up on Brownsville's mean streets, although those same streets have produced opera stars, authors and even a stray sports writer or two.

Psychologists will blame the absence of a father.

Greg Garrison, the prosecuting attorney, in one of the rare mistakes he made all week, blamed America's worship of false idols, saying that the professional athlete has been allowed to become such a mega-god that he no longer is responsive to basic morality.

Garrison said he wouldn't pop any champagne and that's good, because there is nothing to celebrate here.

And even though it took the jury more than nine hours to reach the verdict, this wasn't a tough call.

Garrison said that himself earlier in the trial. Said that if this had been "some kid from the projects" it would have been a two-day affair.

Well, it was some kid from the projects. Some kid who did time in a reform school where Bobby Stewart taught him to fight, which led him to Cus D'Amato, which led him to become the youngest heavyweight champion in history.

"Cus used to tell me," trainer Matt Baransky once told me, "'If I get a good heavyweight it will put 10 years on my life.'

"And then he told me he got that heavyweight. He turned him pro, and after five or six fights he said that if it wasn't for the fact Jimmy Jacobs had so much money invested in the kid, he'd can him right then, tell him to walk and to keep going.

"And then Cus said, 'This bleeper is gonna take 10 years off my life!'"

Baransky was there at the start, when D'Amato rescued Tyson from reform school, when Cus predicted greatness for the thick-necked, strong-armed teenager.

D'Amato died before Tyson fulfilled his prophecy, so he's not around to defend himself against the inevitable charges that it is his fault, that he was so obsessed with Tyson becoming the youngest champ ever that he looked the other way when Tyson shattered training rules, when he exhibited anti-social behavior, when he scorned basic morality.

And after D'Amato was gone, was there the same obsessive urge to make Tyson the richest young heavyweight in history that caused Jacobs and Cayton to ignore breaches of basic morality, to buy Tyson's way out of trouble?

How much fault can be assigned to Kevin Rooney, who trained Tyson until King started calling the shots?

Rooney was close enough to be kissed before each fight, distant enough to settle for lectures on the evils of booze and drugs.

There are those who believe that boxing is thinly disguised savagery and they will be howling today about the sport encouraging violence and we will listen to slurred rebuttals from Muhammad Ali and Joe Frazier and a righteous sermon from George Foreman.

Tyson caused Tyson's downfall. Too stubborn to seek professional help for his torment, too weaned by the sycophants around him to seek instant gratification, smart enough to study boxing history, ignorant enough to ignore it.

There was that scene at The Mirage at dinner. I'm there with Ali, his wife, Lonnie, his longtime friend Gene Kilroy.

Tyson struts in, surrounded by his bodyguards in their sharkskin suits and their sharklike scowls.

Tyson pulls up a chair without waiting for an invitation to join us. The bodyguards stand, arms folded, eunuchs at a harem door.

Earlier, while Ali signed autographs in the lobby, Mrs. Ali had talked about how her husband was reluctant to offer advice to other fighters because he had been badgered to conform all those years.

And then, during dinner, Ali had leaned close to Tyson and, in a hoarse whisper, warned the fighter to be careful with women because of "what's out there."

Tyson cackled, put his paw in his pocket and removed the only contents, a packet of condoms, and flipped them onto the dinner table.

"I'm always prepared," he giggled, while Mrs. Ali's eyes squinted in discomfort.

I first encountered Tyson in Texas, at the Olympic boxing trials in 1984, saw him lose a decision to Henry Tillman, heard D'Amato whine about a conspiracy to keep Tyson off the team.

I did a brief, sympathetic interview with the beaten boxer. Years later, Tyson said he remembered it, remembered me for being kind.

Tyson might have been fibbing when he told me that, the small lie being part of some hidden agenda. You never knew with Tyson, so moody, so cranky, so belligerent, such a short span of attention.

Who knows if professional help would have steered him off the path that led to the slammer?

I saw him in a later column as the emperor with no clothes, deceived by the sycophant tailors around him into believing he had new garments, spun of gold.

The column made him angry, not enlightened. We never had a satisfactory dialogue after that.

So Cayton will blame King and King will blame white America and the rhetoric will turn ugly.

And many women will applaud the verdict because it ends a distressing streak (Clarence Thomas, William Kennedy Smith) and you can't have women afraid to speak out when abused and no should mean no, whether the rapist is a plumber or a former heavyweight champion.

All that heat to be generated, debating the decision to send Mike Tyson to the slammer, from which he came.

Who's to blame? Wasn't there someone out there, strong enough, tough enough, determined enough, caring enough to teach him right from wrong?

Tyson will have plenty of time to ponder the questions, grope for the answers. The odds of getting good advice in the slammer are slim and none, and Slim just got paroled.

There's a wakeup call for America in all of this, but America will be too busy arguing to hear it.

Frazier's Win over Ali Stands Test of Time

Philadelphia Daily News
March 8, 2011

JOE HAND remembers the ferocious left hook Joe Frazier launched in the 15th round. Remembers it thundering into Muhammad Ali's jaw. Remembers Ali toppling backward, hitting the canvas with a thud.

"I was shocked that Ali got back up," Hand recalled the other day, sitting by the pool in Belleair Beach, Fla. "I remember the tassels on Ali's shoes. I remember thinking, 'Everybody's got an angle' and that Ali must have thought the tassels made him look faster."

Ali was faster than Frazier, tassels or no tassels. Just not fast enough in the final round of a brutal, primitive fight to avoid that lethal left hook, the one Frazier said he "reached down home" for.

It is 40 years to the day and Hand has vivid memories of what he calls "the greatest sporting event of all time."

He was a cop back then, one of the original investors in Cloverlay, the syndicate of local businessmen who owned shares in Frazier. He looks back in awe, at the furor the fight generated, at the gaudy crowd the fight attracted to Madison Square Garden, at the damage the fight inflicted on both fighters.

"I had a train, an Amtrak train, eight cars," Hand recalled. "To take the Cloverlay people to New York. All the men in tuxedos. Ringside was formal. I had 500 tickets to distribute.

"I remember charging $25 round trip and I still made a fistful of money. I hired two detectives to provide security that night. Told 'em they had to wear suits. Stuffed all the money in their pockets.

"You looked around that night. . . . Burt Lancaster, a terrific movie star, was doing color commentary on the broadcast. Frank Sinatra was taking pictures for Life magazine. The Kennedys were there. Nixon was there.

"Ringside tickets were $150. I had a ticket for [mayor] Frank Rizzo, ringside. And three more for his staff, not ringside. Rizzo said, 'I can't sit in front of my friends.' He wanted three more ringside seats. There was no way I could get 'em. He handed back his ticket and said there were no hard feelings.

"And then I heard from a Cadillac dealer in Delaware. He wanted two ringside tickets. Get 'em, plus $2,000 and I could come to his showroom and pick out any Cadillac I wanted. Never could get that other ticket.

"Last minute I hear that Leonard Tose and John Taxin need tickets. I come up with two tickets. Tose said, 'Any time you wanna see an Eagles game, call me.' I never went to an Eagles game where I didn't pay my way in. Taxin said, 'Any time you want to eat at Bookbinders it's on me.' I never ate at Bookbinders where I didn't pick up the tab."

Hand remembers Frazier's dark mood leading up to the fight. "He got mean, he got nasty," he said. "I was the guy who showed up bearing bad news.

"He goes to training camp and his phone bill the first month is $500. The Cloverlay people go nuts. They pick me to tell him he can't do that. Here, we were gonna make all this money, and they were worried about a $500 phone bill.

"Then there was the motorcycle, which he loved to ride. They want me to tell him he can't ride it. He gives me the name of a Chevrolet dealer, tells me if he can have a Corvette he'll trade in the motorcycle. He got a $4,000 car for a $600 motorcycle.

"That night, you just knew Frazier would win. All that anger he'd built up from Ali's insults. There was no way in the world Ali could beat him that night.

"When it was over, back in Joe's dressing room, two guys came in and took everything Joe had worn, the green and gold robe, the boxing trunks, the gloves. Left him with a jockstrap and socks. I don't know what happened to all that gear."

He does know what happened to Frazier in the days that followed. "Got home, checked into St. Luke's Hospital," Hand said sadly.

"His blood pressure was sky-high. If it got any higher they said it would cause a stroke.

"I stayed with him through the night. Yank Durham went off on a trip to Europe. Bruce Wright, the attorney, he had someplace to go. I was the only one. He was my friend. It hurt to see him so beat up.

"Both fighters were never the same after that night. I don't see much of Joe but they tell me he's limping, walking with a cane."

There was one more memory, one I'd never heard before. "Cloverlay wanted to build a playground in Beaufort [S.C.] to honor Joe," Hand said. "I talked to the mayor, told him what we had in mind, flew down there.

"I call the mayor, they tell me he'll meet me at Howard Johnson's. He walks in, walks out. I was sitting there with two of Joe's sisters and I figure out later he did not want to sit in a restaurant with two black people.

"I start asking around about how they'll organize the teams to play on the ballfield. They tell me they'll drive around town with a loud-speaker and tell kids when and where to sign up. I ask 'em how many black kids will be on these teams. I don't get a real answer.

"And that day I get a phone call saying maybe I'd better leave town and forget about the playground. I get in my rental car, I see two guys parked nearby. I'm carrying a gun and glad of it because I've got to drive down a dirt road to get to the airport.

"Nothing happened, but the playground never got built."

Stan Hochman poses for a story.
(*Philadelphia Daily News* File Photo, October 23, 1967.)

Perhaps not an athlete himself, Stan Hochman could
nonetheless manage a chin-up.
(*Philadelphia Daily News* File Photo, February 13, 1968.)

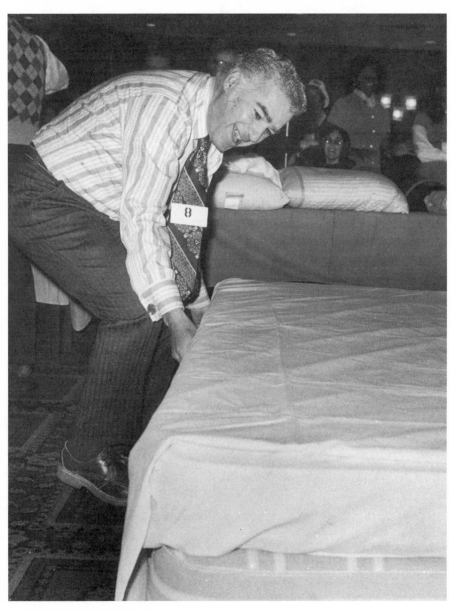

Stan Hochman competes in a bed-making competition for a story
at the Marriott Hotel in Philadelphia. He won.
(Myers/*Philadelphia Daily News* File Photo.)

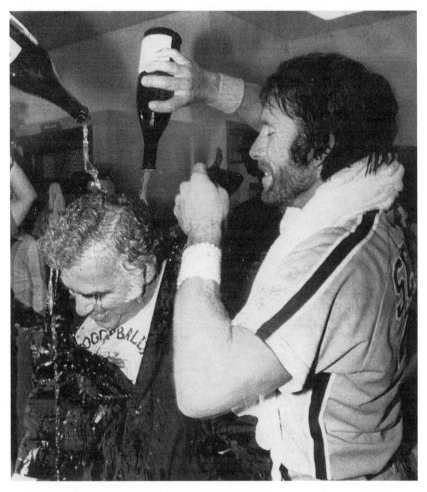

The Phillies' Mike Schmidt douses Stan Hochman with champagne
in the dressing-room celebration after the Phillies clinched the 1978
Eastern Division championship.
(jjh/Mike Feldman, UPI, September 30, 1978.)

FACING PAGE:

TOP: Stan Hochman sits in the left-field stands in Atlanta Stadium
during a Braves-Padres game. (ry/lg, UPI, September 16, 1973.)

BOTTOM: Stan Hochman weighs in
as part of a story on health.
(*Philadelphia Daily News* File Photo.)

Stan Hochman takes the microphone,
flanked by Wilbert Montgomery and Ron Jaworski.
(*Philadelphia Daily News* File Photo, February 19, 1982.)

Stan Hochman, a premier horse-racing writer, poses
alongside a horse with his daughter, Anndee, in 1983.
(Hochman family collection.)

A scene from the movie *Rocky V*, filmed at the Philadelphia Civic Center, features Stan Hochman in the role of a sportswriter. ("ROCKY V" © 1990 METRO-GOLDWYN-MAYER STUDIOS INC. ALL RIGHTS RESERVED. Courtesy of MGM Media Licensing.)

Stan Hochman and Muhammad Ali attend a formal affair.
(Photo by Webster Riddick, © 1991, Frazier's Golden Gloves, Inc.
Courtesy of Weatta Frazier Collins.)

Stan Hochman dons Dr. J gloves to write one of his columns.
(Bob Laramie/*Philadelphia Daily News* Photo, February 24, 1991.)

FACING PAGE:

Stan Hochman peruses his natural environment, the newsroom.
(© Brad Nau.)

At an event for the Philadelphia Police Athletic League, Stan Hochman poses with a police officer and a group of children. (Kelly and Massa Photography, January 20, 2000.)

At a book signing, Stan Hochman shares the stage with Bernie Parent. (Yong Kim/ *Philadelphia Daily News* Photo, November 14, 2012.)

Stan Hochman dances with his granddaughter, Sasha. (Hochman family collection.)

Anndee, Stan (who often referred to himself as "the third-best writer in [the] family"), and Gloria Hochman sit poised at their typewriters in a family holiday greeting card. (Hochman family collection.)

Happy Holidays

Peace and Love,
The Hochmans

Stan Hochman dances with his wife, Gloria.
(Hochman family collection.)

PART IV
Football

Introduction

RAY DIDINGER

DUANE THOMAS DIDN'T TALK during the 1971 NFL season. He didn't talk to his coaches. He didn't talk to his teammates. He certainly didn't talk to the media. But he talked to Stan Hochman. It was just another example of how Stan was able to get the stories no one else could.

It was after Super Bowl VI, after Thomas played a starring role in the Dallas Cowboys 24–3 win over Miami, that Stan approached the sullen running back. Thomas wore the same scowl he had worn all season as he waved off any attempt at conversation. Most writers had stopped trying to talk with Thomas, but not Stan.

"Duane, you don't look happy," Stan said.

Thomas tapped his chest.

"Happiness is in here," he said.

So Thomas had his Super Bowl ring, and Stan had his scoop. The fact that Thomas spoke was the most interesting angle of an otherwise ho-hum Super Bowl. If there were a game ball for writers, Stan would have won it. That was true most days.

When Leonard Tose met with NFL commissioner Pete Rozelle to discuss the gambling debts that would ultimately force him to sell the Eagles, Stan wound up riding in the limousine with Tose on the way to Penn Station. His account of watching Tose gulp down one scotch after another while insisting everything was fine took the *Daily News* readers right to the heart of the story.

"I think you guys [writers] orchestrate this," Tose said. It was a portrait of a man in denial and headed for certain ruin. We all wrote the story of the owner's demise, but Stan—with his up-close-and-personal reporting—allowed us to see the pain behind those words.

Stan bonded with Buddy Ryan over their mutual love of horses. Stan didn't bond with Ryan's boss, Eagles owner Norman Braman, who was more interested in making money than winning football games. Stan called the owner Norman "Bottom Line" Braman, and the name stuck.

Football is a complex game with many layers of strategy. For a writer, it is easy to lose the reader in statistics and jargon. Stan never did that. He focused on the people—the coaches and players—because he understood that the people were more interesting than the Xs and Os. His account of Dick Vermeil's emotional meltdown as coach of the Eagles, which is included in this collection, is a vivid portrait of the pressure these men live with as they prepare for each Sunday's game.

Whether the Eagles won or lost, there was one thing the fans all agreed on: they wanted to see what Stan had to say about it in the Monday sports section.

Vermeil Listens to Own Advice— Leaving the Eagles

Philadelphia Daily News
January 11, 1983

SPASMS. DICK VERMEIL would be sitting there, staring at the gray-and-white game films, looking for some lard-assed enemy linebacker he could exploit, and suddenly his body would twitch convulsively, like a guy who had clutched a live wire.

"I could start feeling it last year," Vermeil said yesterday. "I'd be sitting in the darn staff meeting, projector on, looking at films.

"All of the muscles in the back of your neck would stiffen. And then, you'd feel like you'd had eight cups of coffee. Quiver. From the intensity.

"And then you've got to run the film all over again because you didn't see what you think you were seeing.

"Your concentration span is poor. And your mind wanders. With me, it was my emotions. I embarrassed myself sometimes. Some of the things I did."

Some of the things he did, some of the things he said. Some of the things he doesn't remember doing or saying because he overloaded the circuits and the lights went out in the ballyard of his mind.

It happened at least twice this year, and Vermeil could feel the wires fraying. So he put himself on the injured-reserve list yesterday. Said he was burned out, which is the kind of thing that can happen when you're clutching high-voltage wires for a living for 23 years.

He was a lot like the ballerina in the film "Red Shoes." The projector whir was music only he heard, and he could not stop dancing. But he did not want to fall off a parapet in front of a screeching locomotive. He did not want to collapse some Sunday with his earphones on and a clipboard in his hands in front of 67,000 yowling strangers.

So he walked away. He will try television for at least a year. He said that if he finds he cannot live without coaching he will be back, next time trying to muffle the spasms by delegating more responsibility, by quitting at 3 A.M. instead of 6 A.M.

Eddie Sawyer quit as manager of the Phillies after opening day, 1960. Said he was 49 and wanted to live to be 50.

But Sawyer had a wretched team to manage, with a hippo named

Pancho Herrera playing second base and a pitching staff that was either too young or too old.

Vermeil is 47, trim, dapper, movie-handsome. The scars are all inside. He got here in 1976 and took a mediocre rabble of a football mob and transformed it into a Super Bowl team five years later.

This year the team stumbled through a woeful 3–6 season. The strike disillusioned him, but that isn't why he quit. The owner's snarling post-strike stance disenchanted him, but that isn't why he quit. His best friend, Bill Walsh, will abandon the sideline demons to concentrate on being San Francisco general manager, but that isn't why he quit. The money is good in television, the hours are short and a color commentator doesn't have to worry about what a cameraman is shoving up his nose in his spare time, but that isn't why he quit.

"Last spring I did some public service announcements for Blue Cross and Blue Shield," Vermeil said. "With the message being, 'Take care of yourself, you belong to you.'

"I've decided to take my own advice and step down, out of coaching. I am emotionally burned out. I'm going to get out for a while and see if I can live without it."

That's it. No muddy controversy, no murky intrigue. The Eagles played lousy so Vermeil worked harder, because that always was his answer. But this time it came up dark and gloomy as an empty blackboard.

"When I started coaching 23 years ago," he said, "I told myself if I ever questioned it I should get out. The head coach should be the tempo-setter.

"I've made a lot of mistakes. The most vivid is that I set a tempo it may not be possible to keep through a 10-year pro contract."

Later on in the emotional press conference Vermeil said his biggest mistake was listening to too many people who said he was too demanding of his players and of himself.

That was his strength. And his weakness. He cared so much about winning, he figured his players would care just as much. He worked so hard, he thought they wouldn't bitch if he worked them almost as hard.

The workaholic image was no sham. I spent a week with the Eagles in 1979 as they prepared for the Steelers. I arrived at 8:03 that first morning and found Vermeil glaring at his wristwatch.

Later in the grinding week, Thursday or Friday, he shrugged his hunched shoulders, troubled by an episode he was willing to share. "I know I've been pushing myself too hard," he said. "I found myself eating a hoagie in the john the other night. You can't work that many hours that you wind up doing that."

The Eagles beat the Steelers and Vermeil did not slow down. He got rid of the squawkers, and he kept a core of guys who had been through the early '70s hell. But the new guys had not known the ugly days, and wouldn't sacrifice enough of themselves to avoid slithering back into that unfamiliar swamp.

For all the changes, the Eagles still had too many journeymen players who had to play out of their skulls on Sundays to beat the good teams. When they stopped playing out of their skulls, Vermeil did not blame them. He blamed himself, and that acid ate away at his insides.

"I hope very much my players can understand where I'm coming from," Vermeil said, the words filtering through sobs. "I love those guys. And it's not easy to say goodbye to them."

He was beaten by the one guy he couldn't whip, Dick Vermeil. He is too intense, too dedicated, too determined just to tap-dance his way through a season. He had no other interests to distract him, no hobbies to soften the pressures of the job.

He blamed the struggle with himself on his personality, a personality forged in Calistoga's Owl Garage, working for his dad.

"My environment was an intense environment, in terms of work," Vermeil said. "Nothing was ever good enough unless it was done his way. And even then, sometimes it wasn't good enough."

He quit the garage job many times, but always shuffled back to it. Now, he is walking away from coaching, because he has bankrupted his energy, his enthusiasm.

Leonard Tose, who has weathered other post-season blues, was stunned when Vermeil decided to pack it in. The players had a warning.

"I told the squad right before the (second) Washington game," Vermeil said, "that if I couldn't get them playing up to their ability again, I might be the first guy I'd waive."

He wasn't much for empty threats. Al Chesley went from starter to the waiver wire when he couldn't or wouldn't conform. He loved his players, but the passion had limits.

Tose saw him swaggering across his television screen, whipping old Woody Hayes in the Rose Bowl, and hired him in 1976. He soared across the South Philly skies like a meteor and it was exciting.

And now he is fading into the blackness. Like a meteor. Burned out.

On the Road with Leonard Tose

Philadelphia Daily News
December 19, 1984

NEW YORK—Leonard Tose says we've been wrong, wrong, wrong, 13,000,000 times wrong when we keep saying he's $40 million in hock.

"You keep saying there's $9 million in personal debts," Tose muttered as he angled across Penn Station's cluttered waiting room, heading for the shelter of the Iron Horse Bar and a chance to douse the fire in his belly with a Dewar's and water, with a twist.

"There is no $9 million in personal debts. There is nothing in personal debts. How could I get $9 million in debt?"

"How" I asked, "could the Philadelphia Eagles be $31 million in debt?"

"Bullbleep," Tose grumbled, startling a benchful of passengers. "The whole debt is $27 million. That's what it is. I don't know where you guys get your numbers."

We had ridden from the Waldorf-Astoria to Penn Station in Tose's rented limousine. Tose, his daughter Susan Fletcher, his attorney Larry Shaiman, his publicity man Ed Wisneski. And me.

What was I doing in the front seat of Leonard Tose's limo? Blinking in disbelief, mostly.

When the emergency meeting of the National Football League owners had finally broken up, Susan Fletcher and Shaiman had scurried up the mezzanine steps of the Waldorf-Astoria to use a pay phone to call Mayor W. Wilson Goode.

Shaiman did the talking, reassuring the mayor that everything had gone splendidly, describing the meeting as very positive. As they started back down the steps I asked Susan if she intended to make the 7 o'clock Metroliner.

She glanced at her watch, said, "No, we'll have to make the 7:30 train, and if you need a ride you can join us, just hop in the front seat."

We all then walked briskly across the cluttered hotel lobby to the Hilton Room, where commissioner Pete Rozelle and Tose were in the early throes of a press conference that had all the style and substance of mud wrestling.

Tose denied that he had a $12 million Crocker Bank loan due by January 1. "It's due in March or April," he said hazily. And then he glanced at his watch and said he had to catch a train and left Rozelle standing there to catch the flak of tough questions about what it was the owners had decided after five hours of meetings.

We darted out of the hotel and found the long gray limo at the curb. Tose, Ms. Fletcher, Shaiman scrambled into the back. As Wisneski crouched I asked him to double-check about having me as a passenger. He leaned in, leaned out, and said it was OK.

The owners had pledged to help Tose, the commissioner seemed elated, Tose had promised to keep the team in Philadelphia. The conversation on the way to Penn Station seemed strangely out of synch.

Susan did most of the talking. About the balmy weather, about a fur coat, about an upcoming trip to Acapulco, about a lovely summer years ago when she broke up with her boyfriend and her father whisked her through the New York scene after telling her that in two weeks she wouldn't even remember the guy's name. He was right.

At the station, Susan headed for the ticket windows, to swap her Metroliner tickets for the less-expensive club car seats on the regular train.

"What are you gonna do?" Tose asked. "Save me a buck? You go swap the tickets, I'm gonna get a drink."

And that's how Tose came to tell me that his debts were exaggerated, and how I wound up sitting with him at the Iron Horse Bar, while he gulped down three Dewar's and water with a twist in a 45-minute dialogue.

"I'm not gonna give you a bleeping exclusive interview," he snarled, while Wisneski clutched his ribs and whispered in Tose's ear, begging Tose to open his mouth only to inhale the scotch.

Tose had not eaten all day. He said he had not eaten in four days. There were some things I wanted to ask him before the Dewar's skidded through his system. I wanted to know how he would be able to live with the city's anger, with the backlash of fury stemming from the aborted move to Phoenix.

"The anger you perceive," Tose said, while Wisneski did a flamenco dance in the background, "is totally different than what I perceive. You should have been in 30th Street station this morning. People coming up to me, wishing me luck."

"But what about the barbershop scene, the schoolboys booing you?" I asked.

"Arrrgggh," Tose gargled. "A couple of kids. A friendly reaction. They weren't unfriendly. I think you guys orchestrate this. I don't think it's out there."

"The test will come," I suggested, sipping at the Jack Daniels and soda Tose had bought me, "when it's time to sell season tickets."

"The phones are ringing off the hook," Tose countered swiftly. "And I'm quoting my ticket manager."

Susan joined us, fanning four tickets. There was a problem with getting four club car seats. She had one confirmed and three maybes. I moved to the stool on my right to make room for her next to Tose.

"I didn't know who you were," she said sweetly. "If I had, I'd have told you to take a cab. You got in, I said, 'The gentleman needed a ride.' My father said, 'That's Stan Hochman.'"

Tose didn't know when a $12-million note was due, his daughter didn't recognize a columnist who has been with one of the two newspapers in town for 26 years. There is a Twilight Zone quality to this story of a thwarted team napping.

A lot of people think Susan Fletcher is the villainess, that she's the one who choreographed the botched sale to the Guida group, that she was so eager to get to Phoenix she registered her teenage daughter in a school there.

"No," she said. "You listen to James Monaghan, you're in trouble."

Didn't all that harsh criticism of her role trouble her?

"I'm not angry or bitter about it," she said. "Leonard Tose is the boss. He always has been the boss. He always will be the boss. You've known him for a long time. Does anybody make him do something he doesn't want to do?"

Wisneski said I was harassing them, that they had earned the chance to get loose after a trying day. The Jack Daniels had affected my hearing. I wanted to know from this attractive little woman's own lips if she thought the citizens of Philadelphia would forgive and forget her machinations to move the team to Phoenix.

"Yeah," she said, after ordering a Dewar's and soda. "We made a lot of sacrifices. Leonard Tose made a lot of sacrifices to stay in Philadelphia.

"No, I don't think time heals all wounds. But sometimes a little controversy is healthy. If you take something for granted, you never realize how valuable it is. Now, people realize how valuable the Eagles are.

"My father quoted from Shakespeare the other day and it was beautiful. 'If you can laugh in the midst of adversity, it is much better than laughing later.'"

"No," Tose interrupted, "that isn't what I said. What Shakespeare said was that the true test of a man is to laugh when going through adversity."

Would Tose use that thought as his shield against a withering storm of criticism?

"Leonard Tose is a survivor," Susan said. "If he wasn't, he would have surrendered a long time ago. We talked this morning about trying to describe what my dad is. And we decided he is very unique.

"Compare him to the other owners in town. Is there anybody else you can write about?"

It was conceded that Tose had spent considerable time in the limelight. "He's earned the right to be in the limelight," Ms. Fletcher said.

Tose scowled up from his glass. "I don't know what more I can say," he said. "I am not gonna move the team."

There was talk about Susan's trip to Acapulco, and some jesting that that would start a fresh round of rumors that the team was moving to Mexico, and she told an anecdote about a preseason game in Mexico City where the tickets didn't correspond to the stadium seats.

It was time to board the train, and as we joined the milling crowd at track 14, a fat man shook Tose's hand and wished him luck.

"See," Tose chortled. "I told you people are pulling for me."

"Why," I asked the fat man, "are you pulling for a guy who wanted to move the team to Phoenix?"

"Nahhhh," the guy answered, glancing at Tose. "If you moved the team to Phoenix, then you couldn't eat at the Knife & Fork Inn (an Atlantic City restaurant)."

"You're right," Tose said, grinning. And an argument erupted about the charm of that restaurant and its pan-fried flounder.

I hunted down Shaiman on the train. He was properly, lawyerly mum as I tried to clarify the mystery about how much Tose owed. Finally, he volunteered to consult with Tose, returned, and said, "There are no loans due until Jan. 1, 1986."

At 30th Street station, while passersby gawked, Tose paused for some final words. "I got confused on the podium," he said. "When they asked me when the loan was due and I said March or April. Actually, there is nothing due until Jan. 1, 1986."

So, what's the urgency to refinance, to relocate?

"Long-range planning," Ms. Fletcher said. "Provision," Tose echoed.

"And," he said, "I'll tell you something else. The 45 days the league has given me, we'll get it done in 15."

I may have had stranger days in the last 26 years, but I cannot recall them. Maybe it's contagious.

Buddy System Can Be Tough to Swallow

Philadelphia Daily News
March 24, 1986

TAMPA—The first official gathering of Eagles was still three hours away when the words started grinding out of Buddy Ryan's mouth like barbed wire off a screechy spool. Ryan told the media that "Maddix, the fullback, looks like a reject guard from the USFL, he's so damn fat."

There was some giggling and a murmur that sounded like "Same Old Buddy" because he had mangled Michael Haddix's name while ripping a first-round draft choice. That's what the headline said in the Tampa paper the next morning: "Same Old Buddy."

And if it gets shortened to the initials SOB, that won't bother the stubby, earthy, outspoken new coach of the Philadelphia Eagles either. Names can never harm him, but overstuffed, uninspired football players can do him in.

"It's the borderline guys who get you fired," Ryan explained before waltzing through a radio show with Ron Jaworski. "The guys who look like players but can't play worth a damn."

Smart, belligerent guys earn a place in Ryan's lineup and in his heart. Dumb, timid guys get branded by Ryan's barbed-wire mouth.

The danger in this kind of quick-draw, shoot-from-the-hip approach is that you may "lose" an intelligent, sensitive player when you whip him publicly.

"Nahhh," Ryan muttered. "I never lose a player. They find out that sulking don't pay.

"If you're not in shape I'll let you know. If you can't play, we'll let you go.

"Great players are players who show up in shape. Intelligent guys understand the problems and get 'em ironed out. Dumb guys sulk and pout.

"You never see smart guys pout. The guys I've had problems with are dumb guys. They'll be what you let 'em be."

Ryan demands that chin straps be buckled at all times on the practice field, either under the chin or behind the back of the helmet. He once saw a player lose the sight in one eye when a dangling chin strap flicked through his facemask.

So there is a swath of compassion somewhere inside that pudgy body. He will do his best to keep it concealed while he teaches the Eagles to play the game his way.

"In July, that's when it's gonna be tough," Ryan warned. "Instead of 20 up-and-downs the linemen are gonna do 50.

"But when a guy can't do 10 now, you've got to worry about that guy.

"So you rip him in the media and you see which way he goes. If he shows up at the next minicamp 15 pounds lighter, terrific. If he shows up sad-eyed and bloated, you find somebody else to play in his spot."

Marion Campbell never did that. He never raked a guy in public even if the guy couldn't recognize a blitz from a blister. He thought his players would respond to kindness.

"If these guys were all All-Pro, Campbell would still be here," Ryan sneered.

It would be foolhardy to suggest to Ryan that you catch more flies with honey than with vinegar. He's not interested in catching flies. He is obsessed with catching up with the rest of the league.

His manner is abrupt, his language earthy, his methods crude.

The depth chart for his Tampa minicamp was fascinating. Linebacker Joel Williams, who was used for one play from scrimmage after a bitter holdout, shows up on the first defensive unit.

"We had to go back to the '84 films," Ryan explained. If it was designed to show Williams he is wanted, it didn't work. He still wants to be traded.

Reggie Wilkes wound up on the third unit, which means Ryan was not dazzled by Wilkes's outstanding performance in the last game of the season.

Herm Edwards lost his starting job sometime in January in the film room, which seems unjust.

"I evaluated the talent," Ryan said. "I figure if he had any questions he could come and see me. I don't have a lot of time to spend with a player. I'm busy."

Terrific. On Wednesday, Same Old Buddy ripped Leonard Mitchell for being overweight. On Friday he said Mitchell has a chance to be All-Pro.

He praised Mike Reichenbach's performance at middle linebacker, a vital position in Ryan's "46" defense. He called him "Rock-em-back," which is a wonderful name for a linebacker.

Almost as good as Singletary, the guy who played the position in Chicago. "There's only been one Singletary ever made," Ryan gushed. "With his dedication, ability, smarts. He even had looks."

Handsome is as handsome does. The folks in the 600 level are going to love Ryan because they are weary of players who are pampered, praised and overpaid. And of coaches who make excuses for them.

Ryan will call a stiff a stiff and they like that. The players will have to adjust to his harsh mouth and the fodder it provides for the critics in the 600 level.

"Hey," Ryan said bluntly, "they are paid very well. If they don't do the job, somebody's gotta get on 'em.

"Tough town? Well, I'm a tough coach so we oughta get along great."

Maybe, maybe not.

Chicago was a competitive media town, but Philadelphia makes the Chicago scene look like a day at the beach.

The media won't mind being used as a messenger for Ryan's sermons, just as long as we're not abused. We won't play his game if he's gonna mark the cards.

For weeks now, he has been damning Jaworski with faint praise. He talked about bringing in a veteran quarterback to compete with and inspire Jaworski. He bolstered his own image by describing a meeting with his quarterback as "short and sweet," summing up the thrust of it as a warning to get "his butt to minicamp."

The cordial meeting lasted almost 45 minutes. The offensive unit knows that because they sat there, twiddling their thumbs until it ended.

We are all aware of Ryan's harsh standards, his barbed-wire mouth, without him twisting the facts to look even tougher, meaner, or to demean a guy who has played hard and played hurt for a lot of years.

"When you win, it's the players," Ryan said, mocking a view held by many writers and players. "When you lose, it's the coaches."

Ryan fidgeted through that call-in stint on WIP like a guy who would rather be getting root canal work done.

He was more curt than charming, more grumpy than gregarious. And when a caller suggested, "You don't need three quarterbacks," Ryan interrupted to say, "I don't really worry about what you think. I've been doing this for 35 years."

Saturday morning, in the lobby of the Ashley Plaza Hotel, Same Old Buddy shook hands and warned gently, "I'll be reading your stuff and I'm gonna grade it."

Coach, I don't really care what you think. I've been doing this for 35 years. Give us the truth, the whole truth and nothing but the truth and we'll get along just splendid.

Roughly Speaking, Jaws Enjoyed Himself

Philadelphia Daily News
September 15, 1986

CHICAGO—The Fridge fell on Ron Jaworski and Jaworski's lights went out.

When the lights flickered back on, the trainer was thrusting smelling salts under his nose and asking him tough questions, like what town was he in.

Jaworski wasn't even sure what sport he was in.

"It was," he said later, "like going 15 rounds with the world's champion and losing in the last 10 seconds."

For a guy whose legs were still wobbly, it wasn't a bad description. The world-champion Bears beat the Eagles 13–10 in overtime, in a heavyweight scuffle that had all the hype of Hulk Hogan vs. Sergeant Slaughter, all the bitter fury of Ali-Frazier.

"It was a great game," Jaworski said, his gaze still glazed with that thin sheen that a knockout punch drapes across a fighter's eyes.

"All that hitting, all that jabbering, the finger-pointing. It was a fun game."

Fun is in the glazed eyes of the beholder. It was a game littered with high-speed collisions, with startling surprises, with wrenching twists and sudden turns, with baffling strategy.

The crash that turned the game inside out happened with 74 seconds left in regulation, and the Eagles chugging upfield.

Jaworski rolled right, a screen pass unraveling. He could hear the thunder of pursuit, and he hurried his throw, lofting it past Ron Johnson and out of bounds.

"I thought the ball was gone," Jaworski recalled. "And that's when he (William Perry) laid it on me.

"I'm not sure I was already out of bounds. That's one of those plays, if you get the call, fine. We didn't."

"Mike Singletary got hurt on that same play," Buddy Ryan said, once he got his throat unclogged and his tear ducts behaving. "He was in-bounds. Our guy was out of bounds."

The Bears are Jaworski's hardhearted utility company, always putting his lights out, turning his Christmas decorations dark. It happened once before, when Mike Hartenstine rattled his spine, causing the short circuit that's a concussion.

"Look at the films," broadcaster Stan Walters pleaded before yesterday's game.

"Harold Carmichael was supposed to run an alley-oop to the end zone. A guy tackled him, the ref threw the flag, Jaws started to back up, to scramble, since he had a free play.

"Maybe it was supposed to be a five-step drop and now Jaws went back eight. I turned around and yelled, 'Whoa.' First time in my life I ever yelled.

"And then I dived. Came up 5 yards short. If I'd been Carl Lewis, I'd have come up short. Hartenstine lowered his head at the last second, and speared him. And now, everybody remembers it."

It will be overshadowed now, blotted out by what happened here yesterday, when The Fridge plopped on Jaworski after he had released the football, after he had scurried past the sideline.

"He's 300 pounds," Jaworski said. "At that point, I was playing with little cobwebs from the (third-quarter) scramble where I'd hit my head on the turf.

"This one made me lightheaded. If I went back I would have hurt us. But if we'd gotten the ball back in overtime, I was going back in."

Matt Cavanaugh replaced the groggy Jaworski. Threw three passes, all of them caught, two by Chicagoans, one by a teammate.

The Bears bobbled the gift and it shattered, with kicker Kevin Butler coming up short on a 55-yarder with seven seconds left.

The Eagles won the toss and Jaworski squinted at the scene, scraping away the last of the cobwebs, as Charles Crawford lugged the kickoff upfield.

"I really got excited," he said. "I saw that crack. The 'wall' did a great job. I saw Charles breaking through. One more guy and he was gone.

"And then, my heart fell to my feet."

Jaworski's heart fell, because the football fell from Crawford's grasp. Vestee Jackson pounced on it, and the Bears handed it to Walter Payton until they got close enough so that Butler couldn't miss, and it was over, and Ryan tried to talk about it, but his teeth chattered and his lips quivered and his eyes misted and he couldn't do it.

The Eagles had held the Bears scoreless in the first half, had smothered the world champions throughout, confusing Mike Tomczak, their jittery rookie quarterback.

Jaworski, meanwhile, was throwing darts on third-and-long, keeping drives alive, keeping the defense off the field, safe from Payton's scythelike legs.

The Bears, meanwhile, were a pitiful 1-for-9 on third-down conversions while the game teetered in the balance.

"We weren't running the ball well enough," Jaworski said. "If we're gonna be the team we can be, we've got to run the ball better.

"I knew what they were doing coveragewise. The first half, I was getting time to pick out the open guy. They ran a safety blitz, and that's the only sack they got.

"They're one helluva defensive team. They keep after you. They play hard, they play tough. Uh, maybe Perry's shot was a little late, but they play clean.

"There's no way you can brace yourself. I could sense someone coming. If it's a cornerback, it won't do that much damage. If it's Perry, or Richard Dent, you're in trouble.

"Hartenstine, he had a good clean shot. On this hit, I was kind of rolling away from it."

Jaworski finished 18-for-30 for 165 yards. He hit Mike Quick on a lovely touchdown pass. He threw one interception that clattered off Mike Haddix's hands, marring a stick-out day, because it landed in a Chicago lap.

And he threw another interception with Dent tugging on his left ankle, toppling him. Threw it sidearm.

"A dumb throw," Jaworski said. "I should have just thrown it away, out of bounds. I thought I saw green grass there.

"It was poor judgment, I can't deny it. But I never saw (Dave) Duerson."

Jaworski had audibled on the play, sending Keith Byars in motion. But the coverage wasn't what Jaworski anticipated, and Byars, who was to be his emergency, layoff target, had darted upfield.

This is a young team that was woeful against the Redskins and wonderful against the Bears for most of 66 minutes. But it's a loss, a demoralizing, disheartening loss that left the coach in tears and most of his players in stunned silence.

"Hopefully," Jaworski said, "it can be a steppingstone for bigger and better things. You go 15 rounds with the champ and lose and it takes a lot out of you.

"Buddy wasn't the only guy who shed some tears when it was over."

Giles: The Voice of Experience

Philadelphia Daily News
November 22, 1988

DOUG WILLIAMS could throw a football through a carwash and not get it wet. Jimmie Giles could catch it, wet or dry, soapy or smooth.

When Tampa Bay played the Bears in the early '80s, Giles would feint his way open, for an instant, and pow, Williams would flick that steel-cable wrist and the ball would be there and the pudgy guy on the sideline in the blue-and-orange sweater would turn blue. And orange.

"I always had great games against the Bears," Giles said yesterday, chuckling at the memories.

"The Bears, they were the team in the NFC Central. If you didn't play well against the Bears, you were gonna get your butt whipped.

"They had a young linebacker then named Otis Wilson. This guy was tough. But he didn't know the system.

"I used to beat him all the time. Then, that young kid grew up. Before he did, I'd look at his eyes, see the nervous shifting.

"He was unsure, while I knew what I wanted to do. And I had a great quarterback, who could get the ball in the crack."

Williams could throw the ball through a forest fire and not get it scorched.

"Coach (Buddy) Ryan never said anything to me," Giles recalled, "but his players would. At the Pro Bowl.

"They'd tell me how he'd show 'em films on Saturday. He'd say, 'This is what he's gonna do tomorrow.' And then, I'd do it."

Ryan has an elephant's memory, to go with his elephant's manners. He coveted Giles and he finally got the tight end, paroling him from the prison that is the Detroit franchise.

This summer, Ryan cut John Spagnola and kept Giles, the oldest player on the Eagles' roster.

"Nobody mentions that," Giles said slyly. "If they did, I'd tell them to line up, and let's go, one-on-one."

Giles is 34, playing backup to rookie sensation Keith Jackson.

"Anybody," Giles said, "who thinks of me as a backup, I'd tell them, 'OK, you and me, let's go, defend against me.'"

He is 34, the oldest man on the roster, and he has not lost a step in the swagger that has carried him to four Pro Bowl appearances.

"I work as hard as anyone on the field," Giles said. "I prepare myself like I have the last 12 years, to go 80 snaps of the ball.

"I'm in a great situation here. I have the opportunity to help a young kid become a great player. I enjoy that."

Giles has caught only six passes all season, but three of them were memorable: the touchdown grab against the Giants when Randall Cunningham bounced off the turf in the ultimate highlight shot; the fourth-down snag against Dallas; a crucial 17-yarder against Pittsburgh.

"Football," Giles said patiently, "is an up and down game. When we win, I'm happy. We win as a team.

"Sunday, I don't think I had any significant contribution, but we won."

Giles is being humble. He did make a significant contribution on Saturday night, presiding at a players-only meeting.

"I don't like to toot my own horn," Giles said, "but I've called a meeting for every Saturday night. I explain what's at stake.

"To me, each game is like a Super Bowl now. If we win, we go on. If we lose, we're out of it.

"It's just the players. We get a feel for each other. It's like a rap session."

Ryan approves. Which is why he singled out a guy who didn't throw a pass and a guy who didn't catch a pass at the start of his Monday press conference.

"Giles and Matt Cavanaugh are the two leaders of this football team," Ryan said. "We've been begging for leaders since I got here.

"They're not political leaders, these are real leaders. And the great thing about it, they're second-stringers.

"Giles has been a positive influence since he got here. I knew he was a great player, from playing against him. I didn't know what a great person he was until he got here."

Tampa went from worst to first while Giles was there, then toppled quickly when Williams, who could throw a football through a jelly doughnut without getting it smeared, left.

"Doug is the best quarterback I've ever played with," Giles said.

"Randall probably will become, and make sure you get this right, Randall will become the best quarterback I've ever played with. Simply because of his great athletic ability, and his knack of getting out of tight spots.

"When I played with Doug, he was more handcuffed in an offensive situation than Randall is. Doug came out of a pro style at Grambling. He threw it like they do in the pros.

"They both have about the same arm strength. Doug had quick wrists. He could flick the ball and get it between the cracks.

"Randall has more of a whip. And he's still just as effective."

That's leadership at work, Monday afternoon style. Brag about your quarterback, but don't bury him with praise.

Giles is 34, the oldest man on the roster, still lusting after his first Super Bowl appearance.

"You can't let an opportunity get away," he said. "It's not that I think the years are running out on me.

"One year, we needed one game to get to the Super Bowl and we fell nine points short. We couldn't make it happen.

"I had a perfect game that day. One-for-one for one touchdown . . . but they called it back.

"It's an opportunity I've thought about. I thought, if we get close again, give me the ball. I think I can do it.

"Been in the league 12 years and haven't been to a Super Bowl. I don't want it to end that way."

Which is what he tells this young team at those Saturday night rap sessions, the ones that precede those Sunday afternoon seances Randall Cunningham conducts, the ones that have Jimmie Giles feeling younger than springtime, even if he is the oldest man on the roster.

To Zubrow, the Battle Can Be Won

Philadelphia Daily News
September 29, 1989

ED ZUBROW was there, Saturday night, when the citizens recaptured the corner of Fifth and Indiana from the enemy.

Marched in midnight's brittle light with the carpenters and plumbers and housewives wearing white hard hats, the symbol of citizens who want to take back the streets from the drug dealers.

Some of the drug dealers have submachine guns. All of the marchers have courage.

Zubrow is the special assistant to superintendent of schools Dr. Constance Clayton. Battling substance abuse is his assignment.

Zubrow gave up coaching football at Penn, where he had won two Ivy championships in three years, to take the job.

"I don't go for that sort of St. George trying to slay the dragon (angle)," Zubrow said yesterday.

He wore no hair shirt, just a button-down white broadcloth with blue stripes.

He wore no armor, only a blue suit.

He has a scowl that could melt a tank, a voice that could stop a jaguar in its tracks, a chin that looks tough enough to withstand dragon fire.

"The thing I'm absolutely convinced of," he said, "is that it's not about people giving everything up, to be saintly. It's people broadening their view of what their community is."

Zubrow is 38, married, religious.

"There are things I believe and faith I have," he said, "but I don't talk about that.

"It's a matter of, you look around and decide what you want to do, and what seems right, and you do it."

And if it involves a challenge, bigger and meaner than Mike Tyson, you rub your hands together and stick that chin out and take your best shot.

"The most fun jobs," he said, "are the jobs where you are dealing with challenges. Challenges that sometimes appear to be, uh, overwhelming.

"Part of the fun and part of the learning comes from taking it, breaking it down into parts and chipping away at it. And making progress.

"Football was that way. I'm not sure there ever was a Monday night, looking at the opponent's film, that I didn't feel . . . this is hopeless.

"I'd think of something, put the next reel on, and bam, they had the perfect counter to it.

"But I didn't put the projector away and say, 'This is hopeless.'

"There are certain things that are plain good fights."

He did not enlist in the fight against drugs. He says Clayton drafted him. He was dazzled by her leadership qualities, by her concern for the children of Philadelphia.

"Where it leads, what it brings didn't matter," he said. "I tried to tell that to the team and to my friends."

That was in March. Now, with the leaves beginning their autumn blaze, with Penn 1–1, he suffers no withdrawal pains, harbors no regrets.

"That first week," he said, "my wife and I were in New Hampshire, visiting with friends.

"They asked if I missed it and my wife started laughing. She said, 'I can tell you what the Penn football team is doing every half hour.'

"I'd been saying things like, 'I guess they're in a staff meeting now . . . first day they hit. . . .'

"Sure I miss it. Being with the coaches, being with the kids. But I have no second thoughts."

The war against drugs leaves little room for second thoughts. Last night, he spent time at the McCloskey School, rapping with teachers, with the cops, with parents weary of being prisoners in their homes while the drug dealers strut on the corners.

"A policeman once told me that the biggest things causing the problem are air conditioning and color television sets," he said.

"With color television, people were content to stay in their air-conditioned living rooms, instead of being out coaching Little League.

"And suddenly, years later, they wake up to discover that they're barricaded in their living rooms. And the only kids out there, in the playground, are dealing crack, and kids being kids, that's an attractive picture, the only ones to model themselves after.

"What we have to do is get away from the barricades, we have to take back the neighborhoods, go back to values.

"We are properly restrained from having religion in the schools. But somehow that message has gotten warped to mean that we can't have values in the schools.

"Television has changed the values of young people. There's no longer the notion of earning honest dollars, having a little home, raising a good family. That's not what television shows as something to be aspired to."

Television has become the opiate of the people. And the real stuff is so damn available and affordable, it threatens all of us.

"In the past, society has responded to the outbreak of a drug epidemic, only when it extended into the mainstream," Zubrow said.

"As long as drugs affected isolated areas, parenthesis, poor people, we haven't responded as strongly.

"The same is true of AIDS. When AIDS was perceived as a disease of homosexual men only, it did not receive the commitment and attention it is receiving now.

"What has changed things is the development of a form of cocaine that is the most addictive drug ever.

"It is also the cheapest drug we've ever dealt with. It is suddenly available to any school child who can afford \$3.

"They are suddenly getting high on something more dangerous than a wine cooler or beer.

"Plus, crack disproportionately affects women. Maybe because it can be smoked and does not involve needles.

"Thus, children are affected in more dangerous ways than any previous epidemic.

"Before, women coming down off a high were still functioning, still able to hug a kid. Crack cocaine makes them ignore their children.

"And now, thousands and thousands of kids are being born as addicts, crack babies."

Zubrow has studied the enemy and the poison it distributes.

"I was as naive as the next person," he said. "Living in West Philadelphia, I was aware of some of the things happening in the streets.

"As a football coach, there was a growing awareness of drug abuse among young people. Not the Penn football team.

"But on our campus, I became aware of alcohol abuse.

"And, in recruiting one youngster I asked him why he'd be interested in going so far away from home.

"He told me that people in his neighborhood wanted him to sell rock. I didn't know what rock was.

"I had kids whose families were touched by substance abuse. I had to call a player in and tell him his uncle had been shot in a drug dispute.

"I hope I'm not sounding like a Johnny one-note. I like kids. What I'd like to be about is helping kids become leaders, reaching their potential."

Yesterday, he carried the message to Allentown, speaking at the Pennsylvania Newspaper Publishers luncheon honoring outstanding newspaper carriers.

During lunch he was asked about using pro athletes to deliver anti-drug messages to school kids.

"There's a mixed message there," he said bluntly. "The athlete comes, tells the kids, 'Study hard, stay in school, get your degree.'

"And the kid sits there saying, 'Hey, the reason you've made it is because you can shoot the jumper.'

"And then, the kid heads back out to the playground to work on his jump shot."

When it was his turn to speak, Zubrow winced through the introduction that lauded him for giving something back to mankind, for giving up all that glory, for taking on the risk of serving the community.

Zubrow aimed his booming message at the carriers. "Praise," he told them, "is like poison. The only way it can hurt is if you swallow it."

He talked about a winning edge, about leadership, about not confusing goals and dreams. He was firm, he was clear, he was moving.

He talked about Karl Wallenda, the high-wire walker and how he died in a fall and how his wife confessed that for three months Wallenda thought about falling.

Ed Zubrow will not squander precious moments, vital energy worrying about failing.

"There's a great unmobilized army out there," Zubrow said. "It needs to be mobilized. People need to stand up and say there is a right way.

"The most valued warriors are the ones with daily interaction with the kids. Teachers, parents, people in the community who do stand for something.

"One thing I learned from my involvement with athletics is that the day you say you can't beat a team, you won't beat that team.

"As soon as you say something is hopeless, then it becomes hopeless. We are not outmanned. This war is not unwinnable."

Lurie Mustn't Lose Sight of Little Things

Philadelphia Daily News
December 29, 1994

WOULD DICK VERMEIL still be interested in becoming Philadelphia's coach, general manager and architect to restructure (that's Jeff Lurie's word) the rubble of a team that lost seven in succession if it had snowed on Dec. 18?

If it had snowed that Sunday, the fans would have pelted Santa Claus with snow and ice, with mud and mice.

Vermeil, at the ballyard to be inducted into the Eagles' Honor Roll, would have looked into the frightened eyes of his wife, his kids, their spouses, and the grandchildren straight out of Central Casting, and told Lurie he was flattered by his interest, but forget it!

Lurie, remember, is the guy who promised us the Eagles would take care of "the little things" on their way to becoming a championship franchise.

It is a tough promise to keep. Impossible if you don't surround yourself with talented, dedicated people who know the history of this tattered franchise.

Lurie knows what George Santayana said, about those who ignore the mistakes of the past being doomed to repeat them.

Vermeil might not know Santayana from Santa Claus, but he feels the same way about mistakes of the past, and is still intrigued by the challenge of coaching the Eagles again.

In case you just moved to town from Cairo, Philadelphia football fans became famous for pelting Santa with snowballs at Franklin Field, near the end of the Joe Kuharich regime.

The regular Santa was snowbound in Absecon, N.J., so someone plucked a grizzled guy out of the stands who always wore a Santa suit to the home game that preceded Christmas.

Plopped the guy in a rickety contraption and lugged him around the track at Franklin Field, expecting him to pitch trinkets into the lower stands.

Guy was too busy ducking snowballs to pitch trinkets and a Philadelphia image was etched in stone, never mind how lousy the team that year, how callous, how inept the management.

Lurie got lucky Dec. 18, final home game against the Giants. Most of the 700-level denizens were still in the parking lots, getting tanked, when Santa appeared before the game, riding the John Deere cart.

Would anyone with an ounce of awareness, with a scintilla of common sense, put Santa on the cart that's used to lug badly injured players off the field?

You hire a Santa to toss Hershey kisses to the crowd, you put him in the back seat of a green-and-white convertible.

Put him in a one-horse sleigh, get some tame reindeer, a fire truck, a double-decker bus, a dog sled, uh, maybe not a dog sled, something, anything, but don't send him out there on the injury cart.

And don't drive counterclockwise if Santa is perched on the left side of the cart, equipped with a weak arm. For every chocolate kiss that reached the stands, nine scattered on the Astroturf. The quintessential candy arm?

Somebody gave it a little thought, perhaps, sticking a woman in a shabby gray wig out there, too. Who's gonna pelt Mrs. Claus, even if the Eagles had lost five straight?

How tough would it have been to hand each cheerleader a pillow-case full of goodies and have them prance through the stands, scattering gifts?

And speaking of cheerleaders, how difficult would it be to furnish the "honorary" cheerleader each week with a video, showing two basic cheers, so the kid doesn't have to stand there, like a lamppost, for a funless hour?

Lurie said he'd handle "the little things" and it's a full-time job. Which is what troubled me about Stu Bykofsky's column the other day suggesting that Lurie is partying hearty these days.

Stu also wrote that Christina Lurie is expecting and that's nice. Has there ever been an Eagles owner with a pregnant wife? And does dealing with Randall Cunningham prepare Lurie for changing diapers?

Vermeil seems willing to handle the football stuff, free agents, the draft, trades, waivers, game plans, clock management. He already has his two-point conversion chart memorized, rain or shine.

That leaves the little things for Lurie, which might account for the delay in signing Vermeil.

On the day Lurie fired Rich Kotite, burying him with an avalanche of praise, the owner said he would give one mandate to the new coach, and that would be to run a strenuous training camp.

I caught the retraction in 4.35 seconds, a Philadelphia record. Lurie said, in the very next breath, the intensity of the training camp would, indeed, be up to the new coach.

Lurie also said everyone's job was in jeopardy after a seven-game tailspin, but he has to deepen his voice a little when he wants to portray anger.

Maybe reach down to his brown suede shoes for a macho growl. Maybe not.

The point of this sermon is to offer a little comic relief to the gush of concern for Dick Vermeil's mental health, should he choose to return as coach and general manager.

I think Vermeil will be just fine, because he has exorcised some ghosts from his past, because he is 12 years older, and a lot smarter.

Surely, Lurie researched Vermeil's first go-round with the Eagles, and asked all the right questions.

Surely, Vermeil was only kidding when they had lunch the first time and a salsa splash left a stain on the tablecloth and Vermeil peered at it and said, "The weak safety should have rotated out of zone coverage. . . ."

Maybe Vermeil wanted time to concentrate on his Sugar Bowl gig for ABC before hammering out a contract with Lurie.

Maybe he wanted some more time to check Lurie out with his UCLA connections.

Vermeil doesn't mind dealing with the media, planning the pre-game meals, making trades and hiring a strength coach and polishing the quarterback of the future, but he has to be sure somebody else can take care of the little things.

Lurie has made some dreadful rookie mistakes. Norman Braman made rookie mistakes, Leonard Tose made rookie mistakes, Jerry Wolman made rookie mistakes.

It goes with the territory. But Lurie has to learn from his mistakes. Santa Claus is making a list, and checking it twice, gonna find out who's naughty and nice.

He Lost a Lot, but He Loved the Game

Philadelphia Daily News
April 16, 2003

LEONARD TOSE was the best-dressed guy at the trial, the one where he sued the Sands Hotel & Casino for getting him drunk while they raked in his millions at their blackjack tables. You couldn't tell what the judge was wearing under his generic black robe, but you could safely lay 10-to-1, Tose was better dressed than the judge.

Tose was busted and his handsome home in Villanova had been stripped of most of its furniture by an ex-wife, but he showed up in court each day in expensive suits and silk ties and shirts spun of Egyptian cotton.

He lost. He lost even though there was testimony from a cocktail waitress swearing that her job description was "to keep Mr. Tose's glass filled." A monogrammed glass, courtesy of the casino, which she kept filled with top-shelf scotch, while he shoved stacks of black chips behind the four or five hands he fuzzily played at one time.

He lost, even though the jury got to see the markers he signed through a long, bitter, expensive night of high-stake gambling, $100,000 at 9:20, another $100,000 at 9:45, another $100,000 at 10:05, his signature deteriorating into a splotchy scrawl as the booze muddled his brain, dulled his reflexes.

The casino wanted to get paid and Tose didn't have the scratch.

So he sued and the Camden courthouse jury decided against him. Maybe because he showed up so well-dressed. Maybe because there was no evidence of a casino employee holding a gun to his head, compelling him to hit on 17, to split 8's, to double down even with the dealer showing a jack of diamonds.

There was evidence that his wife at the time, his friends at the time, caused a ruckus some nights, snarling at the pit bosses, beseeching Tose to quit hissing his money away. Tose knew he was a lousy gambler, even sober, yet he kept thinking his luck would turn the next time the dealer shuffled the cards.

And now, there will be no more next times. And if I choose to begin my memories of Tose with the pathetic testimony of that trial and the way it played out, it is because his hair was groomed just so each day, and his handsome shoes gleamed, and it was obvious that appearances mattered, even while confessing that he had squandered millions while his mind was fuzzy with free booze.

That was only one chapter in a life crammed with adventure, with free spending and philanthropy. He inherited a trucking company from his father and he ran it with a clenched fist when dealing with the unions and an open hand when dealing with his employees. He married early and often, the way some people in Chicago vote.

When Jerry Wolman was forced to sell the Eagles after a skyscraper project crumbled, Tose was the high bidder, a record $16.15 million.

He made rookie mistakes as an owner, and the fans sneered at his lifestyle, and the mediocre team he put on the field, but he showed up at the Red Lantern tavern, with sawdust on the floor, and bought drinks for everyone in the joint, when the owner wrote to say he might cancel his season tickets and the Sunday bus trip to the ballyard.

And then he gambled on a handsome, fiercely dedicated college coach named Dick Vermeil. The religion that is Eagles football gathered new converts and Mondays glistened after a victory, were shadowy after a loss.

Vermeil's work ethic had been hammered into armor in his dad's Owl Garage in Calistoga, Calif. He cajoled a band of overachievers into an NFC championship in 1980 and a trip to the Super Bowl. Tose took high hopes and a colorful army to New Orleans, including a cardinal (John Krol) and a comic (Don Rickles).

Rickles tried entertaining the team before the game. At halftime, the Eagles hopelessly behind, Cardinal Krol said softly, "Leonard, sometimes you don't always get what you pray for."

Losing that game was a wound that never healed. Vermeil remained loyal, supportive through the years when Tose was chasing old friends with his anger. He had come within a blink of selling the team to an Arizona guy who would have moved the Eagles to the desert, and some never forgave him.

And then, hounded by the bankers, he sold the team to Norman Braman, a Miami car dealer. Braman eventually wearied of the scrutiny that comes with Philadelphia's passion for its football team. He sold the team, at an exorbitant profit, to Jeff Lurie and we are still waiting for the first of those championships Lurie promised.

Tose's Villanova house was sold at a sheriff's auction. But before he lost it, there was that night where he tried to learn to dance to please a sweet new girlfriend. He paused every 5 minutes or so for another swallow of scotch. No one had to move any furniture to create a dance floor; the big dining room was barren.

He was broke, but he tipped the dance teacher, Harry Watters, $100, and you could see your image in his polished shoes. Appearances.

He took his girlfriend and her family on a cruise. They sat in the "smoking" section at dinner and they could barely hear the ship's orchestra. Someone grumbled about that, and Tose approached the band leader and peeled off some Ben Franklins and pretty soon, the orchestra was playing in their part of the dining room.

Remember what you choose, the weaknesses or the strengths, the reckless gambling or the funding for the first Ronald McDonald House. Me, I hope Tose is somewhere peaceful, elegantly dressed, his glass full of top-shelf scotch, poured by a pretty young woman with a genuine smile, sweet music playing in the background.

PART V
Hockey

Introduction

BERNIE PARENT

I COULD HAVE ASKED MANY SPORTSWRITERS and columnists to write a book with me, but Stan was the one I wanted. What he could do with a story, take it to a level no one else could do. He was a magician. It was beautiful!

Together, we wrote *Unmasked*, a story I could never have put together without him. What was so incredible about Stan was how creative he was. You could give him one word, and he could take you on a trip.

He was blessed with a great imagination. I remember Einstein saying that imagination is more important than education. There is a ceiling to education; with imagination, you could go to the moon.

Stan went to the moon and back. He had a passion for the work he did and the people he knew. He taught me that if you love what you're doing and you love people, it comes back to you a thousand-fold. That's what Stan was all about and what made him special.

There are people in life, you look at them and you say, "I wish I had a little piece of that man in me." That's the way I felt about Stan. He changed my life for the better, and I'll always be grateful to him. I learned from him that if you want to succeed, always look at someone you consider successful, see what he or she did, and apply some of it to you. What you need is a purpose. You have to get rid of the fear, be willing to take risks. A lot of people are struggling. They're lost in the woods. I was there. I temporarily lost vision in one eye; my career ended suddenly. I hit bottom. Stan taught me to look in the mirror and see a human being, not just a hockey player.

And as I worked with him, I found out that there was nothing wrong with my asking him how I could improve my life. I learned that it was in his nature to look at each individual and approach each one in a different and appropriate way. He knew how to read a person. That's why people loved him. He was a beautiful person.

Schultz's Shrink Wouldn't Believe Him on the Rink

Philadelphia Daily News
May 7, 1974

DAVE SCHULTZ assembles model airplanes in his spare time. Delicate, painstaking work. A guy has the patience, the dexterity, the hand to put together model airplanes . . . how come he uses those same hands to punch people in the head at the drop of a hockey puck?

"I've just got something in me," Schultz said yesterday after the Flyers zipped through a workout at the Penn rink. "I have to psyche myself up. I'm not naturally like that.

"Sometimes being known for that makes me mad. And yet, as far as winning hockey games, I'm glad I have it.

"I went home Sunday night and I lay there in bed, and I started thinking about Dale Rolfe. I felt sorry for him. Here's a guy who doesn't fight . . . a good, honest hockey player.

"And there, in front of all those people, and in front of a national television audience, he got the hell beat out of him. He must have felt awful.

"Something just changes me on the ice. It's not easy for me. Not like it's easy for a guy like Steve Durbano. A guy who fights in the street, a guy who likes to scrap. It's easier for a guy like that."

Bernie Parent's brother, the psychiatrist, would have his couch full with Schultz. "Ah yes, Mister Schultz, you seem like such a nice, well-mannered young man. . . . I noticed you took your skates off before getting up on the couch.

"Tell me, Mister Schultz, what happens to you when you slip into that uniform with the short, black pants? Does it remind you of sumzing that happened in your childhood, sumzing terrible, sumzing that makes you lash out with your fists?"

The guilt feelings afterwards would intrigue a prattle of psychiatrists. They intrigue guys like Larry Merchant who used to commit his Freudian slips in this space and who now does his probing for the *New York Post*.

Do not invite Dave Schultz and Larry Merchant to the same city. Larry has decided that Schultz is some sort of Pavlovian dog gone mad, who froths at the mouth and savages people when the bell rings. Larry implies that Fred Shero whispers "Fetch" to Schultz and Dave scampers onto the ice to bring back an enemy player between his teeth.

It is a description that is going to rattle Schultz, who resented a "wrestling bear" analogy used to describe that wretched third game in New York. The next day Schultz made a figure-8 in the air four inches from a writer's face with the business end of his stick. At least it looked like a figure-8 between blinks.

Afterwards, with the uniform off, Schultz discussed the issue calmly, as he did yesterday, when he was asked to explain how he had vanished in the sixth game of the brutal series.

"It's psychological," he said, "I'm not too fast, and I have not got that much talent. I get the puck and all of a sudden some guy's on me, time after time, pretty soon, I'm saying, 'I can't even move' and I slow down more.

"The thing is, if a guy keeps pushing the whole way, he's gonna score. That night I never even tried to carry the puck. And I didn't get involved in a fight, because I knew I'd end up with more penalties than the other guy for instigating it.

"I felt I'd let the team down in New York. I came out Sunday, and I wasn't gonna go looking for something. But if it happened, I thought it would be against Butler. Or maybe Ron Harris.

"I figured I might as well try to kick hell out of Harris. He's supposed to be their tough guy. Not that he really is, but Emile Francis puts that pressure on him, saying he's the guy. And that's why I was happy he got a couple of goals to show he can do something else."

Schultz can do something else besides beat up people. Just ask the guys who play with him, Orest Kindrachuk and Don Saleski. They spent most of Sunday afternoon encamped in the New York zone.

"Everybody looks at Dave as a fighter," Saleski said, "but he scored 20 goals. He's got a good shot, he's not afraid to carry the puck. Dave Schultz–fighter is a bad mark, but a good image in a way."

Schultz's reputation is like a cushion to the compact Kindrachuk, who was the closest eyewitness to the demolition job on Rolfe. "The big lummox," Kindrachuk said of Rolfe. "He wouldn't go down. He went down once and got up. Most guys would have stayed down.

"The best thing about Dave, he's got a real good wrist shot. Maybe the best wrist on the team. I always tell him to shoot, shoot, shoot."

Schultz doesn't shoot, shoot, shoot. He doesn't even shoot, shoot. But the "Action Line" of Kindrachuk, Schultz and Saleski has scored five goals and seven assists against Boston this year.

That's the sort of thing that punctures those theories about Shero keeping the snorting bull around to inspire other members of the herd who might be Ferdinands and prefer to smell the flowers. But that still doesn't explain what happens to mild-mannered Dave Schultz once the game begins.

"He's such a quiet guy," Kindrachuk said. "Until he pulls on that sweater . . . and then he's a different man."

Maybe he's allergic to the wool? Or maybe it's psychological? Whatever, the Flyers want to keep him away from Bernie's brother, the psychiatrist, until after the Stanley Cup runneth over.

Even Now Shero Cups His Emotions

Philadelphia Daily News
May 20, 1974

BOBBY CLARKE'S DADDY remembered that trip to Winnipeg. Long, scary trip, because the doctors were going to check out his son for diabetes.

"All the way from Flin Flon," Bobby Clarke's daddy said, through the champagne mist in the Flyers' clubhouse. "He'd never seen the bright lights of the big city.

"It was just before Christmas and they had the Christmas lights up downtown. I said we'd take him downtown to see the lights, but he already had his skates on. He was going for a skate on some rink on the outskirts of town. Hockey . . . it was always hockey."

The Christmas lights shone in Bobby Clarke's eyes last night. He put his arms around his dad's waist and he led him up to the table and he helped them tilt that 35-pound silver trophy and he watched as the champagne cascaded out of the Stanley Cup and ran in sticky rivulets down his daddy's chin and onto his gray suit.

The Christmas lights twinkled in Bobby Clarke's eyes, bells jingled in his ears, harps strummed in his chest. A dream fulfilled?

"Nah," said Clarke, "you can't even dream a dream like this."

The Flyers won the Stanley Cup yesterday. Beat Boston, 1–0, in a lovely classic of a hockey game . . . crackling action . . . frantic patterns forming and shattering . . . masked gymnasts waiting to smother the puck at either end.

Were Christmas lights glinting in Fred Shero's eyes? All those years in the minors, all those spine-jangling bus trips, and now, hockey's greatest prize, awash with champagne, was in his team's locker room.

Shero stayed in his cramped little office. It was hard to tell what was glinting in his eyes. He wears tinted glasses and he squints hard before he answers tough questions. He toyed with the writers. But his voice was bland as tapioca and his face a mask of stone.

Maybe he did shed a tear in the muddle of players after the game ended? Maybe, when he got home, and isolated himself in his den, he took the shackles off his emotions and allowed himself a triumphant shout? Maybe, but probably not.

Shero appears to live in a shadowy neighborhood where someone waits around every corner to rob you of a prize. Don't laugh, don't gloat, don't brag, and no one will steal your joy. It seems like a lonely, friendless place, and that is too bad, because Fred Shero kept this crippled team together and led it up the side of the steepest sort of mountain. At the top, he is entitled to laughter, to tears.

"You're never gonna see Fred show emotions," said assistant coach Mike Nykoluk while family and friends swirled in damp clots in the clubhouse. "He's just not that way.

"Even if, God forbid, Bobby Clarke got hurt and I went into his room to tell him. He'd ask, 'Can he play?' But he wouldn't show emotion or anything. Me, I'm the other way, all emotion."

"He doesn't show emotion," said Don Saleski, who shook off a woeful late-season slump to perform well in the playoffs. "I went in and I said, 'Thanks, Freddy.' He shook my hand, said, 'Thanks, Don,' and he smiled.

"For him, that's showing emotion. And I'd rather hear that from him and see his smile than have people jumping up and down, hugging and kissing me."

Fred Shero does not even do that within his own family, jump up and down, hug and kiss. His own son, tormented by his apathy for athletics, rooted for the opposition until recently.

"I got this letter from a lawyer that pretty much tells the way I am," Shero said, pointing to a letter on his desk.

The letter included the phrase, "I am most happy with my own company" and it quoted from a Janis Ian song about, "Stars, they come and go."

He is a complex, introspective, sensitive man. During the playoffs, he praised New York and he praised Boston. If his team wanted praise they would have to earn it. On the ice.

He would not weave an escape ladder of alibi for them when Barry Ashbee and Gary Dornhoefer got hurt. And he did not encourage them to think they could overcome adversity simply because Someone up there likes them.

So much for "team of destiny" jazz. And so much for Kate Smith. It is fist-swingers, not ballad-singers, who win hockey games. And, if people are wondering why the championship did not put a smile on Shero's face, he reminded people that he had won championships before.

"In the minors," Shero said, "one year we beat Quebec with only 10 men. I said then, 'This team will live forever.' And at a meeting, I mentioned every one of them. And I said, 'We're gonna be the same way.'"

That is hockey they play in St. Paul and Omaha and Shawinigan, the same test of skill and courage. Sure, the skill is greater in the National Hockey League, but courage is not measured by the size of the arena.

And now, having won a championship in every league he has coached in, Shero talked about a series with the Russians, building a new challenge for himself, moments after planting the flag on this mountain top.

The photographers conned him into the clubhouse and posed him behind the Stanley Cup and begged him to smile. "Aw, c'mon, Freddy, smile," they pleaded.

The players smiled their gap-tooth smiles in the background. They know how much Shero meant to their success. "When he came here," Clarke explained, "he didn't ask Ed Van Impe to carry the puck out of his own end.

"He gave us a system that was good for Ed Van Impe, good for Dave Schultz, good for Bobby Clarke. Everybody could play it. He didn't try to change the players.

"Maybe other teams had more talented athletes," said Saleski, "but we had Freddy's system and we worked, worked, worked. We reflect Freddy's philosophy of life."

The philosophy is laced with hard work. Before the final 20 minutes began, Shero spoke in the tense clubhouse. "Make sure this period will live forever," he said, and then stalked out of the dressing room.

The Flyers played inspired hockey. They respect this complex, sensitive man. The whole town may be baffled by him but they love him. Aw, c'mon, Freddy, smile. Please.

Ziegler's Plan Isn't Worth a Red Cent to Snider

Philadelphia Daily News
December 4, 1987

MIAMI WILL FREEZE OVER before the Flyers play a Russian hockey team in a game that counts in the NHL standings.

Dave Brown will win the Lady Byng Trophy before the Flyers play a Russian hockey team in a game that counts in the NHL standings.

Gorbachev will defect and choose to live in Detroit before. . . .

"It won't happen," Flyers president Jay Snider said last night. "We won't play it.

"I believe there's more to life besides hockey. There's human lives. And I don't want to go through my whole life sitting on the sidelines.

"Here's an opportunity for us to make a statement. There's big money involved if the Flyers played a Russian team: sellouts, television, promotions.

"I don't care. And my father (Ed, Flyers owner) doesn't care."

If the league went ahead with its tawdry scheme of importing four Russian teams to play games in the 1989–90 season that would count in the standings, the Flyers would consider forfeiting their match.

League president John Ziegler's mysterious mission to Moscow apparently resulted in this ugly arrangement. Snider flips the pages of the NHL constitution angrily, confident it would take a unanimous vote to approve those games.

Siberia would become a summer resort before the Sniders would consent to match the Flyers against the Russkies. Glasnost be damned.

"Glasnost has not filtered down to the average Russian," Snider grumbled after last night's romp over Hartford.

"For example, in the area of dissidents and refuseniks, they've allowed a few top-level people to be free or emigrate.

"Yet the total emigration is still trickling lower and lower each year since 1980. It's almost at a standstill.

"Real openness would mean the borders would be open. And has that happened? Not at all.

"Afghanistan is a country being annihilated by these people. A sovereign nation being annihilated. Yet, if we sneeze toward Nicaragua we're condemned worldwide and by our own people.

"The Soviets have annihilated one-third of the population of Afghanistan. They booby-trap little toys; not meant to kill, but to maim children.

"They're inhuman.

"Inviting them to come here to play hockey is elevating them to the status of an equal partner, in the world, in life, in hockey. I don't consider them to be my equal morally."

The Flyers played the Russians in 1976. Bobby Clarke set the mood when he told me, "I hate the bastards."

Eleven years have added a thin coat of diplomacy, but the venom bubbles through.

"I don't like playing the Russians," Clarke grumped. "To me, they're coming over for one reason. For the money.

"Yeah, I got to know (Red Army goalie Vladislav) Tretiak, and he seemed like a good guy. But their whole life, their government is against what we believe in and stand for.

"Their goal is to rule the world. This country is made up of a lot of people from a lot of countries the Russians have overrun.

"Do you think the people from Czechoslovakia, or the Jewish people, are gonna be happy if we play them?

"They shouldn't be. I know I'd be hissed off if the Russians had overrun Canada and now wanted to play hockey games here.

"If it was a substitute for the Canada Cup, maybe you'd consider it. I like the Canada Cup idea, once every four years. I don't like what happens to players after the Canada Cup is over."

Politics make strange linemates. Toronto's curmudgeon owner, Harold Ballard, said, "Anyone who votes for this should be sent over there to live."

"I doubt if he's ever said two words to me," Snider said. "Oh, he's probably had some words with my father. Shouted them."

But the Sniders and Ballard agree that they don't want the Russians coming, whether they're wearing hip pads or tutus.

"I don't believe in the Bolshoi ballet coming," Snider said. "Cultural things, sports, are an extension, a reflection of one's society.

"Doctor J was an artist on the court. Bobby Clarke was an artist of sorts on the ice. Just as Nureyev was an artist in Russia at one time.

"If we have cultural exchanges we are saying we have mutual respect for each other's society's artistic expression.

"We're saying they're just a little different than us. No worse, no better. I don't want to grant them that stature.

"If you read the testimony (before Congress) of Anatoly Shcharansky, he pleads with us not to have these cultural exchanges.

"He says we don't understand that by doing it, we're helping to bury the people even further."

There are those who would argue that the country without sin should throw the first puck. They point to bigotry, oppression that blotches segments of our society.

"The very most fundamental thing about freedom starts with human rights," Snider said.

"You can see how they oppress their society. They believe human beings are merely fodder for their cannons. I think they are a direct threat to us. I believe these people are our enemy."

And Snider does not believe in playing games with the enemy, does not believe in sweetening the Soviet treasury with gate receipts from hockey games in Philadelphia.

He is baffled by Ziegler's arrogance in negotiating for the games, then bringing the idea before the Board of Governors, which meets in Palm Beach this weekend.

"I think he's going to have to explain himself in Florida," Snider said grimly. "If you want to talk about this, you do it behind closed doors.

"From a public relations standpoint, what he did was pretty stupid. It makes the league look bad.

"Maybe he thought it wouldn't take a unanimous vote to approve, because he knows Ballard and us won't vote for it.

"But article 3.1 of the league constitution says that each club will play a regular schedule of championship and playoff games with teams of the other member clubs.

"It lists the member clubs. In the voting guide it says that amendments require unanimous consent of all the members."

We are a nation of laws, not men. Maybe Ziegler can explain that to the Russians. Or, if he's too timid, Jay Snider would be happy to do it for him.

The Flyers will not play a Russian hockey team in a game that counts in the standings until Antarctica melts. You can bet all the snow in Siberia on that.

Give That Man a Stick: Clark's Finding It Difficult to Vent His Frustrations

Philadelphia Daily News
February 27, 1990

BOBBY CLARKE played like a guy wearing barbed-wire suspenders. Like someone had smeared Ben-Gay on his athletic supporter.

"When I was a player," Clarke said the other day, "I was always angry.

"I played better angry. I liked being angry. I'd use it on the ice.

"Now, if I get angry, what am I gonna do? You need patience.

"Get mad, what can you do? Yell at a player? That doesn't make the player better. So, there's some frustration."

Bobby Clarke, the player, splintered a forest full of sticks in anger. Bob Clarke, the Flyers' general manager, takes another swig from a pint carton of milk, and turns the other scarred cheek.

The Flyers have 16 games left in a dreadful season. Time enough, given the appalling mediocrity of the Patrick Division.

It ain't easy being general manager of a Flyers team under .500, a team that's 1–21–1 in games it has trailed entering the third period.

It's even tougher in Philadelphia, because if you telephone the Flyers and they put you on hold, you don't get something mellow, like Montovani.

You get WIP radio. In the mornings, that means Angelo Cataldi's "eye-dears" delivered in a tone as cold and nasty as a New England winter.

Last Wednesday, you got a sound bite from goalie Ron Hextall scolding his teammates for looking "lackadaisical" and Cataldi saying, "Isn't that Paul Holmgren's fault?"

The folks who own the Flyers own WIP. Great for ratings, bad for morale. It used to be, mixed emotions meant watching your mother-in-law drive off a cliff in your new Cadillac.

"It bothers me," confessed Clarke, who has taken his share of call-in slashes lately. "You wouldn't be human if it didn't.

"Everything is hindsight. They can look back three years and say you screwed this up, you screwed that up.

"We're all geniuses when we look backward. And we're all geniuses when it's not our neck on the line."

No one's neck is on the line at the moment as the Flyers baffle critics with their inconsistency.

President Jay Snider is happy with the job Clarke is doing. And Clarke is happy with the job Holmgren is doing. Stability has been a Flyers trademark.

Recently, though, two episodes rumpled that glass-smooth pond.

"About three weeks ago," Clarke recalled glumly, "Jay Snider had a little thing in the paper where he said we're gonna bring up these kids and hopefully it would push the veteran players.

"Someone asked me about it. My own feeling was, I was a veteran player, and a veteran who has played 8, 9, 10 years in the National Hockey League should know how to motivate himself.

"Shouldn't have to be motivated by outside sources.

"And, two weeks later, Paul happened to sit out (Ken) Linseman and (Brian) Propp. To motivate them.

"Guy said something to me, I said I expressed my feelings two weeks ago. That's where he got it from.

"I don't have any disagreement with Paul doing it. If that's what he thinks works. He's the coach, he's got to make it work.

"All of a sudden there are headlines. Paul and I have been best friends for 15 years. Winning or losing a hockey game isn't going to change whether we're friends or not."

"We agree," Snider said. "I wasn't talking about motivation. Reporters were asking me about the future.

"I made the point that there are some guys 31, 32, 33 who are not gonna be around. That's factual, and we have to replace 'em.

"What delays the replacing is if they're still at the top of their game and the kids aren't better.

"If there's a drop-off, which we're having, it speeds up how quickly you bring the kids in."

You can go from worst to first in a week in the Patrick Division. You can finish at .500 and make it to the Stanley Cup semifinals, which is what the Flyers did last season.

"Last May," Snider said, "we were one of three teams still playing.

"In this business, you expect to feel the heat. What counts is what have you done for me today.

"I couldn't say that everything Bob Clarke has done has been perfect. He's learning. He's six years into the job.

"Sometimes, you learn more from bad times than you do from good."

People forget, because losing erodes memory, that the very first trade Clarke made involved good friend Darryl Sittler.

They wrap that one in false colors when they suggest that Clarke was delivering a message that no one was untouchable.

"He traded a guy (Sittler) he thought might be out of hockey in a year for a fine young player (Murray Craven)," Snider said.

"Any general manager who makes moves to send a message couldn't work for the Flyers."

"There was no hidden message," Clarke sighed. "Two young players for a veteran, an awfully good guy and a pretty good player who at the time was 34 years old."

And now, six years later, Dave Poulin for Ken Linseman somehow gets described as a "wake-up call."

"Dave had been really good to our club," Clarke said. "We were pretty good friends. Same situation, you end up losing friends.

"We were trying to get a centerman we felt was gonna create some more offense. We'd lost 17 or 18 one-goal games.

"We wanted playmaking (in exchange) for a checking centerman."

Linseman is another thirtysomething guy who might be gone when the Flyers contend again for the Stanley Cup.

Critics badger Clarke for allowing the Flyers to get too old and he resists the temptation to mention injuries to key players (Hextall, Tim Kerr, Mark Howe) that would devastate any team.

There isn't much at Hershey or he would have been shuttling those players to the Spectrum. He won't knock underachievers by name because he believes in his heart that that is counterproductive.

"A coach gives a team bleep between periods," he said, "and they come out and play like bleep the next period.

"They react to the crowd the same way. Last Sunday (against the Islanders) the crowd cheered them and they responded."

Let the record show that in the next game, they coughed up six goals to the Penguins minus Mario Lemieux. Hextall, sitting in the press box, saw "lackadaisical" effort.

"We're all great players when we're winning," Clarke said. "Great managers, great coaches, great players.

"When things are really tough, it tells you something by whose play rises and whose falls off.

"There's no problem between Paul and myself. To me, the worst thing we've found out is that there are people who continually seem to want to create a problem so that somebody gets fired."

Beat the Islanders, lose at Pittsburgh, romp at St. Louis, get stomped in Chicago. The roller coaster continues.

"We've been up and down the last few years," Clarke said. "But somehow we survive."

There still is time, before the March 6 trading deadline, before the magic number for playoff action vanishes, for Clarke to pull the trigger on a major trade.

Clarke, the cynics say, is happier searching for the grinder rather than the flashy center because that's the kind of player he was, wearing those barbed-wire suspenders.

"I think," he said, "the one thing our organization has to acquire is the big center, the dominant-type center.

"We're not gonna get a Mario Lemieux or a Wayne Gretzky.

"Our centers are all quality, competent players. They work hard, give you everything they've got.

"But when we were successful, we had (Rick) MacLeish with 50 goals and 100 points. And myself in the middle. And Orest Kindrachuk, who was a checker and a hard worker.

"Our team was offensively better down the middle than we are now. And that's what we have to get.

"I don't want to sound critical of our own players. Because the guys we've got work their tails off. Great people.

"But we've got to get a big centerman for when you need the goal or the big play.

"We've always been able to develop goaltenders and the defense has been solid through the years."

Snider's office is not equipped with a panic button. The artwork is big-picture.

"I can't speculate on a trade," Snider said. "We have never believed in trading for the sake of trading.

"Sometimes you get another team's problems. The key is to build from within.

"For us to make a move, acquire an older player, to help us get into the playoffs, we're not going to make that kind of move.

"We don't make trades to make the playoffs. We make trades that will help us win the Stanley Cup.

"We've got to operate with an eye toward the future. We are going to have to have a youth movement. And the future is bright."

As a player with an active stick, Clarke looked like a guy who wanted to win at any cost. But he fired an excellent coach named Mike Keenan because he felt Keenan was crushing the players with verbal abuse.

Winning had a price Clarke wasn't willing to pay as a general manager. And now, with the Blackhawks playing well under Keenan, the talk shows yammer with criticism.

Clarke likes the college kids the Flyers drafted and the Finn and the free agent scoring a ton in Kamloops.

He loves the game despite the way expansion has diluted the talent, despite the presence of fainthearted players and their greedy agents.

He shuns the negative and squirms in the spotlight and longs for the days when he could splinter a stick after a loss or enjoy a beer or two after a victory.

Now, with the game changed, and the season staggering to a close, and the critics baying like bloodhounds outside his window, what's he gonna do? Hang up on Angelo Cataldi?

Behind the Marks of a Living Legend

Philadelphia Daily News
October 22, 1992

ALL THOSE YEARS, Bernie Parent wore a mask the color of sunshine. Painted smile. Twinkling eyes. Arched eyebrows. His "Some fun, eh?" motto scrawled across a wrinkle-free forehead.

That was off the ice.

On the ice he wore a generic white mask with the Flyers' logo at the temples, a mask to deflect pucks, a mask to hide the terror he kept deep inside him.

"Goaltending," Parent said yesterday, "it's not a pleasant career."

They honored Parent at the Spectrum last night as a "sports legend." Honored him for his back-to-back Vezina trophies, for his 55 shutouts, for the pucks he stopped with the hockey mask, and, yes, for the "Some fun, eh?" mask he wore the rest of the time.

"The hockey fades away," Parent said, groping to explain why he is still so adored 16 years after the second Stanley Cup parade.

"A new generation comes in. Little kids ask me for my autograph, I say to them, 'How do you know about me?'

"And they say, 'My dad told me about you.' And that is the best feeling of all.

"You have to look at the whole picture. The Flyers, the organization, the Stanley Cups we won, the way the crowds went crazy.

"In addition to winning, the guys were popular. Bobby Clarke, Bob Kelly, Bill Barber, Rick MacLeish, they all had charisma.

"And, because of the way we won. People loved us because Philadelphia people are contact-oriented. And we had a good-hitting team."

They had a good-hitting team and a captain named Clarke who gripped his stick so hard he'd leave a trail of sawdust across the ice.

And, in goal, in his prime, quick, slick Bernie Parent, explaining one particularly nasty purple bruise on his chest by saying, "My wife bit me in a fit of passion."

Last night, Clarke recalled the moment in the sixth game of the championship against Boston, the Flyers clutching a 1–0 lead.

"We had a high-strung right winger out there named Simon Nolet," Clarke recalled. "Ten minutes left, 1–0 game.

"Bernie calls timeout, calls Nolet over, starts talking to him. Nolet waves him away. He gets back to the bench, we ask Simon what Bernie wanted.

"Nolet said, 'That crazy bugger . . . he's got some new golf clubs and he said he wanted to play when this was over.'"

Jesting, is that how he survived so long, all those years in a "not pleasant" career, long enough to become a legend?

"To play well," Parent said, "to do the job you're supposed to do, you have to exit the world. You have to be in your own little world.

"Maybe 'selfish' is not the right word, but you have to be within yourself at all times. You can't expand yourself.

"Goaltending has its own pressures. If you're a quarterback and make a bad move, there are people to help you.

"A pitcher makes a bad pitch, maybe someone catches it.

"A goalie makes a mistake, it's a score.

"It requires a lot of discipline. You have to program yourself. You have to have a good system.

"What's a system? It's the understanding of what you're doing out there. And once a goaltender understands why he's making certain moves, it's easier to be consistent."

He is all gray now, pudgier, mellower, still self-effacingly witty.

He is a senior vice president with Rosanio, Bailets & Talamo Inc., an up-and-coming communications marketing agency in Cherry Hill.

Which means he plays a lot of golf with prospective clients, takes them fishing on his 42-foot Viking off Cape May, schmoozes and shakes hands and lures new business, which ain't easy in this bleak economy.

"What I try to teach young goalies," he said, "is never be realistic in life. I know it's not realistic to say that.

"But reality has too many barriers. I don't care if we're going up against a billion-dollar agency, I compete, show them what we're capable of doing."

The adoration Parent generates is fascinating because the Flyers traded him once, to Toronto, in 1971; because he jumped leagues and wound up with the Philadelphia Blazers in '72; because he bailed out at playoff time in a contract hassle in '73, then found his way back to the Flyers, the quintessential prodigal son.

"I have two main memories," he said. "One bad, one good. I'll tell you the bad one first, because maybe that will help young kids.

"I'd come back to the Flyers from the World League. The papers were saying that Parent was back in town and would help them win a Cup.

"First exhibition game, I get on the ice, I receive a standing ovation, ta-da, ta-da. And 10 minutes later, the New York Rangers have scored eight goals against me.

"They pulled me out. People wondering, 'What the hell is happening?' We came back and won the Cup that year.

"I share that story with people to prove that if you don't give up, if you believe in yourself, the sun will shine again.

"The second memory involves the two championships. That's what you live for, as a little kid.

"The second one was better. The first one, I was numb. The second, I was able to sit back and enjoy it."

There was something so warm, so earthy, so satisfying about that team, it is no surprise that the Philadelphia Sports Congress built its first "sports legend" fund-raiser around Parent.

Dinner guests were promised an evening of fun, eh? What they got was a bonus, Parent sharing his thoughts about life outside the rink.

"The way you keep improving," Parent said, "is to continually change your goals.

"As a kid, my goal was to play in the National Hockey League. I reached my goal, after 10 years, and they called me a rookie.

"My goal had to change. I had to decide, 'What did I want to accomplish?' I thought about team-oriented goals, about individual goals.

"The one thing I keep telling young kids is, you just don't graduate, not as a goalie, but in life.

"You cannot stand still. You must go forward. Otherwise, you'll go backwards."

The Puck Stops Here

Philadelphia Daily News
October 5, 1995

THAT AIN'T A BRAHMS LULLABY Flyers goalie Ron Hextall is playing when he pounds his stick against the net, bang-bong, bong-bong. It's not meant to be.

Some nights it's "The 1812 Overture," and pretty soon the cannons roar and the cymbals clang and there's the kettle-drum thump of bodies splattered against the boards, and the Spectrum crowd is loud enough to rattle windows in Camden.

And that's nice. But if Flyers general manager Bob Clarke wanted a guy who played the pipe organ, he'd have hired Larry Ferrari.

Clarke plucked Hextall from the Islanders last year to stop the puck, not because he's fiery enough to melt the ice in his crease, not because he's as lean as he is mean, not because he never sold his house in Voorhees, not for all those intangible reasons that make for warm, fuzzy stories.

"The main reason we traded for Hexy," Clarke said bluntly, "is that we feel he can stop the puck. That's his job. To stop the puck.

"Part of the personality is his work ethic and his competitiveness that I find attractive for a team.

"But, if you work hard and you don't stop the puck, what good are you? I don't think you can ever get the order of importance mixed up.

"The job is to stop the puck. No matter how nice a guy you are or how hard a worker you are, you don't stop the puck, you're not a lot of value to a team."

Clarke can be that way, colder than Flin Flon (already buried in snow), making tough decisions with his head, not his heart.

He has improved a team that got to the Eastern Conference finals last year. And he is sending it out to play a full schedule starting Saturday with a 31-year-old goalie who didn't make the top 20 list of goaltenders recently published in the *Hockey News*.

"A gossip magazine," Clarke sneered. But he couldn't be coaxed into ranking Hextall on his list because anything he said might be held against him in the next contract negotiations.

"I view a goaltender as part of your hockey team," he said, in that icy tone he saves for the media. "Part of the 20 guys you ice every night. If you rely on one person, whether it's a goaltender or a player, to win you games, I think that's a high risk."

Clarke has surrounded Eric Lindros, the best player in the game, with a talented bunch. Best team ever to wear orange-and-black? Clarke turns ice white at the suggestion.

"Noooo," he moaned. "The best teams I've seen are the ones that won the Cups. To be great, you've got to win. That's professional sports.

"This team hasn't been to the finals yet. Mike Keenan took a couple of teams to the finals. Pat Quinn took a team to the finals.

"It's nice to say we're good, it's nice to say we could be better. But you still have to do it. Everything's in front of you. You want to be great? Then win!"

Just win, baby. When you are 31, you can line the bottom of your bird cage with the *Hockey News* and you don't need the general manager to light a fire under you, because the thermostat is already on high.

Hextall looks around the locker room and measures the talent with a gauge sharpened by nine years in the league.

"This is the best team I've ever played with," he said. "We had a lot of skill the year I was in Quebec, but we didn't have the team we've got here.

"And, obviously, we didn't have the big guy."

For those just back from Patagonia, the big guy is Lindros, who whacks Hextall vigorously as part of a pregame ritual.

There are more really big guys on the Flyers than on the Sixers this year. Big, talented guys. Does that change the way Hextall plays the game?

"It doesn't affect the way you play," Hextall said. "You're not beating yourself up after making a mistake because your teammates, in time, are gonna make up for it. That allows you to just do your job.

"Other years, at times, I tried to do too much. Now, if I do my job, we have a good shot at winning."

There are times he wields the stick like a machete, a habit that obscures his puck-handling skills. He ventures far from the net. His style is not classic.

It isn't that he will gamble even more, hoping his teammates will erase reckless mistakes.

"It's not necessarily that I will gamble more," he said. "It's more like, on a two-on-one, I'm gonna play the shooter instead of trying to play the shooter and the other guy.

"You do that and you wind up playing neither guy and they score, one way or the other. I have to do my job and my job is the guy with the puck.

"The guy without the puck is one of our defensemen's job."

Hextall was the young, fearless goalie when the Flyers got to the Stanley Cup finals in 1987, losing in the seventh game to Edmonton. That ominous sound may be a clock ticking.

"The clock ticks for everybody," Hextall said firmly. "Every game you play, every year you play, is one less game, one less year on your career. But I feel I have some good years left."

Some guys just get older. Hextall is getting wiser, too. He was 8–2 in the last 10 regular-season games he played as the Flyers scuffled for playoff position last season.

And when coach Terry Murray came to him before the playoffs and asked him to scrap some of the energy-sapping parts of his pregame behavior, he accepted the suggestions.

"As you mature, you should be able to evaluate who you are," Clarke said. "If you think you can be better by doing things a certain way, you've got to change.

"Was all that jumping and hopping and bouncing around helping you? If it is, then keep doing it.

"There were times, between faceoffs, the emotion was so high, what did it accomplish? Prior to games, Hexy would be bouncing around. His job was to stop the puck."

"I changed some things last year," Hextall said. "I did a little less in warmup. I think it helped. When you're 20, you've got extra energy to burn.

"The older you get, the smarter you get. It was good advice from somebody who'd been through it.

"Banging the pipes? I'll keep doing that. That's something I've done since I was a kid. Makes me feel good."

PART VI
Basketball

Introduction

JIM LYNAM

THIS COLLECTION NOT ONLY IS a great read but for many will also serve as an entertaining trip down memory lane. For many younger readers, it will present a glimpse into some of the most memorable events and personalities that form the backbone of Philadelphia's fascinating sports history.

Let me state at the outset—unabashedly—that I am a huge Stan Hochman fan. As a senior at the legendary West Catholic High School, I was the topic of one of Stan's articles. It was the first piece ever written about me—I WAS HOOKED!

My love affair with Philadelphia sports started during my very young preteen years. While I was a fan of all the area teams in my early years, my interests were about to undergo an abrupt change.

As I entered my freshman year of high school, my captivation with the local basketball scene and the game itself was already well underway. Those of us who grew up in Southwest Philadelphia followed our favorite teams either on the radio or through the local newspapers (the *Bulletin, Inquirer,* or *Daily News*).

That Philadelphia basketball was unique in countless ways was obvious even to the casual fan. Norman Wilton Chamberlain, the greatest force ever to play the game, was "growing" before our very eyes at Overbrook High School; La Salle College, with All-American Tom Gola, won the 1954 NCAA championship (having won the equally prestigious NIT championship only two years earlier); and the Big 5, although in its infancy, was in the process of establishing itself as one of the truly unique institutions in the history of college athletics.

Add to this the titanic battles between the Boston Celtics and the Philadelphia Warriors that featured Wilt Chamberlain going against Bill Russell, two of the greatest big men ever to play the game. The two teams met twelve times a year—during the regular season!

History reflects that the talent displayed on a nightly basis was not limited to the on-court play. For years, the city of Philadelphia was a virtual pipeline to the NBA for coaches and officials. It would be hard to overstate Philadelphia's impact on the game during this period.

A group of writers that more than equaled the world-class talent of the athletes and coaches they covered chronicled this incredible sports era. It wasn't until many years later, when I traveled the country as an NBA coach, that I came to appreciate the true excellence of Philadelphia sports writing. Philadelphia sportswriters were in a class of their own.

Stan Hochman stood at the head of this impressive group. His style was beyond unique; his insights were incisive, witty, and informative. If I am accused of hyperbole, so be it. We miss you, Stan. You were truly one for the ages!

PRO

Julius Erving: A Man for All People

Philadelphia Daily News
February 13, 1981

EMOLLIENTS.

Julius Erving is serious medicine. He has emollients that protect against the winds of envy and the cold of boredom. They also act as a sunscreen, warding off the harsh heat of bigotry, no matter what direction it comes from. Emollients, that's the word Julius Erving uses in that Dr. Chapstick commercial. That's the word that sets it apart from other commercials, the hook, the grabber.

It's a terrific commercial because it works. But more important, it breaks new ground for Erving. Chapstick's spokespersons until now were whiter than rice . . . Suzy Chaffee, Catfish Hunter, Bucky Dent.

"I view myself as a crossover athlete," Erving said yesterday, at his elegant shoe salon on S. 2nd St. "There are maybe a dozen athletes in the country who can really cross over ethnically.

"I have that feeling, that belief that comes from the mail I get from parents and kids. From people coming up to me from all types of backgrounds, saying, 'I really like what you stand for, what you say, how you handle yourself, and I'd like my son to grow up to be like you.'

––––––

"AND THAT'S A WHITE FATHER talking about his son.

"That Chapstick commercial was designed to give them entry into the black market. . . . Is that manipulation or is that opportunity?

"The narrow-minded thinker thinks, 'If I can't get ahead, why should you?' You may climb out of the pot, but instead of giving you a hand, he'll pull you back into it. He'll think it's manipulation. Then there's the person who realizes there's enough out there for everybody. As long as you handle yourself in consistent fashion, as long as you conform to truth-in-advertising laws, they'll see it as an opportunity.

"As much as they wish they had had it, they're happy that you got it. By you having it, it does open things up for them. I can deal with both schools of thought and not lose any sleep over it."

Emollients. Erving can deal with anything short of mayhem on the court without losing his poise. And he can deal with anything short of death of a loved one without shedding tears.

"There have been times I have felt moved to confrontation," Erving said, recalling episodes with M.L. Carr, Mike Bantom, Elvin Hayes. "There's several reasons for the way I act on the court.

"When I was in junior high school I got into a fight with a player. I won. My coach reprimanded me. His name was Ray Wilson and outside of my mother, he was the single most influential person in my life.

"HE REPRIMANDED ME and I was really upset about it. He told me there were other ways to get the job done. Ways to take care of resolving a problem without using fists.

"He said fighting was a stupid way of doing it, a cannibalistic way of doing it. He said I shouldn't be about that. He planted the seed. I accepted it. I didn't question it.

"It was confusing, though. I hadn't started the fight, and I had won the fight.

"And then my brother passed. I was 19, he was 16. He died of lupus. He complained of pain in his joints in February and he died on April 3rd. A short, brief illness that caught me off-balance, by surprise.

"You feel totally helpless. I felt like . . . nothing. I was 19, my whole life was ahead of me. My only brother was gone. A brother I loved and cherished.

"When it came to being a good person and doing good he was 'way ahead of the game. He was 'way ahead of me. And he was taken from us, just like that. That had a real solidifying influence on my family.

"And it goes beyond that. Once I stopped crying and got over the mourning period, for the second time in my life, I became a changed man.

"I became more purposeful, more goal-orientated. And I didn't let things bother me. It just wasn't worth it. To me, I had experienced the worst I could feel as a person on this earth. Nothing could happen that could make me feel worse, unless my mother died, God forbid.

"Well, that did a number on my attitude. All the little things, the trials and tribulations that would upset most people, I wouldn't let them bother me. I came to control my emotions."

TRAC, the Television, Radio, Advertising Club, honored Erving as "Sportsman of the Year" yesterday at a Franklin Plaza luncheon.

"Julius Erving is a remarkable man," Sixers President Lou Scheinfeld said in the lobby. "A master at his sport and a master at life."

"Julius Erving has everything in the right perspective," said GM Pat Williams. "He always says the right thing, he always has time for everybody."

"Right now," said Coach Billy Cunningham, "I have to say he's the front-runner for Most Valuable Player in the league. And when's the last time anybody but a center won that?"

There was more of that at the luncheon, much, much more of it. And a nine-minute tape of Erving dunks. And a scroll and a bowl. And by the time Erving got a chance to respond it was 2:05 and the audience was back-to-work fidgety.

Erving sensed that, but he would not settle for mumbling thanks, because that is not his style.

"I've had success in my career," Erving said. "Most of the 10 years I can look back on and smile about, be very proud of. The last two years Jesus Christ has touched my life and showed me more than I have ever seen before.

———

"HE WANTS ALL of us to be family. And this is one of the many ways this work is being done. One individual cannot unite a whole world. But any time an athlete, whether it's Mike Schmidt or Bobby Clarke or Ron Jaworski, is honored, they do not only represent themselves.

"I represent my Lord and Savior, my family, all the other athletes in the city, all the members of the 76ers staff, and all of the players who have made so many sacrifices."

Later, sitting in the plush, hushed shoe salon, Erving talked about changes in that deep, resonant voice of his.

"Since accepting Christ as my Savior, I am the way I am," he said, "because He allows me to be, and because the things I'm doing glorify His name. Prior to that, the image I had wasn't a whole lot different. It was good, clean.

"During that time I thought I had more control, that I was responsible for what was going on in my life. And my game was the result of hard work, drive, good coaching, all the tangible things I could label.

"And after doing that right through '78, I spent the summer going through rehabilitation of that groin injury and I still kept coming up short, I still kept asking why? Now, I don't have to ask why anymore."

The Ervings are expecting their fourth child in May. They are selling their 17-room house on Long Island and searching for a big home in Philadelphia, with some ground for the kids to romp on. He has other business interests in mind, and he does not want to wait until retiring to put them in motion.

He was at ease, in a corner of the shoe salon, surrounded by expensive leather shoes, tastefully displayed. Bruno Magli and Salvatore Ferragamo gleaming in ceiling spotlights.

"The key ingredient is quality," explained Alonzo Somerville, a long-time friend of Erving's, and vice president of The Doctor's Shoe Salon. "Only leather shoes. And nobody has the quality we have and the quantity."

The stock has become more varied after an initial emphasis on large sizes.

One glance at Erving's feet tells you why.

"I wear a 15," he said. "My wife wears a 10. We like nice shoes. For many years I was denied the styles I wanted. I couldn't be fitted in a conventional-type store.

"What we tried to create here was the concept and feel of going into your home. I wanted something consistent with my family image, my business image, as someone who tries to project class and good taste."

He has what Bill Bradley used to call a sense of where he's at. That explains his brilliance on the court and his grace off the court. Most athletes are content to open stores featuring sneakers and jogging shoes.

Erving smiled at the observation and raised his eyes to the mirrored ceilings.

"Because of the stereotype," he said. "I never wanted to go along with what everybody else does."

Julius Erving marches to a different drummer. We always knew that. Now he marches in supple, leather, size 15 shoes from his own elegant salon.

Hard Hats Win Some Warm Hearts

Philadelphia Daily News
June 3, 1983

THE CITY REP'S OFFICE said 1.7 million watched the Sixers parade through town yesterday. Mo Cheeks would like the guy who counted the people counting his assists. Or steals.

You think Mo Cheeks had quicker hands than Wally "By Golly" Jones? You think Andrew Toney could do more things with a basketball than Hal Greer? You think Marc Iavaroni would survive some of the brutal picks Luke Jackson used to set? And what would Wilt do against Moses in the fourth quarter night after night after night?

It has been 16 years since the Sixers won a championship with Wilt and Wally and Chet "The Jet" Walker and a red-headed kangaroo-leaping sixth man named Billy Cunningham. Is this year's team better than that year's team?

Argue, go ahead and argue. That's what sports are all about. Nostalgia and sentiment and debate and passion. And every so often a team, rich with talent, thick with character, puts together an awesome performance, wins a championship, and a whole city exults.

Maybe the 1983 Sixers are better than the 1967 Sixers because they play tougher defense and they've got more ways to win. But one thing for sure, the championship parade was sweeter this time.

"We didn't have a parade in '67," said Joe Chase, who is with the city rep's office, and moonlights with Harvey Pollack's statistics crew at the ballgames. (Let the record show he does a better job counting rebounds by Moses than spectator's noses.)

"The parade stuff was relegated to ice hockey. They had this tradition in Canada of taking the Stanley Cup through the streets. So the Flyers had one in '75. Now, it's an acceptable fact."

Terrific. We've gotten something from Canada besides hockey players and cold fronts. That first Flyers' parade was a trifle chaotic, the players trapped in convertibles, pawed at by an overzealous mob. Bernie Parent taking time out at Broad and Tasker to answer the call of nature, as they say in Canada, eh?

We do it smoother now. Players and families on flat-bed trucks, police barricades, the parade ending inside the ballpark where another 50,000 fans can see and hear their heroes.

And so, on the fourth day, Moses parted the rain clouds and said, let there be sunshine. And there he was, waving a kitchen broom as the mob chanted "Sweep, sweep, sweep." It was warm and wonderful, and even if only 875,000 crammed the parade route, that's 875,000 more than celebrated the last time the Sixers won a championship.

"Me," said Mayor Bill Green, half-kidding, when asked for the difference in celebrations.

"I think this city's alive now. There's spirit here. Maybe we're different than we were then. Plus, I think everybody can identify with the way the Sixers proved themselves.

"There was their relentless pursuit, their never-say-die attitude. In our opinion, we probably had the best team for several years, but a slip here, a slip there, kept them from winning.

"This year, they put it all together, and that's a wonderful thing to celebrate."

"Pride," suggested Wilson Goode, the Democratic candidate for mayor. "There's a feeling of pride sweeping the city the last few years. People feel good about Philadelphia.

"You look around this stadium, you see black and white, young and old, saying 'We love Philadelphia' and 'We love our sports teams.'"

Uh huh. But the fans jeered the lovely lady who was introduced as representing Gov. Thornburgh. Some of those fans knew that the next day, when the sunshine faded and the confetti got swept up, they'd be at the welfare office snarling at some bureaucrat who was saying the rules had changed.

"The celebration," councilman David Cohen said, "shows a city feeling good about itself. The sports scene has come a long way since 1967. Plus, Philadelphians have been living with this team year after year.

"So it's a great human feeling, that you can try and fail, and then try again, and finally make it. That's reason enough for a celebration, succeeding after failing many times."

Julius Erving talked about that. He reminded the stadium crowd, "To get to where we're at today we had to live through a whole lot more than four, five, four.

"We have the world championship because after six years of knocking at the door, even though we felt good in our hearts, in our minds, in our souls, we went out and got ourselves a whole cast of hardhats.

"And we got the final piece of the puzzle and that made us complete in every sense of the word. And there was nothing pretty about what we did to the NBA this year. . . . [I]t was beautiful!"

Malone is the hard hat, the guy in overalls, the guy who brings his lunch bucket to the ballyard, the guy still pounding rivets when everybody else is wobbly from fatigue.

Erving is right. It wasn't pretty. Tough defense never is. A lot of guys blotting out the passing lanes, doubling up on people, clawing at them, muffling Kareem and Wilkes and Magic and Nixon, until the only guy left to take the shot is Kurt Rambis.

And Malone dominating the fourth quarter, sweaty and slope-shouldered, grabbing rebounds away from guys who jump higher, who have bigger hands. It ain't nearly as pretty as the championship trophy.

Maybe that explains the gurgling undercurrent of genuine pleasure yesterday. The fans adore Erving and the acrobatic grace he brings to the arena, but Doc didn't play on an NBA championship team until the hard hat went to work underneath. This is a hard hat town.

It was a hard hat town 16 years ago, and Wilt played 48 minutes and Luke Jackson set picks straight out of Jack Kelly's brickyard. Why the difference in decibels this time?

"Pro sports have grown," said Matty Guokas, the keen assistant coach who played on that '67 team. "Now, the media puts it in the public eye. The celebration is a way for people to share in the championship."

"I don't know why," said trainer Al Domenico, who usually has an opinion on anything and everything. "We had a small party then. Friends, relatives.

"Why? That was the greatest team in America and maybe 1,000 people came out to the airport and that was it. Do that many more people have television sets now?"

Barkley Could Star on "All My Children"

Philadelphia Daily News
January 20, 1987

KATE CONFIDED TO CORD that her true love, Patrick, disappeared in the African jungle while they were working on an assignment. Asa rescued Pamela and Pete when a volcano erupted on Malakeva.

I thought Charles Barkley would like to know that.

He had to miss "One Life to Live" yesterday afternoon because the Sixers had the audacity to schedule a game against the Phoenix Suns at the Spectrum, starting at 3.

"These games," Barkley grumped, "interfere with my soap operas."

Barkley did get to see the entire episode of "All My Children," including Angie's tantrum when she found out that Yvonne had been fooling around with Jesse while she was living in Chicago.

"I didn't get out 'til 2," he said. "I thought, 'I can get to the Spectrum in 15 minutes.' I didn't. It was raining. I didn't know that."

So, Charles, the trumpet virtuoso, was late for the pre-concert meeting. Matthew, the leader of the band, kept him offstage for the first six minutes.

When Charles got the chance to play, he rearranged some furniture, delaying the concert for nine minutes. Near the end, he hit some notes nobody else can reach, and the audience went back out into the rain, whistling his praise.

Where does the soap opera end and life begin for Charles Barkley? Will he stay forever "Young and Restless," living in "Another World," without a "Guiding Light?" Or will he drive Matty Guokas into "General Hospital?"

One of Matty's handful of rules is that all the players be in the locker room, in uniform, 45 minutes before game time.

"I feel like I've been coming late for three years," Barkley said. "He says to be here at 7:15, I walk in at 7:15. Done it 50 times.

"I'm not a big believer in coming here, sitting around, getting nervous."

There's an automatic fine for being late, loose change for a guy making $650,000 a year.

Yesterday, Guokas decided to penalize Barkley by removing him from the starting lineup.

"I think," said Barkley, "he was just doing it to let me know he was the boss."

The boss of bosses, Harold Katz, was basking in the glow of television lights, saying how supportive he's been of Andrew Toney.

Julius Erving was in another corner, speaking softly into a cluster of microphones, thrust forward like so many licorice lollipops, explaining how he felt about playing six minutes in the entire second half.

World B. Free glanced around warily like a character in "Twilight Zone," wondering if this wasn't 1976 all over again, more midway carnival than basketball team.

"Everyone is expected to be on time," Guokas said. "It's the one regimentation we have in sports.

"It's the one constraint in the job. If it had been the first or second time, I'd have let it go. It (the benching) is not a major precedent. It's as much a message to the rest of the team.

"It (the fine) is not a major amount of money. If it should become a chronic thing, then some night, you're going to have to say, 'You don't play.'

"It's going to help us in the long run. If we're going to be a good basketball team it's because we're going to play together.

"We've got to do it at both ends of the floor. Your teammates have to rely on you.

"If you're late on a pick, you screw up a play. If you're late helping out defensively and give up an easy basket, it could possibly be the winning shot.

"That's the reason we have these rules. We're all in this together. And we're all expected to be here at the proper time."

Barkley emerged from the shower and edged slowly past the clutter around Katz. Was the owner miffed at Barkley for being late?

"No," Katz said, tenderly squeezing Barkley's bicep. "Charles and I are the best of friends."

Was Barkley mad about being lifted from the starting lineup?

"No," he said. "Nothing bothers me."

That's Barkley, with his sculptured body and his marble head. Does he wonder for a moment if his frequent latenesses bother Maurice Cheeks, who comes to play every night? Or Tim McCormick, who squeezes every ounce of hustle out of that pale body? Or Jeff Ruland, who pounded all those miles on the treadmill rehabilitating that wounded knee as swiftly as possible?

Moving half a ton of backboard support with a thunder dunk, which is what Barkley did in the second quarter, doesn't impress anyone but the television commentators, who have to ad-lib for 8:52.

If strength was important, someone would have signed Arnold Schwarzenegger a long time ago.

"I don't care about fines," Barkley said. Double the lateness penalty every time you invoke it, and Barkley might care before it got to $400.

"I don't care about minutes," said Barkley, who played 37. Cut that down to 12 one night and he'll rattle windows in Camden with his howling.

"Rebounding is my No. 1 thing," Barkley said, crumpling a box score that showed him with 13. "I try to get at least 15 a game."

Will somebody tell him that he can lead the league in rebounds, and if the Sixers get bumped out in the first round of the playoffs, the rebound title and $1.25 will get him a ride on the Broad Street Subway?

"I'm responsible," Barkley said bluntly, "when I step on that court. Other than that I'm a regular human being.

"My job is to play basketball, otherwise I'm Charles."

The Sixers led by a point with 78 seconds left, when Barkley vaulted for an offensive rebound. He got hacked and lobbed the ball at the hoop as he toppled to the floor. It went in.

"Lucky shot," Barkley said. "I thought the ref was gonna call a foul so I just wanted to throw it up there, off the glass. Thank God, it went in."

It happened about an hour after Tony helped a nun, Sister Camellia, who fainted when she saw a photo of Duke in the newspaper. Robin and Anna said goodbye to Robert, who returned to Australia—and Holly, on "General Hospital."

I thought Charles Barkley would like to know that.

Jordan Plays the Game His Way

Philadelphia Daily News
June 12, 1991

INGLEWOOD, CALIFORNIA—Michael Jordan wears sleek, high-fashion $1,000 suits. He will not let us peek inside his closet to see how many he owns.

He will not let us check his pantry to see what he really eats for breakfast.

He most assuredly will not let us poke around inside his head to find out what he thinks about the world beyond the arena. Or even why he plays the way he plays inside the arena.

"You can only see a part of me," he said bluntly. "You see what I want you to see. . . .

"Only my family and friends actually know me, inside, outside."

So he soars past and the earthbound scriveners who cannot jump over the Sunday newspaper they write for check his soles for clay and tell themselves they are checking his soul.

The NBA Finals resume tonight. Chicago lost the first game by two points, when a last-second shot by Jordan rattled in and out and in and out again.

It was one of 24 shots Jordan took that day. He interrupted the sludge of questions about taking too many shots to call his teammates "my supporting cast" and suggest that maybe timidity kept them from taking as many shots as they should have and that jitters kept them from making as many shots as they should have.

"My supporting cast."

You'd think he'd called them wimps or wusses or commie pinko agitators. You'd think he'd swiped a page from the Charles Barkley textbook on team morale.

"I couldn't do it the way Charles has done it," Jordan said. "It's tough to live with a person if he's gonna do it that way.

"It's hard to work with a guy who is constantly knocking you publicly. It's embarrassing, from a player's standpoint, to get embarrassed by one of the star players.

"Because that star player is not a perfect player, either. He's gonna have some faults.

"Charles expects everyone to be like him. But that's something you've got to learn, that we've all got different talents, different desires, different motivations.

"I never point fingers at individuals and say he can't do this, he can't do that. I challenge him to step up and earn respect.

"I've fought with (teammates). Last year, before the second (playoff) game against Detroit.

"One of the guys, and I won't tell you who, had been setting hard picks in practice, but not in the games.

"I told him, 'You do that in practice, you'd better do it in games, too.'"

"Michael," coach Phil Jackson explained, "is not the kind of guy who pats guys on the back. He jabs 'em in the ribs."

So that's what "my supporting cast" was all about, a poke in the ribs, to get faint heartbeats going, to smother those first-game butterflies, to find out if whatever was inside them included the channeled anger to prove they were more than a chorus line behind Mr. Bojangles.

"I've never felt threatened," Jackson said. "Or angry, or disappointed in Michael. There have been times when I felt he could use more discretion.

"Michael was right, after the first game. The coaches thought our guys were very nervous and weren't shooting the ball, and looking to throw it back to him and let him bail them out.

"As a coaching staff, we backed him up. We didn't say it the same way, 'my supporting cast,' but we said, 'You've gotta take the shots.

"'You've gotta make those easy shots, Horace (Grant); Bill (Cartwright), you've gotta find the space to create shots for yourself.'"

Did it work? The Bulls won the next three games and are one coup de grace from finishing off the wounded, weary Lakers.

Game 2, some Lakers whimpered about Jordan's taunting them with exuberant body language. Game 4, they scoffed at a bruised toe that did not keep him from playing 44 splendid minutes.

He is 48 minutes from fulfilling his championship dream, and you cannot wipe that tongue-flapping smile from his fascinating face.

A face you will be seeing more and more of once the city of big shoulders and narrow trophy cases sweeps up after the parade.

Jordan risked some of those commercial opportunities when he snarled and scuffled his way through the Detroit series.

"Phil has encouraged the players to stand on their feet," assistant coach John Bach said. "To say what they mean and mean what they say.

"Detroit had thwarted us, sent us a heavy, heavy message in the past.

That they could physically handle what we were doing, that they could be assertive, cajole and, indeed, intimidate us.

"I think Michael was sending a message that he was prepared to make any sacrifice, even the slight blush on his image.

"If it meant standing up and fighting, if it meant talking trash, he was prepared to give that bit of himself up.

"He had always given up everything he had, physically and mentally. I think he proved he's a leader. And not just a quiet leader."

Jordan has no regrets about the way he played, the trash he talked, about designating himself as spokesman for the world of basketball in bidding good riddance to Detroit's thuggery.

"You can take that any way you want to," Jordan said sternly. "The way I looked at it, if a bully has been bullying long enough, at some point in time, you've got to step up and play him at his own game.

"If they're gonna talk trash, start fights, you have to show you've got some resilience. You can't sit there and take it.

"We didn't want to initiate the dirty tactics, but I felt, those guys were so used to talking trash, let me see if they could take it back, see if they like it.

"If anything, you're going to give your teammates confidence. They see someone standing up and then everyone is gonna stand up together."

The Wheaties folks didn't need a lip-reader to decipher what Jordan said to Dennis Rodman. It's not the kind of stuff you find on the back of a cereal box.

"Don't worry about the Wheaties people," Jordan said, grinning. "Breakfast of champions. We become champions, they'll feel just fine."

Wilt Defends Magic Number: Chamberlain Explains Why He Tallied Bed Partners in Book

Philadelphia Daily News
October 30, 1991

IF WILT CHAMBERLAIN didn't have impeccable taste, if he were braggadocious, or flamboyant, he'd build a 7-foot-high golden arch outside his Bel Air, Calif., mansion, and install a blinking, digital, ever-changing sign in the shape of a smile that said, "Over 20,000 satisfied customers."

That's the number, 20,000. It's in Wilt's new book, "A View From Above."

Points? Rebounds? Assists?

Are you out of your mind? You want statistics, buy the official NBA encyclopedia.

You want Wilt's bedroom box score, it's right there, Chapter 11: "If I had to count my sexual encounters, I would be closing in on *twenty thousand* different ladies."

The italics are Wilt's, as are the quaint formulas used to come up with the magic number, and the justification for including the awesome statistic in the book.

"In the context of my book," Wilt explained the other day, "I felt as though I had to bring it up.

"How could I be involved in something that much of my life, something that helped shape my views on life, without writing about it?

"It would be like leaving out my whole basketball career.

"I could have said, 'Sex is a big part of my life and I enjoyed the relationship of many, many women.' But that wouldn't have been indicative of anything at all.

"The number was not meant to be braggadocious. Just pointing out the facts. My situation was a mutual mind and body thing.

"Our minds wanted it and our bodies did it.

"I came upon the number by random. I went to look at some old things I've kept, appointment books, that sort of thing.

"I'd take a month, like January of '69, how many people might have been with me. Then February '73, then June '84.

"I'd prorate it. Take the numbers, multiply by 12. And come up with the number."

Where was statistician Harvey Pollack when Wilt really needed him? Harvey would never use a short month like February when extrapolating yearly numbers. Even in a leap year.

Anyway, it figures out to 1.2 encounters a day, every day, since Wilt was 15.

Guy never had a headache? He's not likely to get an Advil commercial any time soon.

He's not likely to have Anita Hill furnish a blurb for the back cover, either.

Front cover shows Wilt towering over a photo of the New York skyline. What's that all about? Wilt was born and raised in Philadelphia, played here, once scored 100 points wearing a Philadelphia uniform, set records (while wearing sneakers) that will never be broken.

Maybe Wilt liked the World Trade Center towers, phallic symbols, glinting in the twilight? Don't get the wrong idea about the book. It's not all about sex. It's all about Wilt, who is not a kiss-and-brag kind of guy because he mentions no names, not even the rich and famous, including numbers 11,064, 12,807, 15,456.

"I've had offers to go on the Phil Donahue show," Wilt said, "to talk about promiscuity. I won't do that."

Nor will he do "Geraldo" to compare conquests.

On tour, Wilt will do what he can to turn the dialogue to other topics, other issues.

The book is a smorgasbord, lots of anecdotes and opinions dealing with lots of different subjects, all of them strung like beads with no apparent pattern.

"People get bored very easily," Wilt explained. "Which is why Hollywood doesn't make those epic films anymore. Who's gonna take three hours to watch 'The Ten Commandments?'"

Well, they could leave out a couple, like the one about coveting your neighbor's wife, but that's another story.

To fight boredom, Wilt gives you his views on shamateurism, bigotry in baseball and cruelty to polo ponies all on the same page.

Hopefully, the hubbub about the chapter on sex won't drown out some of the meaningful things Wilt has to say, about the price of fame, about false idols, about drug abuse.

There's some timely reminiscing about Cus D'Amato, the fight trainer who sprung Mike Tyson from that reform school at age 14.

"I knew Cus," Wilt said, "and it was mainly because of Cus that I considered fighting Muhammad Ali.

"If Cus had lived longer, and this man (Tyson) had not changed loyalties and allegiances, he would have had a happier life outside the ring, and maybe inside the ring as well.

"That only goes to emphasize, as I say in the book, that picking your friends is the most important ingredient that you can possibly do in this world of ours.

"Cus was a friend to Tyson . . . and the right kind of friend."

There's one fascinating mistake in the book in which Wilt describes the recent offers he's had to play again.

He calls the Sixers' owner David Katz.

"That's got to be someone else's fault," Wilt sputtered. "I know perfectly well that the owner's name is Harold Katz.

"Oh, David is his son? Well, maybe I will be right ultimately."

That's the quintessential Wilt, sometimes wrong, but never in doubt.

He hates the process used to pick the Olympic basketball team. ("A bunch of old guys, smoking cigars, sitting in a room.")

He scorns star athletes who are multiple offenders in the drug-abuse swamp. ("I would be a very tough commissioner, I don't know if I have enough compassion for the job.")

He did duck the episode involving Michael Jordan in which the superstar shunned the president and the Rose Garden ceremony honoring the Bulls.

"You'd have to ask him why he wasn't there," Wilt said. "Sounds like a snub to me.

"Those ceremonies, they're bull-bleep. Always have been. Gives you the perception that we always want to hallow the winners.

"Maybe both teams should be invited to show respect for what's happened. Both teams are winners to get that far.

"Someone has to win. One hundred and some-odd Kentucky Derbys, you've got a winner for every last one of 'em. What's so special?

"Some of the winners would have finished last in other races, based on times, so what's the big deal?

"This might be better coming from Bill Russell than from me, because I lost more than Bill, but to me, we place too much emphasis on the end result and not how it came about."

The mix is there in the lively book, sage observations tumbling over brash claims.

Wilt doesn't want anyone coming away with the idea that it was all wham, bam, thank you ma'am.

"I saw sex as a joyful activity," he writes, "one that should take a long time and be relaxed."

Wow. All those encounters, slow and relaxed? When did he ever find time to sleep? Or practice free throws?

Magic's Love for Life Clear

Philadelphia Daily News
November 8, 1991

EARVIN JOHNSON tested HIV positive.

Magic Johnson was as stunned as the rest of us.

When you are Magic, HIV positive is something that happens to other guys.

When you can throw a basketball through a rose bush and not get it scratched . . . when your peripheral vision spots Jack Nicholson on one side of the court and Dyan Cannon on the other . . . and the other four guys wearing purple and gold in between . . . when you can run and jump and shoot with guys who were in fifth grade when you won the championship at Michigan State . . . when you've got five NBA championship baubles and a smile that outgleams the rings. . . .

When you're truly, truly magical, some insidious virus does not invade your bloodstream.

"Safe sex is the way to go," Johnson said yesterday, at a remarkable press conference that only reinforced his courage, his kindness, his lust for life.

"Sometimes we think only gay people can get it. . . . And here I am saying that it can happen to anybody. Even me, Magic Johnson. . . . Sometimes you're a little naïve."

Naïve. It was one of the endearing charms he brought to the NBA stage. Wide-eyed, grinning, willing to share his love for the game and the people who played it.

He came grinning into the league in '79, along with the solemn Larry Bird. Together, ebony and ivory, fire and ice, they lugged the game out of musty, half-empty gyms to a worldwide awareness, to prosperity.

Argue if you must about skills, about statistics, about durability, about enhancing the level of play of those around him, but no one can deny Earvin "Magic" Johnson's impact on the game.

Kareem Abdul-Jabbar was there, on the dais, when Johnson told the world about testing HIV positive, about retiring.

The memory came thrashing back, the championship game in 1980, the day Kareem stayed in Los Angeles with a brutal migraine, and Magic had to play center against the Sixers at the Spectrum.

Scored 42.

They asked him for advice on how to list him in the box score and he said G-F-C. Guard, forward, center.

He could do it all. Especially at crunch time, with the numbers vanishing on the clock, with the crowd gagging in anticipation. Winnin' time, he called it.

He stepped up again yesterday. None of that lurking behind a flimsy screen of lies, as too many Hollywood folks have done.

"I'm going to miss playing," Johnson said. "And I will now become a spokesman for the HIV virus. I want people, young people, to realize they can practice safe sex."

He was magical, able to throw a ball through a picket fence and not get it bruised. Willing to shoot the distant three-pointer, slick enough to find daylight on a crowded path to the hoop.

He was lucky, fortunate enough to be surrounded by splendid players.

"People say I've been lucky to have the cast I've had," Johnson said during last spring's showdown with Chicago.

"I haven't been lucky. What people don't realize is that not everyone could have come onto that team and made all the egos work, and not worry about his own ego.

"Kareem was the hardest to work with. But when I came in, I didn't try to be the star.

"It was, 'Hey, keep Kareem happy. Keep Jamaal (Wilkes) happy. Keep Norm Nixon happy.'

"The next year it was someone else. The next year it was James Worthy.

"Then it was my turn. They told me it was my team and I got a chance to score, which no one thought I could do. So I've had the chance to do everything, to play every position. That's fun."

No one knew he was writing his own eulogy at that moment. He talked of playing another year or two. He was genuinely giddy about making the Olympic team, of playing with Michael and Charles.

And always, he spoke of someday owning a team. He said it again yesterday, delivering a message the way he delivers a pass, swift, chest-high.

What he was telling youngsters was that they need not limit their dreams to 12 feet off the ground, to dunking, but to reach beyond the rim, beyond the court.

He picked up the torch of elder statesman, ambassador for the game once Julius Erving retired. He handled the role with grace, with zest, with a joy that transcended race, religion.

It will be Michael Jordan's turn now.

Johnson plans to be visible, a spokesman for safe sex, an advocate against drug abuse and the needle-sharing that feeds the disease.

"Life is going to go on for me, and I'm going to be a happy man," he promised.

We all remember Lou Gehrig, dying of amyotrophic lateral sclerosis, hoarsely saying he was the luckiest man on earth.

We remember Babe Ruth, ravaged by cancer, bundled inside that camel hair coat.

Rocky Marciano's plane crashed. Willie Shoemaker's jeep overturned, crushing his spine. Billy Martin snuffed out on a sleet-slick curve.

But they were no longer playing, fighting, riding, managing. Old people, even once great athletes, get sick and die.

But Johnson is 32, just married, a season to play, an Olympic gold medal to be won. Wealthy. An idol. Recognizable in remote places. Loved everywhere.

When he talks, perhaps they will listen, all those young macho kids who think they are immune to the scourge that is AIDS, all of them blinded by that moment's pleasure, ignorant of what's left of a lifetime of pain.

AIDS is spreading fastest in the black community. Black kids didn't flinch when Rock Hudson died because they never watched Rock Hudson movies.

Liberace? A swishy guy in sequins poundin' a piano with a bunch of candles flickering.

News anchorman Max Robinson might have made a ripple because you don't see that many black men anchoring the network news.

But Magic Johnson? Magic Johnson!

"It's another challenge," he said, "another chapter in my life.

"It's like being—your back is up against the wall. And I think that you just have to come out swinging."

Johnson was incredible yesterday, his poise breathtaking, his humor poignant, his message clear.

You can run but you cannot hide from this deadly killer. No one is immune, regardless of race, creed, bankroll, crammed trophy case.

It is winnin' time, and we are lucky to have Magic Johnson on our side. May God bless him.

A Reach Far beyond Court

Philadelphia Daily News
October 14, 1999

"TIMBERRR!"

That's what Muhammed Ali screeched the first time he met Wilt Chamberlain. Timberrr, as in, the bigger they are, the harder they fall.

Some brave promoter thought about Ali fighting Chamberlain. Some brave boxing people told Wilt he'd be too strong for Ali, have too much reach for Ali, that Ali would have to leap like a kangaroo to reach Wilt's bearded chin.

Wilt loved the challenge, loved the kind of money those brave boxing people were prattling about, but he loved life even more. So he passed on the proposition.

Years later, Wilt would say he ran the idea past his father, who was a passionate boxing fan. Talked about the hours he'd have to spend in the gym, getting ready. Said his dad told him, "You'd be better off working on your free throws. "

Wilt could laugh at himself. He just didn't want anyone else laughing at him. Now Wilt is gone, at 63, with so many challenges waiting to be met. He never fought Ali, but he did get in the sulky behind his own harness horses. And he did play World Class Volleyball. And he did coach in the ABA. And he did write three books.

And he did record a song, "Down by the River." And he did own a nightclub. And he did appear in a movie, towering over Schwarzenegger. And he was working on an autobiographical screenplay when he died. And he never stopped working on that sports car he designed.

And he never stopped speaking out for truth and justice.

And none of those things involved dunking a basketball, because he did not want to be defined as a 7–1 behemoth who could slam a ball through a hoop. For those lucky enough to have seen Wilt play, they know that Wilt developed a fallaway jumper and a finger-roll for layups rather than the brute slam dunk.

Wilt spent a lifetime tilting against the windmills of stereotypes. Nobody loved Goliath, he moaned, and then set out to be more than a giant in basketball shorts.

He conquered a persistent stutter to become a wonderfully glib, caustically opinionated television guest. He never ducked an issue, even if his stance would be unpopular with sponsors, with team owners, with players he wished he could buy for what they were worth and sell for what they thought they were worth.

He lent his name and his booming baritone only to causes he believed in. In recent years, if you wanted to trade on his fame, Wilt insisted you contributed to one of his favorite charities.

But one appearance he willingly made every summer was the Stokes game at Kutsher's in the Catskills. The game honored Maurice Stokes, whose NBA career was cut short by a rare disease.

As a youngster, Wilt spent summers at Kutsher's, bellhopping. A fellow named Red Auerbach coached the hotel basketball team and sweet-talked Wilt about attending Harvard, so he could be a territorial draft pick for the Celtics.

Wilt opted for Kansas University instead. And Eddie Gottlieb, who ran the Warriors, already had outslicked the other owners by getting the rules changed so that he could claim Wilt's rights out of Overbrook High.

I first saw Wilt play for Kansas in an NCAA regional game in Dallas. Wilt grabbed a defensive rebound and started upcourt. An Oklahoma State guard drifted into his path, then hit the brakes. Wilt gently thumped the kid from behind.

No harm, no foul, no whistle. Kansas had crushed SMU the previous game, which might explain why the Dallas fans pelted the court with debris, stopping the game for 15 minutes. Maybe that's where Wilt got the idea that nobody loved Goliath.

Wilt toured with the Globetrotters for big bucks, and then came to the Warriors big enough and tough enough and skilled enough to be rookie of the year that first season. They would change other rules to try and keep him from dominating the game.

He had a plush apartment in Society Hill. He was proud of the way he'd furnished it, and maybe he shouldn't have bragged about the rug made from the incredibly soft fur that grows around a wolf's nose. He got a half-ton of mail from the animal-rights folks about that one.

He never wore much jewelry. Instead of glittery chains around his neck, he wore a classic Egyptian amulet of jade, a likeness of Ramses. A gift from an admirer.

He won a championship here, playing on a team that has been voted the best in the history of the NBA. Then he got himself traded to Los Angeles and won another title there.

He settled in Southern California with its gentle climate. Built a custom-made mansion on a hillside in Bel-Air. Spent time in Hawaii, in Florida, in Vegas for the big fights.

His visits to Philadelphia were always special. Once, he stood on the steps at Overbrook High with some former teammates, the only one who could remember the lyrics of the school song . . . "Upon the hilltop's graceful height its spires against the blue; stands a school of legend bright and inspiration true."

He could be loud and argumentative and mule-stubborn with adults. And he could be kind and gentle and dove-soft around kids. On that same visit, Wilt cut right through the mumble of rhetoric involving role models to speak in blunt language kids could understand.

"You choose up for three-on-three," Wilt said, "you look for a rebounder, you look for a scorer, and you look for someone to handle the ball. Well, kids choose up sides everyday [*sic*]. You don't look for a guy with poor habits. And that is what I tell kids. When you go out and pick your friends, and don't let your friends pick you, look for guys who don't have bad habits.

"How much time, when you're growing up, do you spend with your mother and father? They're out there working. We spend most of our time with friends. Pure and simple, choosing the right friends, that's where it's at."

Wilt chose his friends wisely. They were truly lucky ones. The rest of us were lucky, too. Fortunate to watch Wilt Chamberlain in his prime, playing 48 minutes a game, doing whatever he chose to do better than anyone else—score, pass, rebound. He was Philadelphia's greatest athlete of the century. But you already knew that.

COLLEGE

Massimino Making Sweet Music Again

Philadelphia Daily News
February 10, 1988

ROLAND V. MASSIMINO got to perform at City Hall, which is just a long jump shot from the Academy of Music.

Dreamed that dream as a kid in Hillside, N.J.

"I won six awards from the Julliard School of Music, playing the piano," Massimino said the other day. "Took piano lessons for years as a kid from a hunchbacked woman, a great, great old lady.

"Finally, one day, the athletic director at Hillside was getting on me. 'You gotta play football,' he kept telling me.

"I had a piano lesson at 4:30. But that afternoon I went to football practice. At 5:15, my mother and father showed up at the high school, screaming and yelling.

"I remember it like it was yesterday. I just get off the field and there they are. Sam Dubow was the athletic director. He tells them, 'He's better off here than roaming the streets.'

"My mother says, 'He wouldn't be roaming the streets, he'd be playing the piano.'

"Now, I had to make a decision. Play football or play piano. I played piano a little longer and then I quit to concentrate on sports. Wound up being voted the best athlete in the school."

Massimino coulda been a contendah. He coulda been Van Cliburn. Coulda sat there, hunched over a Steinway, white cuffs shooting out from the sleeves of a black tuxedo, playing Chopin or Schubert, those stubby fingers rippling over the keys.

Instead, he wound up coaching basketball. Coaches Villanova, 8–3 in the treacherous Big East Conference, 16–6 overall, battling top-ranked Temple tonight at McGonigle.

Surprised? How many Roland V. Massiminos do you know?

Same guy. Same stubby fingers. Only now he's using them to signal one of the 23 different defenses he teaches, or waving them petulantly at a referee's call, or wrapping them firmly but gently around the back of some sweaty teenager's neck to get his full attention.

It ain't Chopin or Schubert, but some nights it is a rhapsody and it fills the hall with the sweetest sounds he's ever heard. Like the night Villanova beat Georgetown to win the national championship.

Which is how Rollie Massimino got to play City Hall, reciting a famous holiday poem, with the mayor and assorted dignitaries beaming behind him.

"The national championship, that just made him even more aware of the fun he was having," recalled his daughter, Lee Ann, who coaches lacrosse at Villanova and manages his hectic schedule.

"He's a people person. Loves to talk to, to meet, all kinds of different people. And the championship allowed him to do that. He was recognized wherever he went.

"And then, he did ''Twas the Night Before Christmas' at City Hall. Going home, on the train, suddenly, he's up front with the engineer.

"He's in that little booth with him, learning how the train works. The Paoli local. And I'm sitting there, wondering, 'What are you doing now?'"

Massimino, 53, enjoys going first cabin, but he's at home in the caboose, too. He can yenta with a stock boy and lecture to stockbrokers.

"I talked about the disposition to dominate years ago," he said, running those stubby fingers through thinning, graying hair. "And what was worth $50 then is suddenly worth $5,000."

With a national championship comes high speaking fees and great expectations. A contract to endorse shirts and the tight collar of cynicism. Roses and thorns.

"I'm basically a wimp when it comes to that," Massimino confessed. "I worry about what people say, I worry about what people do, and I worry about the lifestyle of everybody."

His own lifestyle has changed dramatically. In 1971 he left the State University of New York at Stony Brook to take an assistant's job at Penn, accepting a jolting cut in salary.

Arrived with a loyal wife and five disciplined kids in a creaky Pontiac with a rolled-back odometer.

He got the top job at Villanova in 1973, rumpled, emotional, sensitive, caring. Doing opera on the sideline.

"Our ties have labels," said Ken Bogdanoff, who has since signed Massimino to represent his Windsor Shirt company.

"When the tie would go flying over one shoulder, we'd look to see if it was one of ours. Now, at least he looks good at the start of games.

"I sit behind his bench. A shot goes up by the opposition, he's steering it out. He's competing, fighting, scrapping.

"I love to watch him, steering. It's a very human trait."

So is eating. Massimino is a lot like Tommy Lasorda that way. Eats when he wins, because he's happy. Eats when he loses, because he's sad.

"I fluctuate 30 or 40 pounds," Massimino said sheepishly. "I've gotta lose some weight. Which is why I'm working with Pat Croce's guys.

"I've got these special, what do you call 'em, yeah, custom suits an Italian designer made for me. It's the only way they'll fit."

He loves "macaroni" (let the yuppies call it pasta), but he will lose the weight to fit the suits so they won't go to waste because waste is sinful. And he will tell that to his players in one of those prepractice sermonettes he delivers about life beyond the court.

He is transparent as a crystal vase. Almost as fragile. Everybody leaves their fingerprints on him. Every bump leaves its scars.

He is one of the lucky ones, which is what the missed piano lesson anecdote is all about. Lucky to have parents who cared enough to rush to school in search of a straying son.

It could have been very different, because he lost two brothers in tragic accidents, but he was not coddled, was not spoiled.

"I got beat up plenty," he recalled. "My father was tough. A shoemaker. Fingers mashed from the hammer. I was 23, 24 years old and he was still staying up until I came home.

"My parents gave me everything."

What they gave him was that rare blend of love and discipline, parenting skills as complex as a vintner's art, creating wine to be savored for generations to come.

"I talked to the team the day after the Providence game," Massimino said. "I told them, 'I give you a finger and you take an arm.'

"My mother used to say that to me. 'I give you a finger and you take an arm.' You have to know limits.

"She used to leave her purse open. I'd say I was gonna take a nickel and I'd take a quarter."

The Providence game, that was the one in which the Wildcats blew a 19-point lead in the second half and came up empty in overtime against a team that had lost five in a row going in.

And when it was over, Massimino told the writers how he felt about the Providence fans who jeered coach Gordon Chiesa in the pregame introductions, and how it's difficult to rebuild and how they ought to feel good about kids tough enough to rally from 19 points down.

"I got booed my first year here," Massimino recalled. "And Providence beat us and (coach) Dave Gavitt did it for me, said I deserved a chance to put things together."

Massimino remembered. He has a long memory and a short fuse, but he no longer gulps Valium to patch shattered nerves. The highs may not be as silvery, nor the lows as black anymore, even though he still cares just as much about winning.

Veal marsala, a couple of glasses of vino at the Blue Chateau in Providence, to ease the pain.

"It's like Rollie always says," said assistant coach Steve Lappas, "'We work hard and we eat good.'"

The 'Cats came back and whipped Georgetown at the Spectrum on a floor as slippery as a city councilman's promises. Kenny Wilson did not start. Afterward, Massimino's vocabulary betrayed him and he said the benching was "for no apparent reason."

That made it sound frivolous, a whim. What he meant to say was that Wilson was not being punished for breaching team rules, but that, perhaps, watching the early flow of the game sitting alongside the coach might be beneficial.

Three days later, he brought Wilson into his cluttered office for a little one-on-one session.

"I had just watched Pitt–St. John's the night before on television," Massimino said. "Pitt's got a freshman guard going zip, zap, dealing the ball off, making plays.

"I told Kenny he was a junior, his productivity could be better, that he was a reflection of me."

Every coach believes that, that the team on the floor mirrors what he is all about, his work ethic, his toughness, his grace under pressure.

"Rollie is one of my favorites," said St. Joseph's coach Jim Boyle. "He's got a way of looking at basketball that separates him from the pack.

"You watch his team play, you know who the coach is. Teamwork, hard work, unselfishness, moving the ball, blending talents.

"I compare it to watching a game on the tube and the focus isn't quite right so you can see the faces but not the name on the jerseys and yet you know who the coach is.

"You look at that, you're looking at genius."

It goes far beyond X's and O's. The great ones scold the players who shatter the pattern, chastise the ones who get selfish or lazy, bench the ones who strut against the grain of team welfare, all without burying them.

The public voice is a broken chalk on the blackboard screech. The private voice is softer, a scratchy lullaby.

"People always ask me," confessed Lee Ann, "'Does he scream as much at home?'

"He doesn't have to. He has that look. You don't want to do something wrong, something that will cause him to give you that look."

It is that rare motivational mix of fear and respect and love.

"Rollie always knows what he's saying," Lappas said. "He knows how it's gonna affect them. He knows when they need to be chewed out, when they need to be stroked.

"My first year, I watched a massive stroke of genius. He takes out the starters against Pitt and we get drubbed. And we come back and beat 'em on the way to the national championship."

"I was coming off knee surgery so I was the only one who didn't play," recalled senior co-captain Mark Plansky, the only survivor of that championship season.

"At halftime, we'd been playing complacently. He said, 'I'm gonna give you three minutes.' Second half started, three minutes went by, he didn't like what he saw, bam, he yanked everybody."

"They beat us by 30," Massimino said, finishing the story later that day. "We come back and beat 'em in Madison Square Garden in the Big East tournament.

"I once sat down Dwayne McClain because he was two minutes late for practice. Sat him down in a game that meant the Big East title. So, how can anyone say I condoned what Gary McLain did?"

It is there, the ugly dent in the championship trophy that time has not yet repaired. The McLain episode, the volatile point guard who scrawled his confession of drug abuse across the front cover and inside pages of *Sports Illustrated*.

"The pain hasn't gone away," Massimino said. "Gary McLain was not a bad person. He was a victim of our society. He was caught in a trap. And to this day I still don't believe everything he said in that story.

"He was bright, he was alert. How could I have known? Depth perception was fine. He wasn't always tired. No signs.

"He was first to arrive and last to leave at practice. On trips, he was the court jester, a killer.

"I still talk to him. Talked to him Christmas Day. He was one of our kids. Family is family."

Family is triumph and tragedy, joy and sorrow, discipline with love.

"He is second to none in terms of what he brings to the arena of life," said Temple coach John Chaney. "He is a class guy.

"He comes down one street. It is not a two-way street. And his team reflects him in many ways.

"When I won a Division II championship at Cheyney, Rollie sent me a Mailgram for every game we won on the way to the championship.

"I was the first to tell him he was going to win the championship the year he did. And I told him that someday when he looked back, he'd be sitting in his car crying and laughing at the same time.

"Laughing with happiness, yet selfish enough to say, 'Why in hell did so-and-so have to leave me when we were doing so good together?'

"And months later, he told me it happened that way."

There was more laughter than tears the next season. Villanova was 23–14, a splendid year that somehow has been forgotten in the clatter that followed.

Last year, a drab 15–16. And then, the loss of two prize recruits, Bobby Martin to Pitt and Delino DeShields to pro baseball.

The folks who have been sniping at him for years about not recruiting local kids had fresh ammunition.

"We have always recruited the top city kids in Philadelphia," Massimino grumped. "And underscore top. We talk about academics, we talk about athletics. There's a difference between perception and reality.

"There have not been that many top kids. It's a myth. I don't want the third-best, fourth-best, fifth-best, whether it's from Philadelphia or Pittsburgh or California."

The experts, seeing a bare cupboard, picked Villanova to finish in the second division of the bristling Big East.

Massimino clipped and saved the stories. He would take last year's puckered grapes and make a good wine, maybe a zinfandel, earthy, peppery, a mouthful to swallow.

Make it the same way he used to make wine with his shoemaker father, grinding, grinding, turning the crank until the callouses hardened.

"He's still the same driven man," said assistant coach John Olive. "He still coaches with the same fervor as ever.

"His assets? One, he's a tremendous teacher. One-A, he's a great bench coach. And One-B, he's an outstanding motivator. The main thing he's taught me is that you have to be yourself."

Olive was Massimino's first prime recruit at Villanova. The story tells you all you need to know about the two men.

"He was recruiting me for Penn," Olive recalled. "Without exaggeration, he must have come to 35 of my games (at Bishop Eustace in New Jersey). A relentless recruiter.

"My senior year, I started making trips. Coming back from Duke, I opened the paper and saw where Rollie Massimino had been hired as head coach at Villanova.

"I called him, told him I wanted to come to Villanova. He said, 'You can't come here. . . . I just spent two years of Penn's money and Penn's time recruiting you and it's not ethical for me to recruit you for Villanova.'

"Finally, he said he'd talk to (Penn coach) Chuck Daly. And Chuck told him, 'Rollie, if the kid wants to come to Villanova, take him. Besides, you're gonna need players.'"

Now, Olive recruits relentlessly. So do Lappas and newcomer Jay Wright. The harvest looks good. A 6-8 forward from New Jersey named Marc Dowdell, a 5-11 guard from Houston named Chris Walker. A shot at a 6-9 blue-chipper from Palatka, Fla., named Townsend Harris.

"Rollie has seen him play," Olive said. "One visit from him is the equivalent of 20 visits of mine."

That's next year, this is this year. Villanova is second in the Big East and the skeptics are eating crow parmigiana.

Massimino turned Tom Greis, last year's 7-2 cream puff, over to fitness guru Croce. He got back a leaner, meaner sophomore.

"We had to teach him how to run," Massimino said. "We have a three-man drill, where you get the rebound, run down, get another rebound.

"As a freshman, he ran it three times, collapsed, twisted his ankle, was out two weeks. He couldn't do finger-tip pushups last year. Now he can do 20."

Massimino worked on Greis's mind, walking that high-tension wire between cruelty and constructive criticism.

"He responded in a way that showed he wasn't a wimp," Massimino said. "It's a risk. He could have gone into a shell."

"Coach Mass is superlative at that," Plansky said. "Keeping guys from going into the tank.

"Tom was MVP of the Jostens tournament and coach told him that was because there were no big guys in the tournament. He told him he should have had 30 points, he should have done this, done that.

"And after coach knocks him down a few pegs I'll talk to him, tell him he hasn't touched his potential ability yet, that he's got to work harder.

"And all that talk about family is real. He sends us home for three full days during Christmas break. Tells us to spend the time with family, the people we love the most.

"That's important time. I know about other programs where you don't see things like that. And Homecoming here is amazing, all those guys who come back.

"We'll beat a Syracuse or a Georgetown and the next day there will be 15 or 20 slips on coach's desk. From Ed Pinckney, from Stew Granger, from guys calling to congratulate him.

"The thing about him is he loves a challenge. That's why the NBA must have tempted him (when he turned down the New Jersey Nets in 1985). Something he hadn't done before.

"And now, we were picked to finish seventh or eighth in the Big East," Plansky said. "He wants to take a team that, on paper, wasn't supposed to do anything, and take us to the NCAA Tournament.

"And maybe further."

Temple-Kansas: Why All the Fuss?

Philadelphia Daily News
May 23, 1988

THEY COULD HAVE PUT the Temple-Kansas basketball game in Moscow on May Day and not created as much fuss.

They could have stuck it in Tokyo on Dec. 7, in Tel Aviv on Yom Kippur, and not drawn as much criticism.

They could have put it in Athens, not because Temple president Peter Liacouras is Greek, but because the Olympics began in Greece and this is an Olympic year, and coach John Chaney likes souvlaki and guard Mark Macon has always wanted to see the Acropolis.

American Express could have sponsored the game, because Kansas coach Larry Brown never leaves home without the card, and he is always leaving home.

Maybe they couldn't agree on the drachma. Or maybe Temple athletic director Charles Theokas said the idea was all Greek to him, except that he understands Greek.

So they put the game in Atlantic City's Convention Hall on Dec. 10 and got a hotel-casino to sponsor it. And then they flinched when a Vesuvius of controversy erupted.

You'd think they'd put the game in Sicily as a fund-raiser for Nicky Scarfo. If the outrage wasn't so funny, the episode would be sad.

The screams fell into two separate categories. The purists screeched about "tainting" college athletics by association with a hotel-casino. The cynics moaned about inconsistency because Temple played Villanova at cramped McGonigle Hall last season and now they were taking a big game off campus, out of town, out of state, bankrolled by a gambling den.

The purists, who might not know a point spread from a bedspread, wailed about point-shaving scandals of the past.

I'd bet that a Temple athlete is in more danger of corruption on the corner of Broad and Columbia than he is on the boardwalk at Atlantic City.

The legalized bookmaker shops in Las Vegas do more to prevent fixed games than the NCAA. Bookmakers do not want "crooked" games, with the action heavy on one side. They lose money that way.

So when the point spread fluctuates wildly, alarms go off in Vegas.

If the NCAA enforced its rules as efficiently and effectively as the Nevada and New Jersey gambling commissions, college basketball would be a healthier, happier place indeed.

"The casino industry is a legitimate industry, highly regulated," said Temple vice president Pat Swygert, who made the decision.

"In fact, the nuclear industry is also ostensibly highly regulated, but I don't know of a casino that's blown up."

Well, there have been pieces of casinos shattered by disgruntled losers, but Swygert wouldn't know about that because he doesn't smoke, drink or gamble.

And how can you expect a man who doesn't smoke, drink or gamble to understand that accepting $100,000 from a hotel-casino to book a game in Atlantic City and a fund-raiser at that hotel-casino will cause a storm of protest?

"Sports, especially amateur sports, especially in an Olympic year, has a very special place in the national psyche," Swygert said.

"There are many, many myths that surround amateur sports. We'd like to believe that our outstanding track and field stars are truly amateurs when we all know how many earn thousands of dollars each year in endorsements.

"We would like to believe the myths we want to hold and cherish. When you associate a collegiate activity with a casino, that myth of amateur athletics is challenged.

"The fact of the matter is that unlike the Olympics, where people receive endorsement income and clearly are part of the process, no member of the Temple basketball team is either on or is part of a casino payroll, or is endorsing the casino.

"There's a greater myth, that financial considerations have no appropriate place in amateur athletics. We know that is not the case. Take the NCAA playoff system itself.

"The NCAA distributes millions of dollars to the successful competitors, the schools.

"Division I basketball can provide for the phenomenon of a $200,000 free throw. Whether the youngster makes the shot or doesn't determines whether or not the team proceeds to the playoffs. That's enormous pressure."

The kind of enormous pressure that creates the atmosphere for shaving points, whether the game is to be played in Memphis, Minneapolis or Margate.

"Is it appropriate," Swygert asked, "for conferences to be under multimillion, multiyear contracts with major television networks? And what that might entail in terms of the networks scheduling the games?"

If Temple's football team could be part of a multimillion, multiyear contract, they could schedule the Owls at brunch in Beirut or midnight in Manila and the Owls would be there.

Swygert means it when he says, "Temple is not in the business of running a sports franchise." Good thing, because the football team would have moved to Indianapolis or Division II years ago.

Swygert says that Theokas has three basic responsibilities, to run a clean program, to make opportunities to participate fair and equal to all students, to see to it that varsity athletes are true student-athletes.

"We have never said, 'You've got to make money for Temple University,'" Swygert said.

The basketball team grossed $1,000,000 last year. School spirit soared, admission applications increased, alumni reached for their wallets.

"One has to keep in mind," Swygert lectured, "that in a perfect society that same enthusiasm and giving and outpouring of support and generosity should in fact accompany work that is being done by our physics department in the area of superconductivity."

You'll have to speak a little louder, Pat, we can't hear you over the hullabaloo over having a casino sponsor for Temple-Kansas.

The hotel-casino bankrolled the game because it thinks it will draw some basketball fans to the shore who will leave enough money at the craps tables to more than cover the fee.

"I'm not sure the majority of people down for the game," Swygert said innocently, "will visit any casinos."

They won't? You have to walk past the casino to get to the bar and the buffet and the fund-raiser Temple has scheduled.

They build them that way. And they keep building more and more of them because there's a sucker born every 30 seconds.

"These are adults," Swygert said. "They will have the opportunity to exercise discretion. If it means they are going to leave our fund-raiser and lose the house and the car, I'm not willing to accept the proposition that necessarily follows."

And wasn't it three years ago that Liacouras, along with three other university presidents, squelched the idea of holding the Atlantic 10 Conference Tournament in Atlantic City?

Maybe all those empty seats and the mildew that is Morgantown, W.Va., has changed his mind?

That's reality, not myth.

Temple, which held its commencement exercises at the Spectrum, can't be playing any home ballgames there, not if it wants to raise funds for an arena on campus.

The sponsoring hotel-casino has gotten puddles of ink, and the game is still seven months away. They did not return telephone calls to offer their reaction to the tempest in a fudge pot.

On Dec. 11, they'll check the pit drop, the bar tabs, the bottom line. If the Kansas folks trudge into town with a plaid shirt and a $10 bill and don't change either of them, we may never have to listen to this hollow debate again.

Rumeal Robinson: He's Taken His Share of Shots

Philadelphia Daily News
April 4, 1989

SEATTLE—Rumeal Robinson was 10, abandoned, alone, wandering the streets of Cambridge, Mass., his eyes hard, his stomach empty, his hopes somehow high.

"Determination kept me going," Robinson recalled last night, surrounded by strangers, his life forever altered because he swished two free throws with three seconds left in overtime and Michigan slashed Seton Hall, 80–79, to win the NCAA basketball championship.

"I was 10, if anything kept me going, the Man Upstairs kept me going. To this day I think I was blessed.

"I was always taught that negative thinking gets you negative results. Think negative, it will be negative.

"I have always had positive thinking drilled into me."

Alone, abandoned, scuffling through the streets of Cambridge, could he have been thinking positive then?

"I was thinking food," Robinson said swiftly.

Only in America.

Only in America could a homeless, hungry kid be taken in by a mailman's wife, loved and cherished and nurtured and sent off to a big university where he is forced by Proposition 48 to use his energies playing intramural ball with law students, conquering his shyness and his homesickness to become a vital part of a team that is jolted by the departure of its coach 48 hours before the NCAA Tournament begins.

And then, in the championship game, forging a brilliant performance, matched against the quick, slick Gerald Greene.

His team trailing by a point, Robinson grinding toward the hoop, knowing Seton Hall would be clustering around Glen Rice.

Fouled by Greene. Muddled movement on the lanes, a timeout, almost four minutes between foul and free throws.

"The ref kept stalling," said Robinson, a 64.2 percent free-throw shooter. "They (the Pirates) were playing little games. (Seton Hall's) John Morton looked at me and smiled. I looked at him and smiled.

"I had the ball. I had the upper hand.

"I had visioned it. Because we'd lost to Wisconsin when I missed two free throws. The most down point of my career.

"I was hoping to get back up there someday.

"The second one was so easy. When it left my hand, I knew it was going in, the way it rolled off my fingers.

"The first one? That didn't feel as good as the second one. But, both of 'em went in."

Both of 'em went in and Seton Hall got one more desperate shot by Daryl Walker that thudded off the glass and Helen and Louis Ford embraced in the Kingdome stands as Robinson, their adoptive son, got swallowed by a swarm of blue and maize.

Ford is 62. He'd been home with the kids (including a set of 6-year-old twins recently adopted) when Bostonians chipped in to pay for his trip here.

Wearing his postal jacket, he flew here Saturday, arriving just as the game ended and the stampeding crowd told him that Michigan had beaten Illinois.

So, how did he feel when Robinson went to the line with three seconds left in overtime?

"Breathless."

And how did he feel when both shots slithered through the net?

"Wonderful."

Ford doesn't believe in long messages. He has carried too many of them.

Does he feel some calling to open his home to abandoned children?

"It isn't a calling," he said. "Because if it was, I'd take in half the world. But this way, I've taken in four, so at least I've got a piece of the action."

Ford had swapped his U.S. Mail jacket for a windbreaker that said "Michigan staff." Mrs. Ford was wearing a sweat shirt that proclaimed her as "Rumeal's Mom."

"He was very determined," she said, recalling first impressions of the starving child she embraced. "He wanted to be somebody. Now he is somebody. He is Rumeal Robinson."

Has there been a better story? Has there been a better, more dramatic championship game? Has there been a hero who has conquered as much as Robinson has conquered?

The learning disability that stymied his SAT scores, the trip to Jamaica to find his natural father, only to discover he had died the day before, the shyness that kept him apart in those first agonizing college days.

"Lots of guys will face adversity," Robinson said. "People are different for different reasons. That's what makes the world turn.

"If people want to look at Rumeal as someone who has handled adversity, I'm happy to be looked at that way."

He is 6-2, 195, seemingly carved from mahogany. Swift and strong and sure of himself.

He had 14 of his 21 points in the first half, taking 10 shots. He took only three in the second half, the only one he made was a Jordanesque reverse slam that followed some conversation with Greene at the other end.

"He told me they were gonna make a run," Robinson recalled. "At first, I didn't know what he meant."

Seton Hall made a run, slashing a 12-point deficit with piranha defense. Robinson kept looking for his teammates.

"First quarter I went at 'em a lot," Robinson said. "After that I wanted to get the other guys into the game.

"I can't try and take the whole game onto myself. It's a team unity kind of thing. It wouldn't be fair for Rumeal Robinson to try and do it all.

"When Glen Rice took that shot (in the final seconds of regulation), I could have taken that shot.

"I threw him the ball. He's a senior. But the game isn't just played on the floor, it's played with your mind.

"You have to choose your times to go to the basket. Sometimes I try and put a player to sleep and then attack.

"So, at the end, they were looking for Glen and I made up my mind to take the shot.

"It (the foul call) could have gone either way. It was kind of weak to call it then. Refs take over a game and I don't think that's right.

"If I was a ref I wouldn't have called it. A game, ending, that means so much, why call that?

"But, it doesn't matter, because if he hadn't called it, I would have scored.

"There was one big guy back there, backing up. I looked at him, he seemed scared."

During the timeout, teammate Mike Griffin walked up to Robinson to remind him of his traditional pregame chatter.

"He is always telling us that God helps those who help themselves," Griffin recalled giddily. "So I told Rumeal that God helps those who help themselves.

"I was nervous, he was calm."

Why not? After those crucial misses against Wisconsin, Robinson had shown up an hour early for every practice, making 100 free throws.

"Repetition," he said. "I bounce it three times, look up, and shoot the shot. My mechanics should be there."

Tuesday's child, so full of grace. Rumeal Robinson, putting behind him those hungry, homeless days to step up to the line, chesty with confidence, thinking positive thoughts, brushing aside the memories of the misses against Wisconsin.

"There are no bad times," he said. "Only good times and times that seem not so good. You don't want things to happen to you. But they happen. Life is life.

"You have to get back up there. Winners get back up there. Those who don't get back up, they're the ones who don't win."

So Close, So Distant

Philadelphia Daily News
January 9, 1997

BOARD A PLANE, Zane. Hop on a train, Blaine. Get on the bus, Gus. Jump in the van, Stan. That just about does it for college basketball teams heading for a tantalizing road game.

Oh, maybe Wagner College rides the Staten Island ferry occasionally. And perhaps the University of Alaska has mushed to Juneau by dogsled. But has a Division I hoop team ever *walked* to the site of a regular-season road game?

Drexel's Dragons will do it Wednesday when they "travel" to play Penn, first regularly scheduled meeting between the West Philadelphia neighbors in 68 years, which might be another NCAA record of sorts, for rivalries renewed after huge gaps.

"I can't tell you how excited we are about this game," Drexel's athletic director, Dr. Lois Marciani, said giddily. "We're holding a pep rally outside our gym at 5 o'clock, and then, weather permitting, the cheerleaders and the students will walk with the team to the Palestra, with a police escort, down 34th Street."

Weather permitting? Drexel coach Bill Herrion looks and sounds like a guy who would walk barefoot through a snowstorm to play a Big 5 team, even if the Big 5 concept has been riddled by greed and self-interest.

"When I go out recruiting," Herrion said, "or when I'm coaching an All-Star team in the summer, they ask me, 'Where are you located?'

"I tell them, 'We're right next door to Penn,' and they say, 'Oh, yeah, I know where you are."

Herrion is bustling into his sixth season as Drexel's coach.

The Dragons went to the Big Dance in each of the last three seasons. Even beat Memphis in an NCAA first-round game last season.

Winning 20 or more every season is nice. Beating those New England schools in the America East conference is nice. But a Big 5 scalp or two would be a big-time boost to the school's self-esteem.

The Dragons lost a squeaker to La Salle earlier this season. In February, they'll meet St. Joseph's for the fifth time in Herrion's six seasons. And now Penn is on the slate, this season and next.

Can overtures to Temple and Villanova be far behind? Herrion gulps. "I'll be honest with you," he rasped, "they're heavy hitters.

"There is a sense, when you're scheduling, you have to remember who you are. When you win, you spoil some people. We won the last couple of years. They think that can happen every year.

"At this level of college basketball, you get a great player like Malik Rose, you ride him for four years. We're not in a situation where I can go out and get another Malik Rose just like that."

For a while, Drexel was the Tim Witherspoon of local college hoops. A tough opponent. But if you won, cynics might sneer. And if you lost, hoo han, you lost to a tiny school that plays in an unheralded conference.

"I'm hoping," Herrion said, "the other schools in the city now respect us enough to know that when you play Drexel, you're going to play a good basketball team.

"I'd like to think we've been a tough team for the last four years. Sure, Penn, St. Joseph's, LaSalle, those games are way more important to Drexel than they are to them. We need those games.

"You keep going to the NCAA Tournament. You win a game in the first round and people still don't know who you are. What do we have to do to get respect?"

Herrion's Dragons have the respect of Fran Dunphy, coach of the Penn team, rebuilding after an incredible Ivy League run that ended last season.

"I think it's great that we're playing Drexel," Dunphy said. "It's a natural. They'll probably walk to the game.

"It's a great rivalry that hasn't been fostered for any number of reasons. The job Bill Herrion has done is extraordinary. A game against them can only help us."

There are maybe two handfuls of guys like Dunphy, fine coach, good guy, passionate about the game without getting his priorities twisted. The last time Penn played Drexel was in December 1988, the season before Dunphy got the Penn job, in the consolation game of the short-lived Josten's Classic at the Palestra.

Drexel won that one. Herrion is 0–1 against Temple, a first-round NCAA matchup. And he's 0–4 against St. Joe's in a series that expanded his awareness of how wonderful the Palestra experience can be.

"I worked in Boston. I worked in Washington," Herrion said. "There's nothing there like the Palestra. No building as loud.

"My first year here," he recalled, like a golfer replaying the final round at Augusta, "we played St. Joe's on Hawk Hill. Got blown out in the second half. Second year, the 45-second clock was still around and we held the ball. Something I'd never done in my life.

"Two-point game with two minutes left and they beat us by five. Next year, Hawk Hill again, we hit a shot at the buzzer to tie and they beat us in overtime. They wouldn't come to our gym, a tough, little place, so we played 'em at the Palestra. A five-point game. So, we've had three wars with St. Joe's.

"You talk about scheduling. First year, my phone was ringing off the hook, people wanting to play us. Last three years, my phone, in the spring, it hasn't been ringing at all."

The Dragons are 5–0 in conference play after being picked to finish behind Boston U. in the championship race that earns an automatic bid to the NCAA Tournament.

"We're a different team this year," Herrion said cautiously. "Last couple of years, we had the pieces, we knew we were good, because we had a great player, an NBA player.

"This year we've got the pieces and we're trying to put them together. We won't know what we've got until February or March. We're starting two freshmen and a sophomore. Play young kids, there's going to be ups and downs.

"Our ultimate goal is to win the league and earn the automatic bid. Everybody wants us to play tougher non-conference games. We played at UMass, we played LaSalle, we played in the College of Charleston tournament, in the Pre-season at Evansville.

"And then you look at the RPI ratings and we're like 20th. The bottom line for us, we've got to win the league."

The Penn game, though, is a fascinating crossroads for Herrion and his program.

"It's good for our players," he said. "It's good for our former players. It's good for our students, the chance to earn bragging rights. It's good for our administration.

"And where else in America will you find a Division I road game where your players can walk to the game?"

Big 5: A History to Celebrate, Warts and All

Philadelphia Daily News
December 20, 2002

HATED THE STREAMERS. Loved everything else about Big 5 basketball games at the Palestra, the window-rattling noise, the clever rollouts, the bass drum, the constant wing-flapping of the Hawk mascot, Yo-Yo shooting halftime free throws with a cigar stub angled jauntily toward the historic roof. Intense coaches. Intense players. Intense games.

Hated the streamers tossed onto the court after the first hoop by each team. Hated them because they blurred the line between players and spectators, shattered the intensity, disrupted the flow. You celebrate at the end of a game, not in the opening moments. Go ahead, call me a purist.

The NCAA agreed in 1988.

Instructed its referees to call a technical foul. In a January 1993 game, Penn coach Fran Dunphy and St. Joseph's coach John Griffin decided to conscientiously object. The Hawks scored first. When the maroon and gray streamers cascaded onto the court and the "T" was called, Dunphy told Andy Baratta to step over the line when he shot his free throw. And Griffin told Rap Curry to do the same thing when the Penn fans tossed their red and blue streamers.

Robert S. Lyons includes that episode in his informative, entertaining new book, "Palestra Pandemonium." It is a terrific history of the Big 5, even if the cover photo features those damnable crepe-paper streamers.

The revolutionary concept started in 1955, a unique invention mothered by economic necessity. Penn and Villanova staged doubleheaders at the Palestra. St. Joe's, La Salle and Temple played major opponents a few blocks away at the old Convention Hall. They were scuffling for the same entertainment dollar and nobody prospered.

Penn's publicist, Bob Paul, came up with the idea of getting all five Philadelphia schools to play under one roof, the Palestra's historic roof. There were some deep old wounds to be healed, ancient grievances to be forgotten. Somehow Villanova's athletic director, Bud Dudley, the quintessential salesman, sold the idea.

The rest is dramatic history and Lyons does a lovely job of blending details of memorable games with the off-the-court shenanigans, how the alliance struggled, then blossomed, how it finally unraveled under the stress of conference demands and the lust for easier nonconference foes and a smoother path to inclusion in the NCAA Tournament field of 64, and a possible big payoff.

In Lyons's view, Villanova's pugnacious coach Rollie Massimino is spared the scapegoat role for the brief demise of the Big 5 round-robin concept.

Lyons pins the blame on a Villanova administration that felt confined by its Big East commitments.

Daddy Mass left for a brief, unhappy fling in Vegas, and is now flying under the radar at Cleveland State. The Big East split into two divisions, the NCAA tinkered with the schedule limitations, and shazam, the Big 5 was reborn, healthy and high-spirited as ever.

Lyons, bless his heart, includes the warts in his portrait. He writes about Jack Ramsay's Hawks scrapping to a third-place finish in the 1961 NCAA Tournament, only to have to forfeit the season when three key players were implicated in a point-shaving scandal. And he includes the clumsy business of Villanova losing to UCLA in the 1971 championship game, and how that achievement was wiped out when it turned out Howard Porter had signed a pro contract before his eligibility ran out.

The rest is mostly fun and games. There is the nostalgia of simpler times, when Temple's legendary coach Harry Litwack recruited kids over a sandwich and milkshake at Mike's Broad Tower, a student hangout on campus. And how George Raveling, when he was recruiting for Jack Kraft at Villanova, found Johnny Jones's name in an item in *Sports Illustrated*. Jones was the Big 5's most outstanding player in 1967–68, and is a member of the Big 5 Hall of Fame.

The book is well-organized, a lengthy chapter devoted to each of the five schools, each crammed with fascinating anecdotes involving coaches and players. And there are compelling photos scattered throughout the text that conjure up memories for old-timers.

I covered Big 5 games from 1959 through 1966, worked as a color analyst on WCAU's radio broadcasts of the Quaker City tournament. I can still hear myself screaming in disbelief when Wichita State's Dave Stallworth was voted MVP one year, even though the Hawks won the tournament title.

Channel 6 carried selected road games, with Les Keiter doing his sparkling play-by-play, sprinkled with ring-tailed howitzers and in-again out-again Finnegan. We did a game in upstate New York, though, where the ref suffered a heart attack and Les vanished for 14 minutes, leaving me to ad-lib over a camera shot that showed an empty floor.

The "bomb scare" is in the book, Keiter clinging to his broadcast post while they evacuated the Palestra. So is the Shakespeare-quoting Paul Westhead and the malapropping Al Severance and the tyrannical Jim Harding who left some scars at La Salle that Tom Gola worked valiantly to heal.

The memorable upsets are in there too, the legendary game-winning shots, the dazzling chronology of great players, many of them successful at the next level. Wali Jones and Larry Cannon and Lionel Simmons and Michael Brooks and the backcourt wizardry of Pickles Kennedy and Steve Bilsky and Dave Wohl, the year Jimmy Lynam's Hawks stunned De Paul.

Only in Philadelphia. No other city or region has managed to create anything like this raucous round-robin. Go ahead, celebrate, throw a streamer if you must.

As AD, DiJulia Perfectly Content at St. Joe's

Philadelphia Daily News
February 24, 2004

DON DIJULIA IS the eye of the storm. Both eyes.

DiJulia is the athletic director at Saint Joseph's University, which means he is the brakeman on this Jamaica bobsled run of a basketball season, the navigator on an undefeated magic carpet ride, the page-turner on the calliope that is coach Phil Martelli.

"He's the godfather of this whole thing," said Martelli. "He's the link between the past, the great traditions, and the present. He's the bridge to this world."

Right now, DiJulia is busier than the Walt Whitman on a Friday night in July. He carries a walkie-talkie everywhere. Gone for 25 minutes, he trudges back to his office to find a clutter of pale green telephone messages impaled on an ominous spike on his secretary's desk.

"My e-mails are up to a buck-20 a day," he said with a sigh. "I answer them late at night, or at 5:30 in the morning. Got a call from Northeast High the other day, requesting a Jameer Nelson appearance. I called back, told them it was the 1,236th request this week.

"Merchandising? Can't keep it on the shelves. Sponsors are calling us to renew for next year. I say, 'Fine, as long as you don't ask for tickets.' There's a waiting list for 2005–06.

"The Villanova game, we could have sold out a domed stadium, drawn 30, maybe 35,000. Temple game, we could have filled Lincoln Financial Field.

"People are holding functions in this room (second floor of the Fieldhouse) with no tickets to go inside. They just want to hear it, feel it, smell it."

It sounds like summer thunder, feels like love and has the incredibly sweet smell of success, 24–0, ranked second in the country. No one uses the word miracle because, after all, this is a Jesuit school, a small Jesuit school on City Avenue. Closest DiJulia comes is saying: "This was not God's plan. This just happened. What were we ranked, 17th in the preseason?

"No school without major college football has ever, e-v-e-r, had a zero after their name at this point of the season. Football, football is the best way to be good in basketball. Why is it? That's another book.

"Meanwhile, you can't find a copy of *Sports Illustrated* in the tri-state area."

Not the swimsuit issue, dummy, the one with Nelson on the cover, little guy from the little school beating everybody. Another first for the Hawks. No one on the Hawk Hill campus is better equipped to put things in historical context than the soft-spoken DiJulia, in his fifth decade at the school.

"I grew up a Temple fan," he confessed. "Loved Guy Rodgers, Hal Lear, Pickles Kennedy. Some people nicknamed me 'Pickles' as a kid. I wore 5, because of lefthanded Guy Rodgers. Went to St. James, where (Jack) Ramsay coached, where Jack McKinney coached.

"Eleventh grade, McKinney and Father Degnan took us to see a St. Joe game at the Fieldhouse. It was love at first sight."

Got there for the 1960–61 season. It was the best of times, it was the worst of times. He watched as Ramsay's team went 25–5, got to the Final Four, got clobbered by Ohio State and then outlasted Utah in four overtimes to take the third-place trophy. Had to give it back when three players were implicated in a point-shaving scandal that rocked the college hoops world.

"At 20, you don't feel the impact as much as the adults," DiJulia recalled. "Now, I know how big that was. And every year, we make sure we talk about it."

Walked away for 3 years to attend the seminary. Returned and played skimpy minutes on a team that featured Cliff Anderson, Matty Guokas and Billy Oakes.

"I was a backup, glad to be part of that team," DiJulia said proudly. "Nobody had ever heard of Anderson. We shocked everybody, going 26–1 (before losing in the NCAA Tournament), out of this world.

"It was a team that believed in one another. Went out there thinking, why couldn't we win every game we played? Dr. Jack instilled that confidence, similar to Phil's approach. The glass is half full all the time."

Ramsay went to the pros. Won an NBA championship in Portland, beating a Philly team that had solid talent and fragile chemistry. He's in the Hall of Fame.

"His presence is still felt here," DiJulia said. "His coaching imprint. Success with class, that was his legacy. We've had seven go on to coach in the NBA, more than any other school."

McKinney followed Ramsay at St. Joe's, and then came Harry Booth, Jimmy Lynam, Jim Boyle and John Griffin. Griffin was the seventh consecutive St. Joe's graduate to coach the team, if you're counting. When he wearily walked away after the 1994–95 season, DiJulia swiftly narrowed the choices to Bruiser Flint and Martelli, a Widener graduate.

"He'd been an assistant here for 10 years," DiJulia is quick to point out. "So that made him a graduate. He'd always loved St. Joe's. He knew what we stand for, what our goals are.

"I told him, 'Let's do the best you can do and hope to do the best possible. Recruit quality student-athletes, and give it a good Hawkwhack.'" Last year, they extended Martelli's contract through 2010, a lovely security blanket. This year's dream season is sure to attract other, bigger schools. What then?

"There is no magical place," Martelli said, "that could come calling."

One less thing for DiJulia to worry about, while he politely fields calls from schools who lust after being on St. Joe's schedule next season.

This is his second stint as athletic director, with time out to be commissioner of the East Coast Conference and then the Metro Atlantic Athletic Conference.

"That helped prepare me," he said. "I worked with eight schools and then another eight. I had an idea of how 16 schools conducted themselves, what they did right, what they did wrong.

"Came back here and put together a 5-year plan, a 10-year plan. I said in '96 when we got to the NIT finals, it can't get any better than this. And I'm sure I said in '97, it can't get better than the Sweet 16. Let me jump ahead. I hope I'm here on this earth if it's any better than what's happened in '03–04."

He talks softly, dresses conservatively, looks old school.

"The people," he said, "the culture, the times on this campus, in this city, in this nation, have changed. To achieve in a team sport, there are certain elements that have to be there.

"The coach and the players have to agree, before the season starts, on what they think they can do. There must be a standard of play, everyone must accept a role. Buy into that. Plus, try to get better every day, every week. That is present on every team that is successful.

"It's a team sport. The whole is greater than the sum of its parts. Phil has this wonderful analogy. He says, 'We're a fist and when you break a fist, it's five separate players.'

"I talked to the team before the season started. I told them, 'What you accomplished last year was terrific. You should be proud, and I'm proud. The reason so many people like and respect you is the way you did it. You competed with character, composure and class.'

"Competing, that's the first thing. This year, men's soccer, first game of the season, going on the road for a Saturday game. I told them I was going to call the opponent on Monday and see if they felt they played against a team that played harder than anyone they'd faced."

That's old school, but it works at St. Joe's, where the mascot is on scholarship and never, ever stops flapping his arms from tipoff to final buzzer. There must be times when DiJulia would like to hide inside that hawk costume, but not just yet. Too many e-mails to answer, problems to solve, well-wishers to thank, an autograph policy to formulate.

"On Jan. 17 we beat Xavier on national television," DiJulia said. "On Jan. 18, a certain football team (the Eagles) lost an NFC Championship Game. Starting on Jan. 19, every week has been Super Bowl week. Take it, square it, and then square it again.

"People started coming, thinking, 'Ah, another little school.' And then they said, 'Whoa, these guys can play!' The other day I thought, is this the Beatles? Are we the Beatles?"

PART VII
Stan's World: Outside the Lines

Introduction

PAT McLOONE

I F YOU ARE THIS FAR ALONG, the journalistic force that was Stan Hochman is no stranger to you.

Maybe you have been reading Stan in the *Daily News* since the late 1950s, or you followed him on WIP SportsRadio or on *Daily News Live* on Comcast SportsNet. Or maybe you are new to this club of admirers, enjoying every word in this collection, lovingly compiled by the love of Stan's life, the equally gifted Gloria Hochman.

Me? I started from the bleachers, as a kid picking up the *Daily News* at Hal's Pharmacy at Third and Duncannon in Olney every day, mostly to read Stan and the sports pages. My view got much better, as I got a ringside seat when I joined the *Daily News* in 1980, eventually becoming Stan's editor for more than twenty-five years.

Maybe you had to be as close as I was to see how well-rounded and versatile Stan was. This section reflects that side of Stan, as he writes about golf, tennis, the Olympics, restaurants, youth, and, yes, the Wing Bowl—subjects as deadly serious as the tragedy of the Munich Olympics and as out there as his trip to Puerto Vallarta to play 8-ball with Richard Burton and stare into the violet eyes of Liz Taylor.

In his "spare time," Stan was a restaurant and theater critic for the *Daily News*. He always looked forward to his annual week in New York with Gloria and came back to the newsroom to tell the good, the bad, and the ugly of that year's plays on Broadway.

The insatiable appetite for fun and knowledge, no matter the age, shines through best, in my mind, when Stan and Gloria took up ballroom dancing. Long-timers at the *Daily News* saw those lessons in action on more than one occasion as they glided across dance floors big and small.

Stan's brilliant writing and mastery of numerous subjects come through vividly in this section's column on the death of Ben Hogan. A young Stan Hochman said he was "greener than the Augusta fairways" when he covered Hogan at the Masters in 1953 (!).

Hogan's passing is used in making a larger point in the column, as Stan plays editor in deciding which athletes merit front-page news when they die. A snippet:

> Willie Mays and Henry Aaron go out front. So does Ted Williams, the Splendid Splinter. Ernie Banks, inside. Reggie Jackson, a tough call, but Mr. October belongs out front because he did attend Cheltenham High.

In the April 10, 2015, editions of the *Daily News*, on the day after the sad passing of Stan Hochman?

Front page. It had to be.

TENNIS AND GOLF

Ben, Arnie and Jack at '60 Open

Philadelphia Daily News
June 20, 1960

FINAL ROUND of the U.S. Open, 1960, Cherry Hills. The dour Ben Hogan, the charismatic Arnold Palmer, the bland Jack Nicklaus, all in contention on the back nine. Old school, new school, prep school. Golf's past, present, future, the drama crackling through Denver's thin air like bolts of lightning.

HBO has ventured into golf for the first time with a sparkling documentary called "Back Nine at Cherry Hills: The Legends of the 1960 U.S. Open." It debuts tomorrow, the night before Tiger Woods and everybody else tees off in the Open at Torrey Pines.

If you're any kind of student of the game, you know how that 1960 Open with its narrow fairways and knee-high rough turns out, but if you're any kind of student of the game, you won't turn away for a moment as the melodrama unfolds.

And if you're new to the game, you will find the story fascinating, how Hogan, from a dirt-poor background, turned to golf as his ticket out of poverty and loneliness; how Palmer, with his grip-it-and-rip-it machismo, finally found the begrudging approval of his groundskeeper father; how Nicklaus, from an affluent Ohio family, melted those extra pounds and the hearts of the cynics with his brilliant shot-making.

Hogan's story is saddest. His father was a Texas blacksmith at a time when automobiles were churning off the assembly lines. Broke, emotionally battered, he committed suicide when Ben was 9 years old.

Hogan lugged clubs for 65 cents a round, got lucky when a club member encouraged him, mentored him. Hit shots off the practice tee until blood soaked his hands, laboring to cure a wicked hook.

Tried the tour, failed. Tried it again with his wife Valerie and their last $1,400. Down to 86 bucks when someone swiped the tires off their car. Hogan hitched a ride to the Oakland course, finished in the money, got a check for $385.

"Biggest check I'd ever seen," Hogan recalled in a revealing 1985 interview. The rest is history. A history that includes competing against guys like Byron Nelson and Sam Snead and Porky Oliver for skimpy prize money. A history that includes that head-on crash with a Greyhound bus one foggy night that left him with a double fracture of the pelvis, a broken ankle, a broken collarbone, a smashed rib and a blood clot.

Returned to win the Open at Merion, his cramping legs swathed in Ace bandages. There's that famous photo of Hogan's follow-through with a 1-iron, the rough clogged with spectators. Author Dan Jenkins called it "the greatest comeback in the history of sports."

Back in those days they played the final 36 holes on Saturday, making it a test of stamina and skill. Now, the Open ends on Father's Day, and the documentary plucks those strings like Heifetz.

Deacon Palmer was Arnie's strict, volatile father. The son rebelled one day, got thrown into a wall, smashing a stovepipe in the process. Ran away, slithered home when it got dark.

Turned to golf, developed his flair after watching Babe Didrikson play an exhibition in Latrobe. She wiggled on the first tee, said she had to loosen her girdle, and then whacked the ball down the fairway. Palmer would hitch his pants, flick away the cigarette, whack it as hard as he could and most of America loved him.

Not Hogan. They played a practice round at Augusta and Palmer overheard Hogan sneer, "How did Palmer get into the Masters?"

Palmer recalled his father saying, "There's no reason you can't be good and be nice."

Nicklaus was a country-club kid. Went off to Ohio State and gained 50 pounds his freshman year, majoring in partying and beer guzzling. Won the U.S. Amateur, beating Charlie Coe on the last hole. Made the Walker Cup team and thought maybe there was a future in golf.

He was 20 when they paired him with the legendary Hogan for those final two rounds at Cherry Hills. Palmer was seven shots back of an unraveling Mike Souchak after the morning round.

Jenkins recalls Palmer wondering aloud if a 65 and a 280 finish would be enough to win. Bob Drum, the Pittsburgh golf writer, dismissed Palmer with some derisive comment about him probably shooting seven birdies and seven bogeys.

Palmer bolted from his lunch. Drove the first hole (364 yards) and birdied it. Chipped in for a birdie on 2. Birdied 3. Drum turned to Jenkins and said, "Care to join me on the golf course?" Palmer birdied six of the first seven holes, finished the front nine in 30.

Nicklaus took the lead on the 12th hole and then squandered it with mistakes spawned by inexperience.

Hogan figured on finishing birdie-par. And then hit a wedge for his third shot on the par-5 17th. It landed on the slope of the green and then trickled back, back, back into the creek.

Twenty-five years later, Hogan confessed, "I wake up at night thinking about that shot. . . . [N]ot a month goes by that that shot doesn't cut my guts out."

Palmer shot his 65, won the Open, his only Open. Dan Jenkins gets the last word. "On that afternoon," he says, "in the span of just 18 holes, we witnessed the arrival of Nicklaus, the coronation of Palmer and the end of Hogan."

Son Crowns the King

Philadelphia Daily News
September 20, 1973

IF BOBBY RIGGS loses to Billie Jean King tonight he is NOT going to leap off the Pasadena Bridge as previously reported. "There's been 386 suicides off that bridge already," Riggs explained yesterday, "so they've got it surrounded with barbed wire and everything.

"And I'm not interested in the Golden Gate Bridge because people die when they jump off that one. I'm going to Lake Havasu in the middle of the desert where my good friend has imported the London Bridge and re-created it and I will jump off that one. I want a chance to survive."

Of course, if somebody put up enough money, Riggs might try the Golden Gate, wearing a parachute, with the bay at low tide. And for an extra $10,000, he will wear advertising on the parachute.

The wry little speech about losing took place at a party thrown by some aftershave people that resembled a bad Bar Mitzvah more than anything else.

The whole schmear . . . ice sculpture, the band in striped jackets, guacamole salad, bartenders pouring cheap bourbon, and Bobby Riggs sputtering like a 13-year-old.

Billie Jean King was probably off staring at some wallpaper someplace and Bobby Riggs was entwined amongst a giggle of cheerleaders, making this incredible speech, thanking everyone in the room.

"This is Loren Brimbleruff," he'd say, "the man who has trained me for this match. . . . And here's Rheo Whaffentramf, the nutritionist who designed my special diet. Would you believe he's 75 years old?

"And here's George McMartinsmff, who co-authored my book, 'The Hustler.' . . . And there's the Major Domino of the Astrodome, Sidney Sumthinsumthin. . . . And here's Hans Yuckapuck from San Diego State College, who's gonna play me for $100 tonight, right Hans?"

Any minute you expected him to roll up the sleeve of his powder-blue windbreaker and offer a couple of watches for sale.

"I like him and I hate him," Ms. King said earlier in the day at a chaotic press conference. "He's great for tennis, but what he says is so ridiculous. Sometimes I laugh and sometimes I get furious."

"And how do you feeeeel about it now, Billie Jean?" Riggs asked, playing Big Bad Wolf to her Red Riding Hood. "We're approaching the zero hour. Me, I don't have a nerve in my body."

Riggs has all the normal number of nerves in his body. But they are 55 years old and people think a 29-year-old tough, determined athlete like Billie Jean has a chance against him. They worry, though, about HER nerves, and Riggs plays them like guitar strings. "She's quick, she's agile," Riggs said, the words swift and damp, like rain on a hot tin roof. "She says she's unpsychable. She says she has as many junk shots as I do, she can play the big match and stand up to pressure. She claims being a woman is not a drawback when it comes to emotional stress and strings."

You could almost hear Billie Jean gritting her teeth in Muleshoe. It is Riggs at work, poking for an edge, the hustler who has maneuvered his skills and his personality into a huge payday ($100,000 to the loser, around $200,000 to the winner).

And what if Riggs loses? Does he leap off the cliff of fame back to obscurity? "I've talked about it with my brothers," Jimmy Riggs said when the Bar Mitzvah band took a break.

"I'm going to be living with him. It'd be tough for a while. But I've got a motto. . . . [T]hings that look grim, two months from now, you'll laugh at.

"Billie Jean has a lot to win and lot to lose. My dad has everything to win and everything to lose. She's a good player, a together chick. It's going to come down to pure skill and I'm gonna chunk it in on my dad.

"I chunked it in against Margaret Court, half of all the money I own. And if I can find King money, I'll chunk it in again, $1, $2, $5, $100. So far, all I've got is five bucks with a girl tennis player in Vermont."

Jimmy is Riggs's 20-year-old son. A hip, flip apple of a lad who hasn't fallen too far from the tree. "He came along at the right time," Jimmy said proudly. "The nation needed some comic relief and he gave it to them.

"He's gonna win. Easy. He's hit more tennis balls over the net than she has. If it were an airplane race, who would you bet on? A World War II pilot or a brand-new guy?

"My big thrill each month is when he plays some singles with me. On a hot, sunny day, if he gets a little sloppy, I might win a game or two. It's like if I were a musician going to play a duet with Van Cliburn. And that's the way it's gonna be with Billie Jean."

Wanna bet?

The Sugar Cane against the Rough: Chi Chi Rodriguez

Philadelphia Daily News
June 22, 1981

IF CHI CHI RODRIGUEZ had won the U.S. Open at 45, it would have been the second biggest thrill of his life.

"I met Mother Teresa in an airport in the Philippines," Rodriguez said yesterday, over the getaway gabble of the Merion Golf Club locker room. "Biggest thrill of my life."

Mother Teresa, who thinks she is tough enough to whip worldwide poverty with a little help from her friends, told Rodriguez about a leper colony she wanted to create in India.

"If I had won," Rodriguez said, "I'd have given the whole purse to Mother Teresa. Hey, there's 50,000 lepers in India. Maybe $50,000 won't get it done, but maybe somebody else sees this nut giving $50,000 so he gives $50,000 and then it gets done.

"I knocked in that birdie putt on four and I felt like she was guiding the ball to the hole."

That put him 3-under and 3 shots back of the leaders. For the next four holes, Rodriguez hit some shots that not even a Mother Teresa could love. Took four bogeys in a row, vanished from the leader boards.

"I was playing aggressive," he said. "I was trying to win. I coulda played it safer, gotten three bogeys instead of four, won a few thousand bucks more. But I was out there to win."

He didn't win, but he chattered through Merion's narrow back nine in 33 blows, finished with an even-par 280 total, in a five-way tie for sixth place.

Mad dogs and Englishmen were indoors or soaking up the sparse shade. But Rodriguez, looking like a raspberry frappe in his red pants and white shirt, whistled through the four-hour round.

"Ninety degrees?" Rodriguez yelped in scorn. "For a Puerto Rican, that's like steak. The way steak was 25 years ago. It gets up to 95 or 100, that's hot . . . when you're cutting sugar cane.

"Ninety degrees and you're playing golf, that's a walk in the park. I feel better than I ever felt in my life. Maybe it's the Vitamin E I'm taking."

"Nah," suggested John Schroeder, who was cleaning out a nearby locker, "he feels better because he's putting better."

"I am putting better," Rodriguez said proudly, forgetting the three-putt agonies on No. 5 that caused the wheels to come off. "I haven't putted this good the last 17 years on the tour.

"In 1964, I was a fantastic putter. I wrote an article about putting. Got paid $50 for it. And I've never putted good since. All I know now is you're supposed to knock the ball in the hole. The last five weeks I've moved the ball towards my left foot. I had a guy check my eye. I'm left-eyed. So I've got to hit everything off my left foot. Charlie Fletcher was the guy's name. He's an expert rifle shooter."

A lot of what Rodriguez says is as sweet and frothy as yam pie. He is an expert bull shooter. He has not won a tournament since 1979 at Tallahassee, but he lures large, passionate galleries because he has enough charisma for an entire foursome of those surfer-blond sour-faced choirboys the PGA seems to stamp out in some California cookie factory.

"I'm an inspiration to everybody," Rodriguez said. "A little guy like me, little people feel a lot of compassion towards me.

"Old guys like me because I'm old. Young guys like me because I act young, dress young, feel young and I'm gonna stay young.

"People have to accept you the way you are. Nobody else can be me. I can't be somebody else. I believe what's happened, is, in the old days, former caddies came on the tour.

"Now, we have college kids, they all have an education. Their coaches in school taught 'em to win, win, win. Winning is great for the ego. But if a person tries his very best, that's winning. If you try to do it with honor, that's winning. Maybe the PGA tour ought to have a school too, to teach 'em a little, uh, P.R."

THAT'S P.R. as in public relations, not Puerto Rico. When he was new on the tour, Chi Chi was as flamboyant as a San Juan sunset. Plopped his straw hat over the hole whenever he made a nifty putt. Spent the rest of the time talking through it.

Not every shtick made everybody happy. Dave Hill once wanted to part Chi Chi's haircut with a 5-iron. And maybe, just maybe, Chi Chi's gabbiness turned the officials against him.

There was that IVB tournament at Whitemarsh in '64, when he was 13-under after three rounds. Took a 42 on the back side the final day.

"My ball was in bounds," Rodriguez said bitterly. "And a guy declared it out of bounds. Twice. The rules man, he called it out of bounds.

"I didn't know what a snow fence was. My ball was between two fences. It wasn't out of bounds. Two out of bounds. Take that away, it meant the worst I could have done was be in a playoff.

"Everything happens for the best. I might have won the tournament, gotten a bunch of exhibitions out of it, gotten on a plane and the plane went down. I don't hold it against him. Only fools live in the past and the future."

At 45, cherishing every moment with boyish enthusiasm, playing the game with youthful endurance, he reminds people of Pete Rose. Rodriguez, a hardcore baseball fan, bristles at the comparison.

"I DON'T LIKE Pete Rose," he said. "He hits people. He put Ray Fosse out of baseball. Hit a Houston catcher last year and the ball was 15 feet away. I don't believe a human being should harm another human being. I know, in football, they get paid to hit. That's why I don't watch football. Somebody gets hurt, I hurt. In football, someone gets hit, his knees bent out of shape, and someone hollers, 'Did you see that hit?' I don't like violence. I understand football players getting paid to play. But baseball is not that way. Mike Schmidt, he's my kind of player."

And Chi Chi Rodriguez is that rare kind of player, who can finish a final-round 72 with a clutch putt and turn his putter into Zorro's sword, thrusting it back in an invisible scabbard, wiping it clean of make-believe blood, and so on.

"I loved it out there," Rodriguez said. "I loved every moment of it. I just thank God for giving me the opportunity of playing in a U.S. Open, playing behind Jack Nicklaus, playing in front of 20,000 people, and for giving me the opportunity of being born in the greatest country in the world, the United States of America. Where a man can work just four days and make $10,000."

He made $9,920. It beats cutting sugar cane in 95-degree heat. Only fools live in the past, but Chi Chi Rodriguez hasn't forgotten.

Tiger Woods: Triumph of the Spirit

Philadelphia Daily News
March 20, 1997

WHAT IS ALL THIS FUSS about Tiger Woods, who has never won a major golf tournament, who has never even *played* in a major golf tournament as a professional?

Sports Illustrated names him "Sportsman of the Year." CBS trumpets an in-depth television profile they will show just before the Masters Tournament. The *Daily News* devotes an eight-page section to a 21-year-old who has never won a golf tournament, who has never even played in a major golf tournament as a pro.

Sure, sure, he won the U.S. Amateur championship three years in a row, and nobody in the whole cockeyed history of the sport had ever done that. Yeah, yeah, he turned pro and Nike gave him $40 million and Titleist forked over another $20 million in endorsement money. Uh huh, he won three of the first nine tournaments he entered.

If you're going to be a superstar at 21, golf is the ideal venue. Think about it. A 21-year-old leftfielder facing Randy Johnson for the first time is overmatched. Fastball at the belt for strike one, fastball at the chest for strike two, slider below the knees, ball one, futile swing at a shoulder—high fastball for strike three. See ya.

Or a 21-year-old defensive back trying to cover Michael Irvin. Bites on the post fake, suffers windburn as Irvin streaks past, down the sideline. Touchdown.

Or a 21-year-old trying to defend Michael Jordan, and who was that blur curling in the layup?

Even in an individual game like tennis, the 21-year-old has to get his sweaty backhand on a Pete Sampras serve trailing blue sparks.

In golf, the ball just sits there, on a tee, or on some lush Kentucky bluegrass. Drive it long and straight, feather a 9-iron, second shot onto the green, zap in a 12-footer, birdie, move on to the next hole, awash in polite applause.

In golf, you're playing the landscape, you're playing against par. Sure, there are times you will have to improvise a shot, under some ominous tree branches, over some yawning sand trap, but nobody is going for your knee trying to bust up a double play, nobody is putting a forearm in your face, or swatting at your ankles with a hockey stick.

At 21, you are facing the same scenery, the same yardage, the same par numbers as everyone else in the tournament. The ball doesn't ask your age before you strike it. What is so remarkable about a 21-year-old winning three of the first nine tournaments he enters as a pro?

I'll tell you what's so remarkable. It took Jack Nicklaus 25 tournaments before he won his third title. Twenty-five!

Ah, but Nicklaus came along when Arnold Palmer's army was in full whoop. They demeaned Nicklaus as "Fat Jack" and they jiggled coins when he hovered over a putt. Things are different for Woods, because he has lured an army of passionate fans and they surround him with love and they chant encouragement.

Who is king of the hill now? Is it Greg Norman? Isn't he the Australian guy with the big straw hats, the bloke who blew a six-shot lead on the last day of the Masters last year?

Right you are, mate. And didn't he get an avalanche of sympathetic mail? And didn't he come back from a five-month layoff to lead at Doral after two rounds, bragging about his revamped swing, lusting for another shot at the lovely but cruel Augusta National track, before throwing a pair of 74s and fading from contention?

And didn't Norman say that he "welcomes" Woods' presence on the PGA tour? And didn't he plant the seeds of doubt in Tiger's handsome head by saying, "I feel sorry for Tiger in a lot of ways. I think he doesn't have a life for a 21-year-old"?

And didn't members of the golf media remember that when Woods met them when he turned pro, he said he was planning to play in Norman's Shark Shootout, ignoring the fact that the shindig is by invitation only and that Norman hadn't sent out any invitations, and that the two haven't spoken since?

And didn't Mark O'Meara, who lives near Woods in Orlando, Fla., share some significant bits of dialogue when he told the world about Tiger's audacious comments during a one-on-one match at the Isleworth club, Woods saying, "I'd love to come down the stretch head-to-head with you in a tournament"?

O'Meara says he told Woods, "Bud you might hit it 50 yards farther than me, and you might have the perfect swing, but I'll find a way to clip you."

And then, O'Meara made it happen at Pebble Beach, finishing birdie-birdie par to squelch Woods.

The mostly nameless, faceless tour guys in their late 30s say they don't resent Woods, but they do. It's nothing personal. It's just that he got all that up-front cash from Nike and Titleist. And that makes it just a little easier for him to go for the green on some twisting par 5 than it is for a guy with two kids and a harsh mortgage, trying to keep his PGA card.

The envy, the petty jealousy won't stop Woods. He seems oblivious to that. What might hamper him is the loneliness, the boredom, and those outrageous expectations his father has handed him, like a red-hot anvil.

Earl Woods brags that Tiger will transcend the game of golf and bring to the world a humanitarianism that has never been known before. "The world," daddy says, "will be a better place to live in."

Talk about baggage. And then Earl gets toppled by a second heart attack, and there's quadruple bypass and some subsequent surgery, and Tiger skips Doral and Honda to stay close to his dad.

So he doesn't get to play Doral and Honda and he doesn't get to meet quietly with Norman and he doesn't get to reply to the inevitable media question about how tough it is to be out there, alone, at 21.

Woods is such a phenomenon that the media horde now includes the television-tabloid piranhas and lots of folks who don't know an eagle from a bogey. They all want to get up close and personal, though.

So when some inquiring mind at the Nissan Open asked if Woods had a girlfriend, if he went to the movies and who he was as a person, Tiger just ducked, saying, "Well, that's just for my friends to know."

They went to his caddie, Mike "Fluff" Cowan in search of insights.

"Tiger is just a young man who plays pretty great golf," Fluff fluffed. "He's truly pretty much a kid until you put him on the golf course. And then he becomes a much older person than someone who's 21 by years."

Woods has the tranquil genes of his mom and the competitive rage of his dad. He's got the management support team to organize his schedule. He's got his own army of passionate young fans.

And he would seem to have the perfect approach to this humbling game. "It comes down to one thing," Woods has said. "I've still got to hit the shot. Me. Alone. That's what I must never forget."

Go ahead, roll the presses, whir the cameras. Bet on him to achieve greatness even though he's only 21 and he's never won a major championship. Yet!

Front Page Reserved for Greatness

Philadelphia Daily News
September 18, 1997

SQUINTING THROUGH a dense Texas fog, Ben Hogan saw the head-lights of that oncoming Greyhound bus at the last instant. Threw him-self in front of his wife Valerie seconds before the head-on crash sent the steering post through the driver's seat, shattering his left collar-bone as it hurtled past.

His left ankle snapped like a twig, his left leg was mangled, his sev-enth rib fractured. That was Groundhog Day 1949.

A year later, Hogan limped onto Merion's beautiful acreage to com-pete in the U.S. Open. Shot a 72 on the first round. Scorched through a 69 on the second day, trailing Dutch Harrison by two strokes.

The field played two rounds Saturday, Hogan's legs screeching in pain. By the 13th hole of the morning round, he contemplated quit-ting.

Legend has it, his caddie said, "No, Mr. Hogan, you can't quit, be-cause I don't work for quitters."

Hogan finished the round with a 72, still two shots behind the leader, Lloyd Mangrum. In the afternoon, Hogan staggered to 18 need-ing a par to snag a playoff spot with Mangrum and George Fazio.

Hit an incredible 1-iron shot to the green, the image frozen forever by photographer Hy Peskin. The rules limited golfers to 14 clubs in those days. Why did Hogan have a 1-iron and no 7-iron in his bag?

"There are no 7-iron shots at Merion," Hogan said bluntly.

Made his par, won the next day's playoff by three shots when Man-grum picked up his ball on the 16th green to blow away a ladybug and drew a two-shot penalty.

In the moments after Hogan paid his caddie, someone stole both his 1-iron and his golf shoes.

Hogan was a mysterious man, dour as a Russian winter. The Scots called him "The Wee Ice Mon" when he won the British Open. Curt Sampson has written a fascinating, warts-and-all biography called "Ho-gan" that sheds some light on a golfer who practiced until his hands bled.

I was there for his Masters victory in 1953, but I was greener than the Augusta fairways, and didn't realize I was in the presence of greatness. I was puzzled when no one approached him and Valerie as they ate a wordless dinner at the Bon-Aire Hotel one night.

Sampson quotes Jimmy Demaret's one-liner, seeing Hogan sitting alone at the Champions Golf Club in Houston: "There's Hogan, with all his friends."

That Open triumph at Merion, so soon after that brutal head-on crash, just one of 63 tournaments Hogan won, should have been enough to put his obituary on the front page when he died recently at 84.

Perhaps he was too cold, too aloof, perhaps he'd been off-stage too long, because most newspapers placed Hogan's death in the sports section or in the obituary columns and not out front.

The *Washington Post* was one of those papers that buried Hogan inside. And that caused columnist Tony Kornheiser to ruminate on Hogan being relegated inside, when actor James Stewart, explorer Jacques Cousteau and Supreme Court Justice William Brennan made front-page news when they died around the same time.

Kornheiser wondered what the future held for aging sports figures. I wonder too, so I'm stealing the concept. You might remember, this is the newspaper that bannered Joe Frazier's knockout loss to George Foreman the day Lyndon Baines Johnson died.

The same newspaper that put together a memorable keepsake section devoted to Richie Ashburn, in less than 24 hours. Remember, too, that the *Daily News* is blessed with one of America's finest obituary writers in Jim Nicholson, a rare blend of sensitivity and skill.

Ultimately, the decision on who goes out front, who goes inside, is made by the editor, who is free to consider or ignore my suggestions.

Arnold Palmer goes out front, for all that he has achieved, for all that his hitch-your-pants and go-for-the-flag charisma meant to the game. Jack Nicklaus belongs out front, too, for his Grand Slam victories and his faultless demeanor.

Robin Roberts goes out front, symbolizing the Whiz Kids pennant, one of a handful of Philadelphia Hall of Famers.

Steve Carlton? Yes, despite his silence. Jim Bunning? No, unless he winds up in the White House. Mike Schmidt? No, even though he is the greatest third baseman ever to play the game, because he has distanced himself from this city.

Willie Mays and Henry Aaron go out front. So does Ted Williams, the Splendid Splinter. Ernie Banks, inside. Reggie Jackson, a tough call, but Mr. October belongs out front because he did attend Cheltenham High.

Hit king Pete Rose goes out front, whether he is reinstated by baseball or not. Frank Robinson made history as the first black manager, and will rate front page in Cincinnati, Baltimore and Cleveland, but not here.

Sonny Jurgensen deserves front-page space in Washington, but he was here too briefly. Steve Van Buren belongs out front and so does Chuck Bednarik, for playing 60 minutes. And for nailing Frank Gifford, who does not get front-page space.

Does Joe Namath belong for his audacious Super Bowl guarantee? No, because he has drifted away from the game. Johnny Unitas steps inside in those high-top shoes. Jim Brown, out front, for his off-the-field newsmaking as well as his on-the-field heroics.

Muhammad Ali is a cinch, an immortal lock, front page, above the fold. Joe Frazier belongs, too, the Olympic gold-medal winner who came back to Philadelphia to joblessness, one more bit of evidence that this is one tough town.

Wilt Chamberlain, front page. Bill Russell, no. George Mikan, ancient history, back of the paper. Billy Cunningham because he played and coached here, out front. Wali Jones, despite his local ties and charisma, no.

Bobby Clarke is the lone hockey guy to rate front page, for his courage, his work ethic. Sorry, Bernie Parent; forgive me, Broad Street Bullies.

Now, it's your turn. Slip on your green editor's visor, put garters on your sleeves, and make the decision. Choose from among Dick Allen, Julius Erving and Tug McGraw and tell me whether your man's life story belongs on the front page or inside the sports section.

Write to me, care of Stan's World, Philadelphia Daily News, 400 N. Broad St., Box 7788, Philadelphia, Pa. 19101. Best letter earns a suitable prize.

Controversial Entry into Hall

Philadelphia Daily News
February 17, 2004

BIG BILL TILDEN was the first American to win Wimbledon. Won it again, 10 years later, at age 37, the oldest player to win Wimbledon. Won every tournament he entered for a 6-year stretch. Played on seven consecutive Davis Cup championship teams.

Tilden dominated tennis in the 1920s, a golden age of sports that included Babe Ruth, Red Grange, Bobby Jones, Jack Dempsey.

Big Bill, that's what the writers called him even though he was only 6-1 and a lean 170 pounds. Called him "a man of mystery" because they didn't want to write that he was gay, prancing to the strum of his own lyre, even when he began traveling with handpicked teenage ball boys.

Tilden, who was born in Germantown, died in 1953. Coronary thrombosis. Maybe all that smoking, all those steaks, all that ice cream, all that stress. Died alone, at 60, in a Los Angeles apartment, battered, practically broke, virtually friendless, $88 to his name. This was after he'd been jailed twice, first for contributing to the delinquency of a 14-year-old boy, and then again, for violating probation, this time with a teenage hitchhiker.

Frank Deford wrote a compassionate book about him in 1975, "Big Bill Tilden." And now, A.R. Gurney has transformed that book into a thought-provoking play called "Big Bill" that is currently in previews at the Newhouse Theatre at New York's Lincoln Center.

Last week, Tilden was among 19 athletes and managers inducted into the brand-new Philadelphia Sports Hall of Fame, an institution, in its own words, "dedicated to honoring those athletes, coaches, teams . . . that have, through athletics, brought pride and glory to the great city of Philadelphia. . . ."

It couldn't have been easy, kicking the doors wide open, first year, honoring someone who spent time in the slammer for molesting a kid, even though the kid had a troubled history and what went on was said to be consensual.

"We debated for over a year," said Hall of Fame founder Ken Avallon. "Eight of us, the board of directors, and the majority didn't feel we needed to be in position to judge people.

"The arguments focused on Tilden and Pete Rose. It was a tough decision, but we decided to make the criteria what they accomplished on the field. It is the Hall of Fame, not the Hall of Honor."

Debate it if you must. Baseball asks its voters to consider character and integrity when choosing Hall of Famers. Football doesn't. No one is sure how basketball's electoral process works.

Deford was not surprised that Tilden was in the first crop of Philadelphia inductees. "If you're selecting them on the basis of quality of play," he said, "then Tilden is going to be at the top of the tree. He's got to be in the top three or four."

And if he were playing today? "People are always making the argument when comparing athletes of different eras, 'Would he be big enough?'" Deford said. "Red Grange, at 5-9, 160, for example. Well, Tilden had all the physical attributes.

"He was dedicated enough, although he smoked, and didn't train that well. But he dominated his era and he'd be just as good today."

And if Deford wrote his book today? "Good question," he said.

"There's a lot more understanding about homosexuality. I had dinner with the playwright the other day, and with John Michael Higgins, who plays Tilden.

"We talked about today's more liberal attitude, and whether the world would be more accommodating today. The thing is, there is much less sympathy for a pedophile.

"I thought I was as sympathetic as I could be in the book. The guy was a tragic figure, a sad, sad man."

"He descended, literally, into hell," said Marilyn Fernberger, the organizer of the Philadelphia indoor championships for so many gaudy years. "It was all part of an era. Acceptance today would be very different.

"He is one of the greatest players ever. He's in the tennis Hall of Fame, and the International Tennis Hall of Fame. The USTA recently honored him as the male player of the Golden Era of the U.S. Open.

"My husband, Ed, and I collect tennis memorabilia. And when some of Tilden's trophies came on the market we bought the runner-up trophy from the Philadelphia Indoor tournament, 1916. After that, he retired from competition for a while and changed his game. Reformed it. And from then on out, he never lost anything."

Developed a twisting second serve to go with his booming "Cannonball" first serve. Studied opponents and beat them at their own game, boxing with the boxers and slugging with the sluggers. Wrote textbooks about the game, including "Match Play and the Spin of the Ball."

There's a scene in the play where a Penn student working on a research paper discovers that the university library has snatched Tilden's books from the shelves. Well, they're back now, and Tilden is in Penn's Tennis Hall of Fame, even if he didn't make the varsity in his first try, in 1915.

His picture is back on the walls at Germantown Cricket Club. And the tennis courts at Germantown Academy, from which he graduated, are named for him.

He was flamboyant, arriving at the court wearing his trademark camel's-hair coat. He never showered with the other competitors and toward the end, he seldom showered at all. He could be kind and he could be cruel.

The bitter side is symbolized in Gurney's play by the episode involving French champion Suzanne Lenglen. Tilden baits her into playing a set with him by bumbling through a warmup with one of his proteges. And then he smokes her, 6–0.

If he won a point on a linesman's bad call, he'd give it back. He fought the stodgy establishment and he was a pioneer on the pro tour, competing into his 50s. Squandered much of his money backing bad Broadway plays. Even acted in a couple. In the play, someone sneers at his qualifications as an actor. Tilden sighs and says, in anguish, "I've been acting all my life."

Game, set and match.

FROM THE HEART AND, BY THE WAY, LIZ TAYLOR

Snow White and the Dwarf

Philadelphia Daily News
September 7, 1972

MUNICH—Somebody gets mugged in the parking lot, they don't shut down Disneyland. Somebody gets raped or shot or stabbed or pistol-whipped, they don't board up Fantasyland or lock up the gates to Adventureland. Nah.

Life goes on. Sure, there are those red-brown splotches in front of Building 31 where Moshe Weinberg bled to death Tuesday morning, the blood coming out of a bullet hole.

Maybe they can get somebody over there when the crowd thins out. Somebody with a scrub brush and a bucket of soapy water. Tidy up the place, you know. Scatter some tinsel. Stick another pastel-colored flag on the nearby miniature golf course.

Eighteen people were killed in what started out as a despicable act of terrorism. So Avery Brundage lowered the flags and raised his voice and padlocked the Olympic Game for 24 hours.

Avery Brundage thinks the Olympic Games are Fantasyland and Tomorrowland and Storybookland and Adventureland. People keep screaming into his deaf ears, that there are some real people involved. They cry when they are sad, they bleed when they are shot, they die when they are blown apart by grenades.

Comic-Strip Characters

Brundage says they're here to run and jump and play games. Brundage treats them as though they are comic-strip characters taking part in some full-length cartoon he is orchestrating.

The trouble is, Snow White is dead. And this time no handsome prince is going to come along and wake her up with a kiss. This Olympics is for lumpy toads, not handsome princes. And it continues after this brief time out for an angry message from Avery Brundage.

More than 2,000 athletes showed up at the magnificent Olympic Stadium for a memorial service for all of the 11 slaughtered members of the Israeli team. There was solemn music by the Munich Philharmonic, and expressions of sorrow, and pledges to seek a better world.

Most of the athletes came in sweat suits and they looked like a Mondrian painting sitting there, slab of yellow, a row of dark blue, a square patch of red. Carl Borrack, a kinky-haired American fencer, was there.

"Brundage," he muttered afterwards. "He had to get up with his small thing and rant about Rhodesia again. Well, I'll tell you what really tears me up. . . . [W]here were the Russians?"

No Hot Line for Condolences

The Russians were conspicuous by their absence. So this was not a symbol of the world united, rising up against this kind of terrorism. No, the Russians kept using the Olympics as a political arena.

"The Russians," Olga Connolly said later, "probably did not get their instructions from Moscow and stayed away."

Olga Connolly was once Snow White, a Czech discus thrower who met and fell in love with American hammer-thrower Harold Connolly at the Olympics. She's got four kids now and she strides about the Olympic Village preaching against killing and nobody mistakes her for Snow White anymore.

She is content to have the Games resume because she knows they are not Fantasyland. "The Games have to go on," she said, "because we can't run away from problems. This way, we can show the world we can handle our own crisis, and not only two people are involved. We have to become tightly knit if we are brothers and sisters in the family of man. There is no question in my mind the Games should continue.

"But I hope we can come up with something more tangible than medals. If it's only sporting competition that continues, then it's shallow.

"If the philosophy is to look at the Olympic Games as a place to have a ball and win medals then it shouldn't even be held. If you are coming to the Olympic Games as a meeting-place of the world, that's different. You should come to the Olympics to reaffirm your trust in the human beings of the world.

"Now, we should say, in the face of adversity and tragedy, we feel sorry for the Israelis and their families. And we feel pity for the Arab nations. We cannot categorize them all as bad guys because they are still our brothers and sisters.

"What we must say is that we'll get together and we'll change the world. Otherwise we'll be locked in the vicious circle of killing and revenge.

"People have to realize the accomplishment of their private goals may have to give in to the overall goal of relieving hatred, mistrust and frenzy that will eventually blow us all up."

Whispers at a Discotheque

Preach peace at the Olympic and it's like whispering at a discotheque. Who hears? Besides, most of the athletes are too concerned with running and jumping and playing games.

"This is my fifth Olympics," she said, "and I do feel that views are not really voiced. Maybe they're not eloquent enough? Or maybe they're so brainwashed that unless you speak about the hop-skip-and-jump or the size of your bleep, you are talking politics."

Someone nudged Olga with the thought that if she could talk politics at the Olympics, how could she then bar extremists like that wretched Black September group from talking their kind of politics?

"I'm not promoting my ideas with machine guns," she said softly. "I'm not opposed to forums. You can't have issues clarified unless you have dialogue. We have to have rap sessions.

"I hate to get back to the golden rule but you must do unto others as you would have them do unto you. That is where my zeal comes from, no matter how corny it may seem."

But, someone persisted, it seems bizarre to jump and run and play when Moshe Weinberg's blood stains the cobblestones in front of Building 31. Olga Connolly's eyes misted.

"Life goes on," she sighed, and pulled her USA jacket tighter. "My mother died last year. My father died three weeks earlier because he did not want to wait for her funeral.

"She died of cancer. And I watched her for a year. I saw her go from 180 pounds to 65. I was with her through the suffering, in pain, like an animal.

"And as I watched her I thought, why do we have the most sophisticated weapons in the world instead of a cure for cancer? The answer is that we do not have the finest minds of all nations working together.

"But the day after her funeral I went to work. Life went on. The kids had to be fed, the house had to be cleaned, the laundry had to be washed. It doesn't mean it didn't leave a scar in my heart.

"I will go to practice today. And I will go and compete. And momentarily I will enjoy myself competing. But it will still be burning inside me, what a terrible tragedy this was. Things have to be done. I have to be part of the change.

"Maybe this will open people's eyes? Maybe something positive can come out of this tragedy. I don't want those people to have died in vain.

"I'm not worried about the Russians not being there to mourn the dead. I can't worry about their minds. I only worry about my mind, and the minds of people who can clearly think for themselves.

"Americans, we have to be the first to reach out. We can change the world. They can't."

Reaching out. Swifter, higher, stronger. Snow White is pale and sickly. She speaks of peace. Will no one listen? Is there time for all of us to learn to live together before we all die together?

Love Story: Child Finds Home
with Area Trainer

Philadelphia Daily News
November 29, 1990

EVEN IN THE RACE TRACK STABLES, where optimism flourishes like grass thrusting through concrete, the infant Thomas seemed a faint-hope longshot.

By Loneliness, out of Despair, born into a world bleak and bureaucratic.

It is damn near impossible to raise a child in a backstretch barracks. The child's mother decided to relinquish the baby.

Carol Ann Murray, 36, single, a trainer on the hardscrabble circuit that is Philadelphia Park, Garden State and Atlantic City, reached out for Thomas with loving arms.

The odds? Carol Murray is accustomed to long odds.

"My best horses," she said the other day, "have always been the ones we expected the least from.

"I'm not thinking of him becoming president. Or even a lawyer or a doctor.

"I want him to have a happy life, to be able to make choices for himself, to have good friends. That would be a success right there.

"Don't make me out to be some noble, special person. I feel lucky to have Thomas.

"I wake up every morning and I say, 'He's my son,' and it's the most exciting thing that's ever happened to me."

A Triple Crown horse, when it comes, will rank a distant second to the joy Carol Murray feels now, cuddling Thomas on shed row, watching him reach out to pet the soft, rubbery nose of a placid filly.

Racing has been blotched this year by sorrow, some of the very best horses in the world, on the track, on the farm, dying too soon.

Carol Murray's story helps chase the gloom. It is appropriate to tell it now, during National Adoption Month, with thousands of other children with special needs yearning for warm and loving homes.

"I'm just the type of person who has always loved kids," Murray explained, at 5-5 and 100 pounds, no bigger than a teenager herself. "I go to family gatherings and I end up playing with the kids.

"I wasn't one of those people, 36, suddenly frantic, haven't had a baby, dying to have a baby.

"I just felt . . . here was a situation, I see a pregnant woman, no home, no money, I felt compelled to help her.

"Here's a kid who needs a place to live. He's welcome with me. My assistant trainer, Sylvester Valentine, looks after everybody on the back side.

"I still don't know how much prenatal care she got. He knew the girl, knew she was going to give the baby away. I thought, 'I'd like to have that baby.'"

The mother talked about taking the infant to her mother's home in another state, but that plan unraveled.

Through Valentine, she was aware of Carol and the firm but fair way she ran her stable. In the spring, 3 weeks old, Thomas's life began anew.

First, there was a mountain of paperwork to climb. Murray sought help from attorney Barbara Ulrichsen, owner of one of the horses she trains.

"Being the mother of two young children who works full-time," Ulrichsen said, "I thought she was out of her mind.

"She knew she was taking a big risk, but I also knew that if she took the child, it would have a wonderful home.

"The mother relinquished custody to Carol and privately placed the child with her. We'll be filing an adoption action.

"Carol is very good at taking on tough projects.

"I sent her a filly that was ridiculous. The proper description is total witch.

"Her first start, she came out of the gate, leapfrogged. (Jockey) Mary Ann Alligood pulled her up and she wound up trotting over the finish line.

"She was very mediocre last winter, running for (a claiming price of) $11,000. Not winning for that.

"And then Carol said she wanted to try her on grass. Ran her for $18,000. I wondered, 'What kind of fantasy land is that?' She got beat by a head.

"Later, moving up again, she finished third in a handicap race and won the feature last week at the Meadowlands. Candice Key, a tribute to Carol's training."

It has been that way since Carol Murray started training thoroughbreds. She gets the lame and the lazy, the brittle and the bowlegged, and she pokes around, inside their fragile psyches, solving riddles, healing flaws.

"I worked for a lady in Virginia," Murray recalled, "who has become my best friend.

"She taught me what I think is the key to the whole thing . . . to see things the way a horse sees things.

"A horse does everything perfect. And here we are, interfering with that world. We have to learn to not be disruptive.

"Horses do things for a reason. Only people do things for no good reason. Horses aren't made that way."

It is part of the fabric she began weaving as a teenager, playing hooky in Syosset, N.Y., to ride the bus to Roosevelt Raceway, a harness track.

"As I got older, I went farther, to Belmont Park," she confessed.

"I was always fascinated by horses. Nobody in the family had anything to do with horses. Oh, my uncle was a bartender at Aqueduct, but that's it.

"I started out as a race tracker. Hot walker, groom. Later worked with hunters and jumpers. Did a little bit of everything.

"My family thought it was the worst thing in the world. Took about 15 years to bring them around.

"Even when I became a trainer, they still thought it was bad. They said, couldn't I just get a job, do something simple?

"And then, when I started winning some races, my father, who's a print salesman, got psyched about it. Now, he's got winning pictures all over his office.

"When I told my mother I was going to adopt the baby, she started laughing and saying, 'I don't believe it.

"'Nothing you do surprises me, but this surprises me.'

"Now, she's crazy about him. He stayed with my folks while I went to the (thoroughbred) sales. After a couple of days, I thought they'd be dead. But they wanted to keep him longer."

Thomas is 9 months old now, a handsome, mixed-race child with big brown eyes and a smile that would melt steel.

Although he is not sleeping through the night yet, in all the other important ways, he has adjusted to Carol's race track timetable.

"I get up at 7," she said, "and I drop him off at the babysitter on my way to the track.

"The days we don't have something running, I'll pick him up as early as I can, around noon.

"If we've got something running at night at the Meadowlands, Jeanette Loder, who works for me, will put him to bed and stay with him.

"He's already eating mashed potatoes and green beans. No baby food, only the real stuff.

"I get so much help from everyone, that makes life easier."

It never gets easy, handling 14 fragile, nervous race horses, but her crew seems close-knit, a rainbow mix of male and female, black and white. Thomas has more doting aunts and uncles than most kids, plus his own petting zoo.

It is a hard life, with champagne highs and migraine lows, but Carol Murray has always been energized by challenges.

"Actually, it was by accident that I became a trainer," Murray said. "Being an assistant trainer to Kay Jensen, I thought that was the biggest thing I could ever do.

"I'd worked for Woody Stephens, for John Nerud, good people. And then somebody sent us a horse that was all messed up.

"Me and Kay argued about what to do with him. Turn to Johnny. I said he needed time to develop. Kay didn't want him sitting around doing nothing.

"I quit, got my trainer's license. I remembered what Mr. Nerud told me, that anybody can get 'em fit, it's knowing when not to run 'em that counts."

New York was grinding, New Orleans was crawfish pie and me-oh-my-oh on the bayou. She returned to the eastern tracks to be closer to a lovely, supportive, free-spirited family.

"My brother married a Cambodian woman," she said. "My sister married a man from South America.

"Race has never been an issue around our barn."

At Atlantic City, in her Barn X office, there was a crib on the floor, a winner's circle photo of Justa Playboy on the wall.

"One of the first horses I bought for Mr. Bob Levy," she said. "Ran him 27 times, finished off the board only once.

"Won short, won long. He was really, really crooked-legged. When he ran he looked like he was carrying a piano uphill. But he tried, against all odds."

Murray has tried, against tough odds. A prejudice against female trainers is slowly eroding. But Levy and a man named Bob Thibodeaux, a Cajun she met while training in New Orleans, are her only male clients.

Levy, who struck gold with Bet Twice and then Housebuster, applauds Carol's spunk.

"He was the last owner I told about the baby," Murray said. "I was afraid he'd tell me I didn't know anything about babies.

"And then he showed up, with his wife, Cissy, who loves kids, at the house in a great big car.

"The neighbors wondered if this was a drug dealer or a movie star. And they came out with a huge supply of diapers and toys for Thomas."

Some nights, she reads herself to sleep. "I like to read," she said. "Been reading 'The First 12 Months of Life' and a book called 'The Magical Child,' which sounds better than it is.

"And I've been reading a lot of Mark Twain lately. Writers ought to love him because he fought to protect against people stealing stuff, and that's how the copyright came about."

The added responsibility has not dented her zeal for training. For the first 10 months this year, she had 80 starters and won 13 races, with 38 horses in the money.

Her best horse, Idea Que, was claimed away from her recently. But she is high on a 2-year-old named Siempre. Often, optimism is misplaced, just as some of the grass that grows through the concrete turns out to be weeds.

"The only thing that worried me was that a stable goes up and down so much," she said softly. "Me, myself, I can live on nothing.

"If our luck turned sour, I worried about how we'd handle it.

"I remember taking him home for the first time, a Friday night. Big bag of diapers, four bottles.

"I was so excited I didn't sleep the first two days. My brother and sister showed up on Sunday, and by then I was exhausted.

"Every checkup, he's been fine. I couldn't imagine him having a serious problem. If we have problems along the way, hey, everybody has problems."

Valentine, with a heart as big as the starting gate, visualizes no problems Carol Murray can't handle.

"She's always on top of everything," Valentine said.

"What she did didn't surprise me. A lot of women have more courage than a lot of men. I've seen plenty of men crumble under pressure.

"I've raised five kids, three of 'em already finished college. A lot depends on encouraging them, talking to them, teaching them."

It takes that blend of courage and kindness to adopt a child with special needs. The National Adoption Center, located in Philadelphia, has found homes for almost 4,000 hard-to-place kids.

"Minority children, white children over 12, children with physical disabilities or emotional problems, siblings," explained Carolyn Johnson, executive director of the adoption center.

"The number of single-parent adoptions is rising. I feel positive about it. People are educated to the trials and tribulations.

"It helps to have a loving family nearby. We did a study on who adopts children with special needs.

"They tend to be people who are middle-class, who have a faith system, a feel for the underdog.

"What concerns us now, is the growing number of crack-addicted babies, of AIDS babies. No studies are available to pinpoint the possible long-range effects."

Carol Murray heard ominous, if well-intentioned, warnings and sprinted past them, her red hair rippling in the wind, her jaw set.

"I figured," she explained, "he wasn't getting a perfect home with me. He doesn't have a father.

"I live a kind of crazy lifestyle, long, tough hours. Why look for the perfect child when I don't have the perfect home to offer?

"But I love Thomas and we'll handle whatever comes our way."

If that isn't perfect, it's close enough to be in the photo finish.

Accentuating the Positive

Philadelphia Daily News
March 13, 1997

BRUCE JENNER didn't like what he saw in the mirror, so he decided to rearrange it. Not the mirror. His face. With cosmetic surgery.

Is that sad? Bruce Jenner won the decathlon gold medal in the '76 Olympics and everyone knew his face, from the Olympic telecasts, from the front of the Wheaties box, from "Good Morning America."

"It was a stupid thing to do," Jenner admits now. "Did it about 10 years ago when I didn't feel good about myself. Had that Bob Hope ski-jump nose, I was by myself in my bad years. Did it help? No!"

You don't read much about Jenner's bad years in his new self-help book called "Finding the Champion Within."

Hey, who wants to hear advice about reaching your full potential from someone who turned a gold medal into brass, who turned love into loneliness, champagne into a sink full of dirty dishes?

Jenner planted his flag at the summit in '76, the dyslexic kid with the fragile self-confidence who reached down deep inside himself to score 8,618 points in the grueling 10 events. The view from the top of the mountain was exhilarating.

"Life is not easy," Jenner replied, when asked about the plunge into the valley of despair. "You have to work at life. Olympic athlete, training 365 days a year, that's not a well-rounded lifestyle.

"I became so obsessed with winning I didn't grow up as a human being. All I thought about was scoring points. At 26, I was still like a kid.

"And then I got thrown into the big, bad world and I was out there, trying to survive. I relied on too many other people to make decisions for me. I got taken advantage of by people. I had nothing left.

"I lost my motivation. 'Why work? You don't end up with anything.' I lost confidence in myself. And then, in 1989–90, I said, 'This is ridiculous.' I knew I was at my best when I was going after something. I decided to take the same Bruce Jenner who won the gold and climb the mountain of life."

Shazam. Six months later, Cindy Garvey introduced him to a woman named Kris. "Greatest day of my life," Jenner gushed. "I'm in love for the first time in my life. That day turned my life around.

"She's my wife, my best friend, my best buddy, my partner. We had a child, and there's another on the way, the 10th between us, and then, I retire. Enough."

Ten, nice number. Ten events in the decathlon. Ten steps in Jenner's plan, 10 ways to grab control of your life and fulfill your dreams.

Would have been a nice touch to charge $10 for the book, instead of $23. Would have been a nice touch if more of the thoughts were original. Jenner borrows freely and heavily from others. In one five-page stretch he quotes Napoleon Hill, Steven Ungerleider and Jacqueline Golding, Steven Spielberg, Jack Nicklaus, Charles Garfield, Muhammad Ali and Les Brown.

When he lectures on focus, he uses slugger Henry Aaron as an example. Says Aaron used to face a pitcher while peering through a small eyelet hole in his baseball cap. How did Aaron ever survive to hit all those homers? Years after he retired, Aaron remembered squinting through his cap while sitting in the dugout, a different slant entirely.

The leap into network television was crammed with terror. They expected Jenner to read cue cards, a frightening task for someone with dyslexia. He has found a way to compensate, perhaps through audio books, because he can now recall chapter and verse of what he considers significant thoughts.

I run Steve Carlton's theory past him, that man is the only species that sets limits on itself, and you can almost hear his invisible Rolodex flipping until he comes to the "Confidence" card.

"I have more confidence in people than they have in themselves," he said solemnly. "I've been able to climb that mountain. I was able to reach down inside my soul and there was something there that enabled me to overcome the obstacles. Every time I needed it.

"Sure, I had doubts. I had fears. I made all those things work for me. Fear is what stops most people. They think, 'What if I fail?' Well, fear is part of the game. The whole key is to make it work for you."

Cus D'Amato said the very same thing. Told it to Jose Torres, who put it in a book. Told it to Mike Tyson who used to quote Cus a lot, before he met Don King. And now, Jenner is carrying, you should excuse the expression, the fear-and-fire torch.

I shouldn't scoff at Jenner. He's a huge success, making piles of money as a motivational speaker, with his airplane company, his food-supplement company. He's joyously married, giddily anticipating another child. And there's some good, solid, common-sense advice in the book.

But I couldn't resist checking out what I wrote in '76 about Chrystie, his first wife, who worked part time as an airline stewardess and washed his lucky socks while Jenner trained 365 days a year.

"That wasn't even close," Jenner said sternly. "That was more of a media story than a personal story. I worked. I sold insurance, helped pay the bills. There was nobody out there helping me. People change and move on. She's doing fine. I'm doing fine. The media just jumped on that story."

They were such a handsome, earnest young couple, can you blame the media for turning the story into a warm, fuzzy trampoline? We all spent a lot of space writing about the pole vault tucked behind the couch, the 42-inch hurdle in their cramped little living room.

Was that a myth, too?

"The hurdle was there," Jenner said. "I didn't just look at that hurdle. It stared at me. The room was too small for me to jump it, so I'd visualize clearing it, all the time slow-motion exercises.

"You have to compete. From the day we're born, we compete for attention, we compete for toys, we compete for better grades. In our society, you have to be competitive.

"And the greatest competition is within ourselves. There are demons we have to deal with. I compete with myself to become a better person, a better husband, a better father, a better businessman.

"I hope to compete every day of my life. You have to. That's what makes life fun. If I stopped competing, I'd just be living one day at a time."

I wished him a good day.

Take Five—Visit These Best Seaside Destinations for Fine Dining

Philadelphia Daily News
July 18, 2003

YOU WANT a memorable shore meal—fine food, smooth service, handsome setting.

You want something more adventurous than flounder stuffed with crabmeat. You don't want to drop $900 at a blackjack table in order to be "comped" at some dimly lit, early-bordello-styled casino restaurant.

OK, so our favorite shore restaurant, Chef Vola's, is in the basement of a house on a dead-end street, raucous as a family reunion some nights. Low ceiling, tomato cans for light fixtures, Sinatra on the stereo, the Sopranos on the wall, autographed. Cash only. BYOB.

You can't get a prime-time weekend reservation from Memorial Day to Labor Day. Weeknights, you've got a shot. Never on Monday, even if New Year's Eve falls on a Monday. Just one of the charming superstitions of Louise Esposito, the Mom in this quintessential mom-and-pop operation.

Louise makes the desserts. Save room for the incredible banana cream pie, still the most fun you can have in Atlantic City with your clothes on.

Louise also greets you, asks about your kids, your grandchildren. Hopes you will ask about hers. Husband Michael is in the kitchen, along with their son Michael. Louis, another son, is out front, opening your wine, scattering one-liners like grated Parmesan, reciting the evening's specials with the lyric fervor of a Venetian gondolier.

The food is terrific, the atmosphere festive, because someone in the room is celebrating a birthday or anniversary. Or maybe it just feels that way. The basic, one-page laminated menu features steak, chicken and veal dishes at remarkably reasonable prices. Everything is a la carte, but those vegetable side dishes will serve four. Or more.

Pay attention when Louis declaims the specials. He has badgered his dad into offering more seafood items like pan-seared red snapper with a peach beurre blanc sauce, or salmon with a pistachio crust.

They recently added a wonderful bean salad, dusted with pecorino romano cheese and sprinkled with a red wine vinaigrette, to an appetizer list that features fresh Buffalo mozzarella, sliced tomatoes and roasted peppers. And Louise has come up with a rum butter cheesecake for folks who don't count cards or calories.

Try for a weeknight reservation or very early or very late on weekends. Persevere. It's worth it.

Diverse Team of Lively 13's on Right Road

Philadelphia Daily News
May 25, 2004

WHEN'S THE LAST TIME a Philadelphia baseball team covered 3,720 miles in a stick-shift double-clutch bus, a bus built in 1947 when a toilet and air conditioning were optional? Sixteen cities in 20 days? South to Durham, N.C., west to the Iowa cornfields, north to Chicago's bleakest neighborhood, east to the emerald pastures of Cooperstown, N.Y., and then back home by way of Harlem?

If you guessed it might have been the Philadelphia Stars, a legendary Negro League team, go to the head of the baseball history class. It's about to happen again, this time a very different Philadelphia Stars team: fifteen 13-year-old kids; five white; five African-American; five Hispanic.

Confucius said that a journey of a thousand miles begins with but a single step. This odyssey began with a passionate dream of Steve Bandura, program director at the Marian Anderson Recreation Center at 17th and Fitzwater. Bandura wanted to honor the hardscrabble barnstorming of the Negro Leaguers, wanted kids to learn about baseball, about each other, about diversity.

"There will be no video games on the bus," Bandura says firmly. "I want them to look at the scenery, to look at America."

And when America looks back at them, it will see this diverse, handsome squad, not one baseball cap worn backward, not a single shirttail flapping, no shoelaces dangling. Nor will it hear profanity, trash talk, arrogant slang.

Bandura is a disciplinarian, not just a dreamer of impossible dreams; Don Quixote with an aluminum fungo bat for a lance, jabbing at the windmills of bigotry; riding a creaky old bus across the landscape, trampling stereotypes along the way. Seven years ago he shepherded a mostly black playground team called the Monarchs on a similar barnstorming trip. That one honored the 50th anniversary of Jackie Robinson integrating Major League Baseball. That was a younger team, on a shorter journey (13 days, 2,000 miles), games being booked on the fly. Same Flxible Clipper bus, the "e" missing, perhaps to make the bus sound swifter.

That trip ended at Robinson's gravesite in Brooklyn. Bandura gave the kids brand-new baseballs and asked them to write a message to be left there. One kid wrote, "Thank you for changing my life."

"Robinson integrated Major League Baseball," Bandura says, "but Little League remains segregated. And that's because neighborhoods in most cities, including this one, remain segregated. Ignorance creates fear, breeds intolerance. On this team the kids learn about other cultures, other lifestyles."

Peter Capolino, president of Mitchell & Ness, bought the bus for $25,000 and turned it over to Bandura. Outfits the kids in snazzy uniforms. Each kid and coach gets a throwback jersey. Hence the name "Throwback Tour."

"I was thinking of calling it 'A Little Exposure Goes a Long Way,'" confesses Bandura, who chose a Dick Allen 1972 White Sox uniform as his throwback jersey.

"Steve Bandura is a saint," Capolino gushes. "This man could have gone on to a lucrative career in marketing, but chooses to work with kids instead. That playground at 17th and Fitzwater is immaculate.

"You know, I never wanted to be in business. I always wanted to be a school teacher. In 1970, when I got out of the Army, my father was not in good health. I filled in at Mitchell & Ness for a short time . . . and I never left.

"I always wanted to have some influence on children. We never had any of our own. The business had been small and struggling for many years. When it started to get successful the people buying my products were young, urban kids from all over the city. I felt I should give back to help youngsters find their way.

"Steve Bandura is probably living the life I wanted to live. He is trying to unify people, to battle racial prejudices. He started in his neighborhood playground and has expanded his horizons. This trip, for these kids, will be like going to another planet. I think it will be a pivotal moment in their lives, and I'd love to see other, bigger businesses jump in to support it."

When the Stars made an early-season appearance at Citizens Bank Park, along with survivors of the original Stars, Phillies Charities, Inc., handed over a $10,000 check. But Bandura is still about $20,000 short of budget for the trip and is searching for a qualified bus driver.

We've established that he's a dreamer and a disciplinarian. Add romantic to the mix, because he proposed to Robin Garland on the pitcher's mound during a trip to Doubleday Field in Cooperstown.

"I took a team up there when they celebrated 'Pride and Passion' week," Bandura explains. "I had my pitcher fake an injury. I went out there and then I waved for Robin to come out of the stands to check the kid out. I proposed and we have it on videotape. It seemed like forever before she said, 'Yes!'"

Robin recalls: "I was totally floored. I had just been accepted to study physical therapy at Jefferson Hospital and when the pitcher got hurt, I thought, 'I'm not ready, I'm not ready.' Time stands still at moments like that, and according to him it felt like hours before I responded."

They have a 5-year-old daughter named Stephanie and a precocious 2-year-old boy named Scott. "Steve is compassionate, generous, selfless, humble," says Robin. She likes that he decided to assemble this roster of dissimilar players. "I wish we could have encompassed more. I know he tried to reach out to the Asian community. The trip is a great idea and the kids will get more from it 10 years from now. Hopefully there will be a ripple effect. Exposure and education are the best ways of breaking down barriers."

Assistant coach Bob Hopkins says winning games is a secondary aspect of the trip. "Our goal is to show that diversity works," he says. "That's the reason this team was put together. You can see how these kids interact. Five minutes after they first got together, it was like they were lifelong friends."

Shawn O'Neill is another assistant coach who has known Bandura for 5 years. "I coached against him with 8-year-olds," O'Neill says. "He asked my son, Shawn, if he'd like to play on the Stars. It was a no-brainer. You look at these kids, you wouldn't know they come from different neighborhoods. They're like the best of friends."

John Bromley, another assistant, recalls competing against Bandura in a softball league in the mid-1980s. "One year our team won the championship and Steve's team finished second," he says. "He was the only guy from his team to show up at the banquet. We're cut from similar cloth and we still play hockey together.

"The one thing he's always stressed is racial diversity. We've got four of my players from the Northeast on the team. I'm tired of the knucklehead mentality that creates prejudice. The world is changing. You get on board with it, or it passes you by. And Steve has been way out in front.

"I've learned more baseball in the last 2 years, working with him, than all the years I've been playing the game. You pay close attention every game, you'll see something you've never seen before. I'm probably more excited about the trip than the kids. We're going to get to see and touch baseball history and that's a lifetime dream."

To recap, Bandura is strict, compassionate, idealistic. Add stubborn to the mix. "It's a player-centric team," says one of the dads.

Bandura explains: "If there's a question about playing time, I'll talk to the player. I will not talk to the parent about playing time.

"The kids are all different, different neighborhoods, different life-styles. And they defy stereotypes."

Tim Vernon lives in Fort Washington, goes to a mostly white school in a mostly white neighborhood. Tony, his dad, is an executive with Johnson & Johnson, who grew up celebrating Robin Roberts's birthday. Wears a throwback Phillies windbreaker to games. Jean Vernon is a first-grade teacher.

Surely, there must be teams closer to home that would welcome Tim, a pitcher/catcher.

"There's nothing that would offer Tim this kind of experience," Jean says. "Living in the suburbs, going to an independent school, you're not really seeing the whole picture. Tim feels blessed to be part of this team."

Anthony Ortiz lives in the Northeast, the son of a retired policeman. His mom, Leticia, is an elementary school nurse. "Steve has a wonderful vision," she says, "and he's working hard to fulfill it. I'm not sure the kids realize the opportunity they have here. It's an opportunity so many kids can't even dream about.

"People should be culturally sensitive. Steve was before his time when it came to that. We all have the same likes and dislikes. We all need a roof over our heads, food in our bellies, clothes on our backs. People fear what they don't know. This team gives the kids a chance to see that other kids are not so different."

Rasheed Stewart lives within walking distance of the Anderson rec center. His dad is a firefighter, his mom, Cherise, a human resources manager.

"There's so much ignorance and prejudice out there," she sighs. "Understanding needs to start when kids are young. We may all have different cultures, but people are people. These kids get along great."

Not all the kids come from stable, two-parent homes. Bandura has coached them for 5 years, thinks he knows them, hopes they will mature into good citizens. "There is always the lure of the streets," he says glumly.

Meanwhile they hone their skills in indoor batting cages. There's a weight room designed for 8- to 14-year-olds. There are Friday night sessions devoted to learning baseball's history. They are the "Good News Bears" and are counting the days until the magical trip begins.

They are eager to step out of Iowa's rustling corn at the Field of Dreams, eager to see the ivy clinging to Wrigley Field's walls, eager to watch them churn out baseball bats at the Louisville Slugger Museum, eager to scan Mike Schmidt's plaque at the Hall of Fame.

Bandura requires each kid to keep a journal. He will keep one, too.

It is the quintessential feel-good story at a time when America is achingly desperate for feel-good stories.

Let the Debates Begin:
Sports Film Fest Here

Philadelphia Daily News
October 1, 2008

THERE'S A STORY behind the story of "The Pride of the Yankees." Ray Didinger dug it up with archeologist fervor, using one of those silky brushes to sweep aside half-a-century of Hollywood debris.

"The movie was made in 1942," Didinger said. "The producers knew that the only people going to the movies were women. The men were all off to war.

"They decided they had to make it a love story, the story of Lou and Eleanor Gehrig. So the poster shows Gary Cooper in a suit, hugging Teresa Wright. No bats, no balls, no gloves.

"The movie is billed as 'America's Greatest Love Story.' When they reissued it in 1946, the poster showed Cooper in Yankee pinstripes, two different campaigns. So it might have been the very first sports 'chick flick.'"

The vignette will be part of a book Didinger has written with Glen Macnow, his partner on a weekend WIP (610-AM) talk show. It's called "The Ultimate Book of Sports Movies."

The book won't be out until next fall, but their top 10 is a relevant list now, with the U.S. Sports Film Festival chugging into Philadelphia, Oct. 23 to 26. The festival's Web site plugs a book by Randy Williams called "Sports Cinema—100 Movies: The Best of Hollywood's Athletic Heroes, Losers, Myths, and Misfits."

Williams ranks "The Hustler" on top. Didinger/Macnow rate it ninth. I have it eighth. And Stan Isaacs, former *Newsday* columnist, an inveterate list-maker, and author of a new book, "Ten Moments That Shook the Sports World," loved "the dingy poolroom atmosphere" and has it third on his esoteric list.

"We've got two lists of 'worst' movies," Macnow said proudly. "Worst original and worst remake. Both Babe Ruth movies are in there, the one with William Bendix and the one with John Goodman.

"We've got the classic, critically acclaimed movies in the book, as well as the stupid comedies, movies like 'Horse Feathers' with the Marx Brothers. People like them."

Yo, they have "Caddyshack" ranked sixth all-time. Aarghhhh! "You can't be on a golf course," Macnow argued, "without someone doing the Cinderella bit, 'This crowd has gone deadly silent, a Cinderella story outta nowhere. . . . [I]t's in the hole, it's in the hole.'"

Inspiration for the book came from someone else's list. "The *New York Times*," Macnow said, "ran this list of 1,000 best movies. I looked for sports movies and looked and looked. There were maybe three, maybe four on the list, 'Raging Bull,' 'Sporting Life,' a rodeo movie called 'Junior Bonner.' No 'Rocky,' no 'Hustler.' It's like they still regard sports as the toy department."

Not in Philadelphia, which makes this the logical site for the first annual sports film festival. It will include all sorts of panel discussions, including a hard look at memorable "sports moments" in non-sports movies.

"We've got a chapter devoted to those," Didinger said. "The football scene from 'M*A*S*H.' The killer stalking a tennis player in Hitchcock's 'Strangers on a Train.' And, of course, the scene from 'Diner' where the Colts fan is quizzing his girlfriend before he asks her to marry him.

"Barry Levinson wrote the original list of questions. Then he showed them to Ernie Accorsi, who was general manager of the Colts. They were way too easy. One question was, 'What are the Colts' colors?' and Ernie changed it to 'What were the original Colts' colors?' which were green and gray.

"Sean Payton (Saints coach) gave us one from 'One Flew Over the Cuckoo's Nest' and it's not Jack Nicholson doing the play-by-play on the World Series. It's when he gets the Indian to play basketball.

"We asked celebrities for their favorite movie, and James Gandolfini picked 'Bull Durham' just for the scene where the manager tells Kevin Costner he's being released. Gandolfini called the look on Costner's face a sublime piece of acting."

Didinger/Macnow have "Bull Durham" fifth. Williams has it second. I have it second. It doesn't even make Isaacs's top 10. Let the debates begin.

TOP TENS

Randy Williams:
1. The Hustler
2. Bull Durham
3. This Sporting Life
4. Chariots of Fire
5. Raging Bull
6. Olympia

7. Rocky
8. Breaking Away
9. Requiem for a Heavyweight
10. Slap Shot

Ray Didinger/Glen Macnow:
1. Rocky
2. Hoosiers
3. Raging Bull
4. The Natural
5. Bull Durham
6. Caddyshack
7. The Longest Yard
8. Slap Shot
9. The Hustler
10. North Dallas Forty

Stan Isaacs:
1. Chariots of Fire
2. Field of Dreams
3. The Hustler
4. The Sting
5. Rocky
6. The Bingo Long Traveling All-Stars and Motor Kings
7. The Natural
8. The Loneliness of the Long Distance Runner
9. Downhill Racer
10. Body and Soul

Stan Hochman:
1. Raging Bull
2. Bull Durham
3. Rocky
4. The Natural
5. Hoosiers
6. Chariots of Fire
7. Field of Dreams
8. The Hustler
9. North Dallas Forty
10. Body and Soul

A Rubberized Field of Dreams

Philadelphia Daily News
May 27, 2009

THERE'S THIS VACANT MEADOW in Churchville. There's this fistful of folks in Northampton Township who want to transform that vacant meadow into a Miracle League baseball field for special-needs kids. A safe, smooth, flat, rubberized field, so that wheelchairs don't topple over first base or get stuck in the sand around second base.

"It all began with Coach Eddie (Bagwell)," said Diane Alford, one of the founders of Miracle League and its current executive director. "He coached a T-ball team in Conyers, which is near Atlanta, and he noticed this kid in a wheelchair who came to every practice, every game, to watch his brother play.

"Finally, he put the kid on the team. And then 35 other disabled kids came out, and we formed four teams, even though we were afraid of what might happen on a regulation field. And that's what happened, wheelchairs toppled and some got stuck in the dirt around second base.

"My brother Dean was a Georgia Tech graduate with a background in engineering. He got together with architects to create a flat, rubberized, safe field for those kids. Through the Rotary Club, they raised a million dollars and built the field. And now there are 220 of those fields, including one in Puerto Rico and one in Canada."

Plus the one on the drawing board in Northampton Township. The one that will cost $750,000 to build, a daunting number that can't be reached solely through cookie sales or car washes or canisters on Wawa counters. Corporate sponsors are needed, even in this wobbly economy.

"We reached out to the Rich Ashburn Foundation, and they responded," said Debbi Katz, a leader of the Miracle League of Northampton Township group. "We hope the Phillies will get involved. In Pittsburgh, the Pirates contributed $250,000 to build a field." Katz has a background as an occupational therapist. She has a brother with Down syndrome, and that led her to get involved with the Special Olympics.

"Access to fields, that's hard," she sighed. "There are 850 kids in sports programs in Northampton Township. The special-needs kids were scheduled from 5:30 to 7 on Sunday nights, and nobody was watching.

"And then Joe Hand Jr. showed up at the township meeting, when the discussion involved what to do with the piece of land adjoining two existing fields. Bill Gannon was there, with the same idea."

"It was 2 years ago," said Hand, a vital force in his dad's company, which promotes boxing matches and has branched out into mixed martial arts closed-circuit action. "The parks and recreation department told us we could have the land, but we would have to raise the money to build the field.

"We had the land; we had drawings. The Ashburn Foundation promotes kids playing baseball. We have talked about naming the field for Rich Ashburn and Harry Kalas. It was a natural fit.

"We joined the national Miracle League organization. Diane Alford has been terrific, offering encouragement. She's coming to visit on June 22 to help us plan the fundraising, recruiting volunteers, spreading the word.

"Meanwhile, we plan to talk to Comcast, to UPS, to the Phillies. There are lots of construction guys who live in the area. They've offered bulldozers when the time comes. Meanwhile, when Cole Hamels got his Camaro as the World Series MVP, the Chevy dealers gave us $8,500 in his name.

"We held a beef-and-beer night that raised $12,000. We're selling bricks with people's names on them. We'll have T-shirts. We're selling tickets to a Trenton Thunder game on July 19. With private donations, we're up to $50,000.

"I went to watch the dedication of a field in Sewell (N.J.). It was an incredible experience, the parents crying tears of joy, the kids with dazzling smiles. Plus, there were these girls, softball players, acting as 'buddies' for the disabled kids. And they were so enthusiastic to be part of it."

No Iowa cornfield has to be leveled, no otherworldly voice has to command, "Build it and they will come." It can be the quintessential field of dreams.

"In the past," Alford said, "it took an average of 18 months from organizing to Opening Day. Now, it's taking 24 months. With the economy the way it is, you just have to think longer, work harder."

"It's a challenge," Katz said bluntly. "Right now, we need more awareness. The outfield fence will be portable, so that the field can be used for soccer, for lacrosse. And it's not just for Bucks County kids, it's for Montgomery County, Delaware County, Chester County.

"These kids struggle day to day, to take a shower, to brush their teeth, to follow directions. When they're out there, on the field, they feel good, they feel happy.

"I'm extremely optimistic. I just can't imagine we're not going to do it."

Shonda Schilling, on Handling Life's Curveballs

Philadelphia Daily News
May 31, 2010

SHONDA SCHILLING has written a terrific book called "The Best Kind of Different." It's about raising a child with Asperger's syndrome. It's about saintly patience. It's about mending a fraying marriage. It's about parenting four kids plus a husband, all with ADHD. It's about life after baseball.

"It's a love story," Shonda said the other day, fresh from another New England book signing. "It's about how I love my kids, how I love my husband, how I love myself."

The kids are Gehrig, Gabriella, Grant and Garrison. The husband is Curt Schilling. Uh huh, the guy who pitched for Boston in a World Series with a bloody sock covering a stapled tendon in his ankle.

Pitched here, too. You remember him as the big, strong, gabby guy who pitched gallantly for the '93 Phillies. Or you remember him as the guy who draped a towel over his head when Mitch Williams pitched the ninth. Same guy!

Enough about Curt. This is about Shonda and Grant and the residue of guilt for not getting him diagnosed properly until he was 7. Kids with Asperger's syndrome, their brains are wired differently.

Malls can be mellow or menacing. Meals can be pleasant or painful. Focus goes from fuzzy to sharp in the blink of an eye. Those early years, Curt would second-guess Shonda's parenting skills in tense phone calls from the road. Bystanders sneered at her, or snickered, or clucked sympathetically, as she wrestled with a seemingly out-of-control child. Screams happened.

And now? "You can look at Grant, talk to him, for 4 days," Shonda said, "and think he's fine. That fifth day? WOW!

"We have had to rewire our brains. That's where the deep breaths come in. And we have to anticipate his reactions.

"He will walk on the pool cover. And encourage a friend to walk on the pool cover until they get wet to the knees. We can't shout at him. We have to take him aside and explain the dangers. Again."

Asperger's kids can be charming and they can be hammer-blunt. "*People* magazine is doing a story on our family," Shonda said, chuckling at the episode. "We explained it to Grant.

"The reporter is riding with us, sitting in the front seat. And then suddenly, here's Grant yelling, 'Who is this person? Why is she sitting in my seat?'"

Curt retired from baseball. Surely, that helped. Another set of eyes, another pair of hands around the house. "It didn't go all that smoothly," Shonda confessed. "Having him around, 24/7. I wanted the house run the way I ran it. I wanted him to parent my way!"

The growling exchanges got noisier, more frequent. They embraced marriage counseling. "You have to keep your eyes open, your heart open, but most important, you have to keep your ears open," she said. "You have to listen to the other person. And now, I'm more in love with my husband than I've ever been."

The Schillings have been deeply involved with the ALS Association, Lou Gehrig's disease. Hence, the name of their oldest son. Shonda spent too much time in tanning salons and reaped the cruel harvest of melanoma. She helped create the Shade Foundation of America.

And now, here she is on the front lines of the fight to spread awareness of Asperger's syndrome. When does she have time for fun?

"I have lots of fun in my life," she countered swiftly. "My family brings me joy. Reaching out to someone brings me joy.

"The first time I spoke in public about Grant and parenting an Asperger's child, there was a woman waiting for me afterwards. She was sobbing, so that I could barely understand her at first.

"I calmed her, I spoke to her. Now she knew she was not alone. I loved standing there with that woman. What is more fulfilling than to help someone? I told her everything was going to be all right.

"We talked as a family about writing the book. I wrote it while the kids were at school. Sure, the laundry got backed up. Yes, Christmas shopping got frantic."

Was there never an anguished "why me" moment? Not even when Gehrig developed anorexia? "No," Shonda said. "For Gehrig it was a matter of control. Eating was something he could control. I'm proud of being a mother, I'm proud of being a wife. You do what you have to do. All this has made me stronger."

That must help with the jumble of dealing with four kids and a husband with ADHD. "Uh," she corrected gently, "I tell people I have five kids!"

Iguana Days and Nights . . .
OH, and Liz Was There Too

Philadelphia Daily News
March 24, 2011

THOSE VIOLET EYES. Those sparkling violet eyes. That's what I remember most about my lunch with Elizabeth Taylor in that hotel dining room in Puerto Vallarta.

I was close enough to reach out and touch her if I dared. I didn't dare.

Those violet eyes were flashing hostility. Why not? She had been through tough times with Eddie Fisher, and he was Jewish and from Philadelphia, and I was Jewish, from Philadelphia, and a writer, and if that wasn't a toxic trifecta, it sure seemed that way gazing into those violet eyes.

Richard Burton was there. He was starring in a movie called "Night of the Iguana."

Deborah Kerr was in the movie, too. Her husband had once had a fling with Ava Gardner, who was in the movie.

Sue Lyon, of "Lolita" fame, was in the movie. She brought along her boyfriend, Hampton Fancher III, skinny as a pool cue, always carrying a book of poetry. I do remember Ms. Taylor snarling, "If he kisses her elbow one more time, I'm gonna throw up."

John Huston was the director. His daughter, Anjelica, was coming to visit, so he had to send his girlfriend home.

And, oh yeah, Ms. Gardner, who had it in her contract that she didn't have to talk with the media, decided to take water-ski lessons from a handsome instructor.

Water-ski lessons? That represented a menace to Ms. Gardner's health and the movie timetable, so two burly security guys lugged the water-ski instructor to the airport and handed him a one-way ticket to Mexico City.

Which helps you understand what I was doing in Puerto Vallarta shortly after covering the 1964 World Series.

I was there to chronicle the madcap behavior of this gaudy bunch of Hollywood folks making a movie based on a Tennessee Williams play.

It was J. Ray Hunt's idea. He was the managing editor, and the price of the *Daily News* was going from a nickel to a dime, so he thought that a series on celebrities gone wild might boost circulation.

He told me to book a flight to Puerto Vallarta.

He didn't tell me that the airport lacked landing lights so you had to fly there during daylight hours.

He told me not to warn the movie people that I was coming. He didn't tell me that I'd find a town without telephones or air conditioning or television sets or newspapers.

I got a hero's welcome from the movie crew. They were desperate to know the details of the World Series.

I told them about Joe Pepitone losing a ball in the background of white shirts, and about Johnny Keane explaining his use of Bob Gibson in game seven: "I had a commitment to his heart."

And if that wasn't enough, Grayson Hall was in the movie. Got an Academy Award nomination for best supporting actress in it.

Her real name was Shirley Grossman, and her mom lived on the Parkway, and she felt sorry for this Philadelphia writer, so she whispered some significant gossip and that helped.

Burton was terrific, a man's man, an eloquent storyteller, a baseball enthusiast (he'd hit a home run in the Broadway show league while appearing in "Camelot" and had fallen in love with the sport).

I taught him 8-ball and 9-ball at the tattered pool room, and wound up predicting that his relationship with Taylor would not last long, which was dumb and wrong.

I got to interview the main characters, except for Gardner, and ached with loneliness, so I headed home two days early.

The *Daily News* trucks were carrying my photo as "Our Man in Puerto Vallarta," so I didn't dare show my face.

I hunkered in our second-floor apartment near the Art Museum for two days before checking in at the paper with the first two installments of the series.

Years later, having dinner with Sheila, who had lived downstairs in those days, talk turned to my Mexican adventure.

I described sneaking home and hiding out for two days, and her face flushed and she shuddered in relief.

"I had heard a man's footsteps," she confessed. "I knew Stan was in Mexico and I thought, 'If Gloria is entertaining someone, well, that's none of my business,' but it's great to hear, after all these years, that it was really you."

They'll Come If, and When, It's Built

Philadelphia Daily News
May 18, 2011

THEY ARE GOING TO BUILD a baseball academy at the Marian Anderson rec center. They said so on Sept. 22. They just didn't say when.

And now, almost 8 months later, nothing. Not a cute photo of dignitaries wearing hard hats, gripping shovels, breaking ground. Not a backhoe, a tractor, a bulldozer at work. Nothing.

Hey, it could be worse. They announced an Urban Youth Academy for Hialeah, Fla., in January 2009 and 28 months later, all they have is a set of blueprints gathering dust.

You can send a sympathy card to Hialeah Mayor Julio Robaina after they start construction at 17th and Fitzwater. But first, why has it taken so long to get started here?

Major League Baseball says it never had a definite timetable, and, besides, we had a rough winter, weatherwise.

The Phillies say it's not that the project is late getting started, it's just that the announcement came too early.

The attorney handling the bidding process says it's complicated when you have this many partners in a project.

"There's nothing sinister involved," said Dave Montgomery, the Phillies president. "The road is paved with good intentions."

Yikes. It's the road to hell that is paved with good intentions. We're talking about an academy that will teach baseball skills while offering tutoring and academic help to ease the path toward college scholarships.

The Phillies have pledged help in maintaining the "show" field planned for FDR Park, and personnel to conduct clinics. They are also responsible for any cost overruns on the project.

"We might take some of the blame for pushing up the announcement," Montgomery said. "We wanted a player there and Ut (Chase Utley) was there."

That was nice, but a kid from Penn Charter wound up stealing the show. Demetrius Jennings talked about his love for the game, his years of playing ball at Anderson, about coming back to mentor kids after he gets his medical degree.

Will the Academy be up and running before Jennings gets his degree?

After a week of prompting, Jimmie Lee Solomon, MLB's executive vice president of baseball development, answered some questions by email.

"Since there was no timetable," Solomon wrote, "we can neither claim to being on time, ahead of schedule, nor admit to being delayed. In addition to our diligent planning, weather has played a factor in our ability to move things along at a quicker pace."

That is pure nonsense. We could have had a tropical heat wave in December and it would not have impacted the start of construction. First, you have to put the project out for bids, and that can be done even if you're up to your armpits in snow. Is the nearly $3 million from MLB, Baseball Tomorrow, the city and state still there?

"The money," Solomon wrote, "that was allocated for the Urban Youth Academy is still available and has remained unchanged."

That's good news in the light of the new governor's cost-cutting approach, in the light of Philadelphia's slashing of school funds, in the light of an economy still struggling.

Maybe we can just blame it on the lawyers? Mike DiBerardinis, the Parks and Recreation commissioner, who is gung-ho for building the academy, has been on vacation and unavailable for comment.

Ed Fagan, a city attorney, in charge of special grants projects, pointed to the complicated financing.

"It's been like a ping-pong ball, going back and forth," Fagan said. "There's the complexity of the financing, so many different partners.

"All of the site surveying has been done, all the practicality studies have been done. We thought it could be handled as a design-and-build project. It turns out there has to be four-part bidding, design is one component, construction is another.

"We were hoping to have the field in the Ashburn complex ready for play this summer. The money is still there."

So, once the t's are crossed and the i's dotted, and ground broken, how long before kids are playing ball?

"Once we have our construction team in place," Solomon wrote, "we'll develop a timeline for completion that will be agreed upon by the bid winner and all contributing parties."

Solomon said construction on the first academy, in Compton, Calif., was started in June 2004. It opened in March 2006.

Steve Bandura, director at Anderson, keeps busy with plans.

"The kids are excited, the families are excited," Bandura said. "I'm asked about it, every day.

"We've talked to people who will run the education side, the SAT prep. And we've talked to people who will handle the strength and agility training. Meanwhile, we're just waiting and waiting."

And what about those kids in Hialeah, the ones who have started shaving since the project was announced? Solomon wrote: "The proposed Academy in Hialeah was a stand-alone, it was part of a huge project that suffered when the recession hit nationwide a couple of years ago. We will get it back on track at the appropriate time. Our money to build this Academy is also still allocated."

The Last Bite

Philadelphia Daily News
January 22, 2012

GUYS KEEP SWAGGERING up to Bill Simmons, aka El Wingador, and say how they could do what he does, how much they love chicken wings. "And I tell 'em, 'This isn't about loving wings,'" he grumbles. "'This is about eating wings! Sure, you'll love the first 50. But what about the next 50? And the 50 after that?'"

What El Wingador does is eat chicken wings. Swiftly, thoroughly, tirelessly. He has won the Wing Bowl five times. Five! And now, at 50, he is determined to win it again when the wing-eating, beer-drinking, boob-jiggling festival erupts at the Wells Fargo Center shortly after dawn on Feb. 3.

Last year, in a heartbreaking, jaw-aching defeat, he ate 254 wings—and lost. Lost by one wing to Jonathan Squibb. The loss would stick in his craw, if he had a craw. "All the years I've competed in Wing Bowl," he says sadly, "when time is up you have 1 minute to finish what's in your mouth. Time was up, Squibb had a ton of food in his mouth. They crowned him, he still had food in his mouth. They interviewed him with the crown on and he still had food in his mouth. People tell me that someone finally walked up to him with a napkin and he got rid of the food in his mouth.

"Ahhhh, Wing Bowl, sometimes they flip-flop on the rules."

Ahhh, Wing Bowl, that orgy of gluttony, nudity, obscenity. A Wing Bowl without controversy is like life without laughter, a day without sunshine, a stripper with her top on.

"My greatest fear in life," says Angelo Cataldi, the WIP-radio morning host and ringmaster of this annual circus, "is that this will be our legacy . . . that we will leave behind naked girls, empty beer cans and a ton of mostly eaten chicken wings. They will look back and say, 'Who started this and who can we sue?' As the years go by, I heap more of the credit on Al Morganti. Because without Al, none of this could have happened."

It was Morganti's idea. "The Eagles would die early, back then," Cataldi's co-host recalls. "I was traveling, covering hockey. Buffalo was wings. I had two staples in my diet: pizza and wings. The Bills kept going to the Super Bowl. They'd lose, but they kept going. The people in

Buffalo had something to watch. We had that dead period leading up to the Super Bowl. Why not steal something from Buffalo? Wings."

The first Wing Bowl was held in the lobby of the Wyndham Franklin Hotel in late January 1993. "We had about 200 people there, watching from the overhang (mezzanine). A guy named Carmen (Cordero) won it."

"And then they asked him what he'd do next," producer Joe Waechter remembers. "And he said, 'Get ready for Wing Bowl 2.'"

"And that," said Cataldi, "was the first time we thought there was gonna be a Wing Bowl 2."

Morganti, the quintessential second banana on the "Morning Show," laterals the credit back to Cataldi. "I had an idea, he ran with it," he said. "It's salesmanship. He is the guy who could sell ice cubes in Alaska."

The venue has changed several times. The prizes, too: $20,000 to the winner, a car, rings and other bling, trips to Mexico for the best entourage, a Harley-Davidson motorcycle to the bounciest wingette.

"It went to another level when that guy from the Mummers came in covered in gold," Morganti says. "Called himself the Golden Buddha. Got us on the front page of the *Daily News.*"

"And then the wingettes became a big part of it, and that ramped things way up," adds Cataldi. "It went from an eating competition to an event. And that's when we had to start selling tickets. We nearly had a riot one year, turning away thousands at 5 o'clock in the morning, the Walt Whitman Bridge backed up."

"The cops recognized me," said Rhea Hughes, a vital part of the "Morning Show." "They were turning away cars, but they let me in. And now, my husband has 30 friends at our house at 4 in the morning, kind of a pregame thing. And then they go to Wing Bowl. It's a boys' morning out."

"Some bad things do good," says El Wingador. "This brings people together. It doesn't make us a bad city. New Orleans has the Mardi Gras and that doesn't make New Orleans a bad city."

His first Wing Bowl was No. 7. "Heavy Kevy was a friend. He won it twice, retired undefeated. He asked me if I ate wings," El Wingador recalls. "I said I wouldn't stop. I'd keep eating until I dropped. They called me 'Chicken Man' back then because I ate chicken every day. He named me 'The Wingador,' but my wife thought it sounded better if we made it 'El Wingador.' I told her I was going to make El Wingador a household name.

"I had to do an eating stunt to qualify. We decided to do a Spanish theme, so I ate 15 Taco Bell chicken burritos in 28 minutes. I walked in, sat down, thought of it as a bar eating contest. Then I looked around, and said, 'Uh oh, this is more than a bar contest.'

"I weighed 262 then. I'll be 330 for this one. I used to eat like I was at a picnic. Now, I eat like I'm going to the electric chair. I got a Liberty Bell for winning that first one, given to me by the mayor, Ed Rendell, at the time. It's on my mantel. And, oh, yeah, a trip to Cancun."

"Heavy Kevy wanted him to pick up the baton," is the way Cataldi remembers it. "Kevy proposed to his girlfriend and vowed to stop eating. So he brought El Wingador into it. He was a godsend; local guy, good eater, good guy. Last year, I almost cried for him. They handed me the results and I tried to hide my feelings. I looked down and Wingador knew right then he'd lost."

El Wingador doesn't talk about revenge, because that's a dish best served cold. It doesn't mesh with his training schedule.

"I get up early, do 2 miles on the treadmill," he says. "After that, I'll eat 10 to 15 pounds of food during the day, a couple of pizzas, some roast-beef hoagies, a couple of pounds of pasta. For dinner, it's mostly protein. And then, after dinner, I go to the gym with my wife, Debby, do the cardio work I need. I go to bed feeling great, wake up feeling great.

"That first year, the only thing that got tired was my jaw. So, down through the years I'd strengthen my jaw by eating frozen Tootsie Rolls. Cram six or seven in my mouth. They don't dissolve, so you have to keep on chewing. I'd go through 10 pounds a week."

He is not a one-trick grazer, like some pro eaters.

"I was a pro in 2003," he says. "I really don't do hot dogs, but I competed in Nathan's at Coney Island. Ate 26 hot dogs, looked over and (Takeru) Kobayashi was at 41. I just shut it down and watched him eat.

"I ate 6 feet of sushi once. Ate 10 pounds of cow's brains at the Glutton Bowl and that got me ranked fourth in the world. They flew me to Los Angeles and I ate 14.4 pounds of cheeseburgers. Nice size. The first six or seven were real good. After that, you don't really taste them."

Winning Wing Bowl five times is hard, becoming a household name is even harder. He worked up a sauce. He has paired with Rastelli Foods with a line of El Wingador products. He has plans for a string of restaurants.

"Wings," he says. "The best chicken pot pie in the world. Mac and cheese. Comfort foods. What people like to eat. Only the best."

He has been pitching a reality television show, seeking America's next big eater.

"I'm looking for someone who can't sing, can't dance, isn't an athlete, but loves to eat," he says. "Start with 100 eaters, narrow the field to 10. Hooters has agreed to host the events. A well-known production company is looking at it."

First, though, will be Wing Bowl 20, with Squibb back to defend his crown against Eaterama, Gentleman Jerry, Boring John and the usual list of suspects. Plus Takeru Kobayashi, the legendary competitive eater from Japan. Kobayashi made a guest appearance last year, gobbling down a cheeseburger in 24.3 seconds.

"Let's face it," El Wingador says, "he could out-eat the table. But I don't think he will do that well in this event. Chicken wings, that involves a bone, and he's not used to that. The time frame is different for him, too.

"He came last year, scouted it. He's thorough that way. He's like me: He doesn't want to go out there and be embarrassed in any way."

Embarrassed? Hardly a word you ever hear at a Wing Bowl. Cataldi and Morganti laugh at some memorable goofs.

"There was the time our vocalist was going to sing 'God Bless America' on a trampoline," Cataldi sighed. "From the first bounce, we knew we were in trouble."

"And how about the time we had two wingettes wrestle in a pit of wings?" Morganti says, chuckling. "They kept getting jabbed with the wings. And then the sauce got in their eyes and they couldn't see. What a mess!"

The screwups, the occasional projectile vomiting ("If you heave, you leave") add still another element to the charm of the babes, the beer, the bedlam.

"I'm in it to win it," El Wingador said solemnly. "But it is a young man's game. I'm 50 and finishing in the top three would be a feat."

Morganti reveals the morning-line odds the day before the event. So will El Wingador be one of the favorites or a longshot?

"I'll figure out the odds when they tell me I have to announce them," Morganti says with a shrug. "Plan is a four-letter word."

Acknowledgments

S INCE APRIL 9, 2015, WHEN STAN PASSED AWAY, I have been fortunate enough to be surrounded by loving family, friends, and even strangers who were Stan's fans, all of whom have helped me navigate my way through his shocking death and the years beyond. I remember a letter I received from Margaret Jackson, a woman who had never met Stan but who had a date with him every Thursday when she tuned in to WIP radio to hear the Grand Imperial Poobah settle the most controversial sports issues of the week. She wrote, "I hope you will write a book about Stan. He had so much still to teach us."

This is that book. I couldn't have written it without the support of this city's distinguished sportswriters, broadcasters, players, and Stan Hochman fans. I especially thank Pat McLoone, Philadelphia Media News's (PMN's) sports managing editor, without whose friendship and sensitivity I could not have gotten through Stan's illness or put together this book, and Ed Barkowitz and Rich Hofmann, who spent weeks identifying and lining up columns for me to include. Ed and I talked almost every week as I wrote and edited.

I appreciate the input and encouragement of my good friends Ray Didinger and his wife, Maria Gallagher, and Angelo Cataldi and his wife, Gail, who have taken this journey with me, along with Steve Bandura, Michael Barkaan, Josh Barnett, Zach Berman, Lorenzo Biggs, Les Bowen, Bob Brookover, Sam Carchidi, Joe Conklin, Michael Days, Don DiJulia, Paul Domowitch, Sam Donnellon, Fran Dunphy, Rob Ellis, the late Bill Fleischman, Weatta Frazier Collins, Big Daddy Graham, the Guv (the Honorable Edward G. Rendell), Paul Hagen, Joe Hand Jr., Joe Hand Sr., Marcus Hayes, Rhea Hughes, Dick Jerardi, Larry Kane, Mike Kern, Coach Jim Lynam, Glen Macnow, Garry and Sondra Maddox, Tom Mahon, Bill Marimow, Jeff McLane, Larry Merchant, Mike Missanelli, the late David Montgomery, Al Morganti, Brad Nowe, Bernie and Gini Parent, Merrill Reese, Fred Shabel, Mike Sielski, Vai Sikahema, John Smallwood, Claire Smith, Zack Stalberg, Jayson Stark, Karl Stark, Dick Vermeil, Cindy Webster, Joe Wechsler, Bill Werndell, Rich Westcott, Bill White, and Marc Zumoff. Thanks go to Stan Wischnowski, PMN senior vice president, attorney Suzanne Mitchell Parillo, and Mike Mercanti for working with me to include the columns and photographs you've seen and read here. I am grateful to the former and current members of the *Philadelphia Daily News* sports staff, who suggested columns and unearthed still another of Stan's "zingers." My gratitude goes to Andy Jasner, Mark Kram Jr., Bob Vetrone Jr., and Deb Woodell. David Luck, my technology guru, held my hand through myriad computer crises.

Thanks also go to Ken Mullner, former executive director of the Adoption Center, who supported me every step of the way.

If you asked Stan to name the sports figure from whom he received the most sage advice, he would say, "Wilt Chamberlain." He always remembered Wilt's saying, "Choose your friends wisely." And that's the message that, from his hospital bed in the intensive care unit, he asked me to transmit to our granddaughter, Sasha. He would have been proud to know that she was the valedictorian of her graduating class at Philadelphia's Central High School and is a student at Barnard College–Columbia University.

The day after Stan's funeral, our daughter, Anndee, and I accepted an award inducting him into the Big 5 Hall of Fame. That honor meant so much to him; he had been talking about it for weeks. I extend my gratitude to the Philadelphia Sports Writers Association, the Miracle League of Northampton, the Adoption Center, and the Pennsylvania Golden Gloves and Joe Hand Boxing Gym, all of which have established awards in Stan's name, and to the anticipated Philadelphia Museum of Sports, which—thanks to Lou Scheinfeld—will house a section dedicated to Stan and will sponsor an annual Stan Hochman Sports Essay contest in the Philadelphia public schools.

I thank everyone in our extraordinary family—our daughter, Anndee, our daughter-in-law, Elissa, our granddaughter, Sasha Rose, who make me proud every day of their talent, their generosity, their thoughtfulness, and their values; my beloved sister, Charlotte, who never left my side the first week after Stan passed away; my brother-in-law, Don; my nieces and nephews, Laurie and Greg, Jill, Jonathan, and Rebecca, Claudia, Cathy, Evie and Tzveka; my always-there-for-me friends Melissa, Fred and Judy, Becky, Carolyn and Don, Joan and Lee, Mady, Marcia and Ron, Nina, Batia and Marty, Gayl and Harold, Harriet, Judy, Carlene and Harold, SaraKay and Stan, Milt, Harry, Polly, Gary Newman, Ed Viner, Louis, Louise and Michael Esposito, and Dorothy Lawton, who soothed me through so many sleepless nights. How lucky I am to have my cousins Joan and Jerry, Ken and Tracy, Deby, Milton, Stuart, Marc, Bob, Jacob, Dylan, Scout, Erika, Ashlee, Margaret, Nancy, and Brenda, who miss Stan's presence, his famous chocolate cake, his way around fine wine, the gourmet meals he prepared, and the love he served with them. So many other cousins, nieces, nephews—Teagan, Andrew, Lola, and Greyson; Joanne and Mark, Howard, Ronna and Bob; Yoav, Boaz, Laura and Jay; Alana and Kira—and friends (you know who you are) lift my spirits every day. My parents, Sarah and Abe Honickman, were Stan's biggest fans, and his mother, Rose Hochman, instilled in him a reverence for learning and writing. I wish his father, Isadore, had lived long enough to enjoy his son's success. His brother, Wally, encouraged him to stay in Philadelphia, for which I owe him a debt I never can repay. The completion of this book is a tribute to their love and support.

Much appreciation goes to my editor, Ryan Mulligan, for his insight, guidance, and confidence in me, and to my team at Temple University Press—Ann-Marie Anderson, Gary Kramer, Irene Imperio Kull, Kate Nichols, Ashley Petrucci, Joan Vidal, David Wilson, and my outstanding freelance copyeditor, Heather Wilcox. Special thanks go to the late Lew Klein and his wife, Janet, who established Temple University's School of Media and Communications. Lew gave Stan his start on radio and presented me with one of the first "Lewies."

In 1959, when Larry Merchant, then sports editor of the *Philadelphia Daily News*, hired Stan to cover baseball, he told him, "Inform 'em . . . entertain 'em . . . and every so often surprise 'em." I hope you felt the flavor of that advice in the pages you read.

Index

Gloria Hochman is an award-winning author, journalist, broadcaster, and popular public speaker. She is the author of the *New York Times* best seller *A Brilliant Madness: Living with Manic-Depressive Illness,* co-authored with Patty Duke; *Heart Bypass: What Every Patient Must Know;* and *Adult Children of Divorce: Breaking the Cycle and Finding Fulfillment in Love, Marriage and Family,* co-authored with Edward Beal. She is also the editor of *The Age for Change: Baby Boomers Defy the Rules of Aging.* Hochman is the Director of Media Relations for the Adoption Center. She and Stan Hochman were married for fifty-four years.